DISEASES AND PARASITES
of Cattle, Sheep and Goats in South Africa

P Oberem | D Claassen | R du Preez | C Shacklock | T Snyman

Published by Afrivet Business Management 2022

Newmark Park Silverlakes Road
Faerie Glen

PO Box 2009
Faerie Glen
0043

+27 (0) 12 991 6416
+27 (0) 860 VEEARTS

www.afrivet.co.za

ISBN: 978 0 620 43028 9

Printer: IngramSpark
Publisher: Kejafa Knowledge Works

Second edition
First print 2022

ii

ACKNOWLEDGEMENTS

TEXT CONTRIBUTIONS
- Didi Claassen
- Riaan du Preez
- Danie Odendaal
- Caryn Shacklock
- Thys Snyman

EDITORIAL ASSISTANCE
Amélia Wassenaar

GRAPHICS
Akhona Salie

PHOTO CREDITS
The following contributors have made their valuable photographic material available to Afrivet for training and education of South African livestock owners:

- Afrivet Training Services (Matthew Carter)
- Afrivet Agents
- Agricultural Research Council (OVI)
- Anipedia Owners (JAW Coetzer and PT Oberem)
- Briza Publishers
- Middelburg Veterinary Laboratory
- Prof Mike Picker UCT (Blowfly –Lucilia cuprina)
- Schering Plough Animal Health
- University of Pretoria, Faculty of Veterinary Science
- Veterinarians and researchers: Drs Danie Odendaal, Abdalla Latif, Ian Southey, Nigel Dumford (WHO), Hans van de Pypekamp and Robin Taylor.
- Tsetse fly images as published in, *Pollinators, Predators & Parasites: The Ecological Roles of Insects in Southern Africa.* Photos © Hennie de Klerk.

Cover photo: Photo Library

My heartfelt thanks to all of those listed above.
Pamela Oberem (Editor).

CONTRIBUTORS

Pamela Oberem is a veterinarian and writer, with field and research experience on infectious diseases, vaccine use and vaccine production. She is the author and editor of many technical publications on infectious diseases.

Peter Oberem is the founder and managing director of Afrivet Business Management. He is an expert in the field of the control of veterinary parasites and the management of tick-borne diseases of livestock, and the development of veterinary products specifically designed for South African conditions. He was formerly president of the South African Animal Health Association and of the Wildlife Ranchers' Association of SA.

Didi Claassen gained broad experience on the control of livestock diseases as a private, and then a state veterinarian, for a number of years. She graduated as a Specialist Veterinary pathologist receiving her M.Med.Vet. qualification. Didi is currently the head of the Technical and Marketing Support division of Afrivet.

Riaan du Preez is a veterinarian who obtained his field experience as a large animal practitioner in the Free Sate. Thereafter, he studied for an MBA and was the President of the SAVA for a number of years. He is currently head of New Business Development division at Afrivet.

Caryn Shacklock is a veterinarian who specialises in parasitology. She obtained her M.Med.Vet degree on the subject of tick resistance. She is currently the head of the Afrivet Diagnostic Laboratory in Howick KZN which supports farmers by monitoring and advising on tick- and parasite control problems.

Thys Snyman is an experienced veterinary consultant on large animal production in particular to intensive large animal units such as diaries and feedlots.

FOREWORD

Water- and food security are some of the world's greatest challenges and South Africa is no exception. The challenge posed by food security is illustrated by some depressing statistics: a typical South African household spends about 70% of its budget on food of which milk, meat and eggs makes up half, but despite this, 25% of our children attend school without a meal during the day (The Empty Plate, Tracy Ledger). Providing food for an ever growing population is a huge challenge for producers, not least because among other challenges such as climate change, South African stock owners also have to battle many infectious diseases some of which can also impact on human health. **So, livestock farming requires all the possible support mechanisms possible to be successful.**

Afrivet Business Management, South Africa's own animal health company has now been in existence for 21 years, contributing to the health and productivity of our national herds and flocks. Our success supports our original observation that in addition to providing suitable products specially formulated for the South African market, stock owners need technical information and support to ensure optimal use of stock remedies. **Diseases and Parasites of Cattle, Sheep and Goats (2006)**, our first technical publication was a huge success, selling 9000 copies (in South African terms this qualifies it as a bestseller!). The demand for the book illustrated the hunger for knowledge among both commercial and developing farmers. By popular demand we published additional books and provided the scientific textbook, Infectious of Livestock Diseases in Southern Africa, an online platform at www.anipedia.org for veterinarians, para-veterinarians and advanced farmers. To ensure that recent research findings are communicated timeously to vets and farmers we published scientific monographs on tick biology and identification, tick control, tick-borne diseases and very importantly in the light of continuous waves of foot-and-mouth outbreaks, a new approach to its control, to allow South African farmers access to overseas markets.

Our company Afrivet is a leader in providing stock remedies and veterinary medicines but we have also expanded our services to training for stock owners. **Afrivet Training Services (ATS)** is a dedicated training arm of the Afrivet which provides courses on stock management and primary animal health care to enable farmers who don't have easy access to veterinarians with assistance, a huge challenge in rural areas. The oral training given by ATS is supported with illustrated manuals which summarise the course contents. In addition to this we provide apps that advise stock owners about animal health and livestock management. And finally, in our view the pinnacle of our contribution to the concept of Sound Technical Advice is the making available to farmers of animal-side diagnostic tests that can give results within as little as 10 minutes.

Encouraged by the positive response to our many books, manuals and monographs in this sphere we have decided that it is important to update our very first publication. We thank the dedicated editor and contributors and know that they will relish seeing the impact of their efforts on the well-being of our nation.

Dr Peter Oberem
CEO Afrivet Business Management

HOW TO USE THIS BOOK

This book is intended to provide and inform livestock owners about animal diseases, parasites and poisonings, in particular those in rural areas where veterinary advice is difficult to access. Nothing can replace the role of the veterinarian, who is a highly qualified professional, trained in many aspects of disease diagnosis, provision of treatment and recommendations on various types of livestock farming. On the farm veterinary advice should always be sought if possible because each farm / property has its own particular problems and circumstances. Therefore, the vaccine schedules and advice on the control of parasites is generalised and should be tailored in consultation with veterinarians working in the area.

The book is prefaced with some discussion on general aspects (management and nutrition) which are vital elements for effective livestock farming. The diseases of livestock are divided into categories according to the body system (e.g. ears/eyes, respiratory), or category of animal (dairy, young animal) which we have found to be the most user friendly method of categorisation. Within each disease section, the conditions likely to be identifiable by livestock owner are discussed. The list of conditions is by no means complete but cover the most common conditions likely to be encountered in ruminants.

We have provided some reference to the registered products sold by Afrivet Business Management which are easily to livestock owners. However, since there is a variety of similar products on the market we would encourage readers to consult widely and search for the best products for their particular needs.

It is our hope that this book can make a valuable contribution to animal health not only in South Africa but also further afield in neighbouring countries.

Dr Pamela Oberem
Scientific Editor

CONTENTS

MANAGEMENT   2

NUTRITION   17

DISEASES   27

AGEING ANIMALS 177

REFERENCES 181

INDEX 183

Management

MANAGEMENT

The good management of livestock is essential for successful farming and economically viable food and animal production. This includes the following elements: the proper planning and execution of the selected production and breeding system, proper fodder flow planning and correct nutrition according to the production stage of the herd, strategic disease and parasite control as well as avoidance of genetic problems. This section gives a broad overview of these elements of management. Note that veterinarians and nutritionists involved in livestock practise have the necessary knowledge and skills to help in structuring herd health and fodder flow programmes so their expertise should be sought to achieve optimum herd production.

SELECTING RUMINANT PRODUCTION AND BREEDING SYSTEMS

The production system adopted by a farmer is selected according to the geographic location of the farm, the food source, the species to be raised and the proximity and nature of the nearest marketing point. A brief summary of the various production systems is given below. For further information on managing or starting up any of these production systems please consult breeder's organisations and the references.

Extensive beef farming

This type of production is carried out on natural grazing (veld) in grassland or bushveld areas of the country. Natural grazing is sometimes supplemented with planted pastures for winter feeding.

Extensive beef production systems produce either weaner bulls or steers (castrated bulls) for marketing. The goal is to maximise growth and reproductive rate while minimising costs of production, which is mainly feed. This is achieved by selecting animals for rapid growth rate and culling non-productive cows. Extensive beef production on range (veld) conditions requires using breeds which are fertile, well-

adapted to the environment and which fulfil the requirement of the selected market. Late-maturing cattle breeds such continental beef breeds, are fast growing and provide lean meat, but appear to be less fertile under these conditions than small- or medium-framed, early maturing animals such as Angus and Hereford. The large-framed animals require more food per hectare than their smaller counterparts and are thus less well-adapted to deal with the nutritional challenges that extensive farming has to offer. In addition, the Angus and Hereford provide excellent meat quality with marbling, but cross-breeding will alter these characteristics.

Indigenous breeds such as Ngunis are easy-care, well-adapted to veld conditions being more tick- and disease- resistant than other breeds, but up to now they have suffered from poor improvement strategies which should be addressed by serious breeders (van de Pypekamp). Nguni's are believed to have enormous potential for beef production if selected properly. Other zebu breeds such as Brahmans have been used extensively for cross-breeding and

are also hardy under SA conditions. Synthetic breeds such as Bonsmara which have been bred for adaptability are also suitable for a wide range of ecological conditions.

Cattle raised on veld are best bred so that their calving season is 30 days before the first summer rains. Heifers to be bred for the first time are put to the bull 3-4 weeks before the main herd, to give them an extra month recovery time before they are bred for the second time.

In general, practical breeding strategies must place emphasis on breeding at a young age and culling non-conceivers, but specific approaches to selection and cross breeding should be discussed with production specialists. Stud bulls must be selected on birth- and weaning-weight, fitness and fertility. Synchronization of extensive beef cows with fixed time artificial insemination (FTAI) is becoming popular in other countries due to certain advantages: the benefits are a concentrated breeding (and thus calving) season, but the main advantage is the weaning of heavier calves, since more calves are born early in the calving season and are thus older and heavier when they are weaned/marketed, with a better return on investment.

Nguni cow and calf on natural grazing

Intensive meat production (cattle/sheep)

Intensive or feedlot systems were established initially to minimise costs and increase profitability, but along with this intensification comes the increased the risk of disease, environmental problems such as waste management and pollution. There is also increased resistance from welfare and animal rights groups to this kind of farming. Raising animals in a feedlot system requires thorough planning, preferably with input from nutritionists and veterinarians to be economically viable, because of the increased risk of disease. Factors that must be considered are the location, topography, water supply, direction of water flow after heavy rain, layout and proximity to markets. Economic factors to be considered are initial capital outlay, economies of scale and a varied supply network. The latter is needed so that an easy switch can be made from one breed to another. The breed to be used will be determined by the maize (feed) price. If the feed is cheap, larger framed later maturing beef types will be preferable because they can be fed cheaply for a relatively long time (> 110 days) without becoming overfat.

The opposite is true when the maize is expensive. Preference is then given to breeds that mature early and are able to become market ready in 90 days or even less. Since a feedlot is essentially a zero –grazing system, feed is bought in and is the highest input cost. The selection of feed formulation, feeding practices and feed bank management must be carefully considered. The use of feed additives including growth promotants, can be considered to maximise feed conversion; allowing adaptation to concentrates is essential to prevent acidosis.

New arrivals at the feedlot are particularly prone to respiratory diseases due to the high stress levels precipitated by weaning, transport, mixing of strange animals, and environmental factors such as dust, cold and wind. Caring well for newly introduced calves is worth the investment: new arrivals should be allowed to rest, eat and drink. This can be facilitated by not overstocking the adaptation pens, ensuring that the same size/weight of animals share a pen and also ensuring that there

is adequate floor- and-feedbank space to comfortably accommodate all the animals in a particular pen. In addition, multiple feeding points should be available to eliminate competition for food. Shelter from wind and cold must be provided, and dust must be reduced to the minimum by using water-sprayers. The use of vaccines, dips, dewormers and vitamin A supplements are some of the additional input costs needed.

Dairy cattle

Intensive, commercial style dairy farming has been described as a multi-faceted enterprise which involves competent managing of the milk herd, the milking parlour, forage provision planning and financial management. This is a complex task which requires a high-level expertise and attention to detail. Most dairy cattle in SA are exotic European breeds that are prone to heat stress. To manage this, cows must be provided with sufficient shade, watering points and in some cases mist showers and fans in the holding area before entering the

Cattle in a zero grazing feedlot

milking parlour. Reproduction in dairy cattle focuses on reconception within 65 days of calving in order to maintain inter-calf periods of approximately 380 days. This is important because a cow's life-time productivity is closely linked to how many lactation peaks she can achieve over her productive life. The udder is under severe stress and mastitis is an occupational hazard for these animals. In addition, several metabolic disorders mostly linked to nutritional stress, also plague these high producing animals. Energy supply can simply not keep up with energy output and many dairy cows end up in a negative energy balance, especially during the first 50 days of lactation, during which time peak production is reached.

The management of mastitis and a nutritional programme to match each production group's needs, is of utmost importance.

Selection for fertility and good udder conformation must also be done by selecting bulls/ semen that can contribute to these

improvements. Supervision of calving is essential as any complications can have a detrimental effect on re-conception. Bulls that sire small calves are thus preferable especially if the bull is to be used on heifers,

Raising replacement heifers requires an efficient calf raising system with the emphasis on suitable facilities, correct feeding, and meticulous supervision. Milk production targets, optimal intercalving periods and acceptable milk somatic cell counts must be discussed with a consulting veterinarian.

Less intensive, small scale dairy models, more suited to African conditions have been successful in countries such as Kenya where cross–bred animals which are more resistant to the climate and diseases, are used. The milk produced by these small-scale diaries is received and processed by co-operatives to ensure quality and freedom from diseases such as bovine TB and brucellosis.

Extensive sheep and goat farming

Small stock are raised mostly extensively in the arid and semi-arid areas of the country, such as the Karoo and the Kalahari. They can be grazed together with cattle in some areas because they utilise different forages. Semi extensive small stock farming is practiced in temperate Highveld grassland areas. The breeds used must be selected for the correct type of enterprise and environment, for example, the Ile de France which is suitable for semi-extensive meat and wool production systems, will thrive in temperate but not in harsher environments, while more hardy breeds such as Dorpers and indigenous breeds are better adapted for harsh climates. Meat production in SA is currently the most important extensive economic activity involving small stock, when compared with the wool and fibre industries which have suffered changing fortunes over the last few decades. The mutton market generally favours the lean carcases

Commercial dairy farms in SA make use mostly of exotic breeds which are heat sensitive.

of late maturing breeds such as SA Mutton Merinos and Ile de France. Goat-kid meat is an underutilised commodity in SA since it is lean and tender, and should be exploited more fully by farmers or marketing groups.

Breeding in sheep, and especially in goats, is seasonal although the length varies with breed: British sheep breeds having a short season, Merinos a medium length season and indigenous sheep can be bred almost all year round. Ewes come into oestrus under the influence of nutritional and seasonal effects, specifically the decrease in daylight length. The natural oestrus period is therefore autumn (April/May), but in practice two seasons can be utilised by management and feeding. The periodicity of oestrus in ewes is 17 days and its duration is an average of 27 hours. The length of the season is usually 5-6 weeks. The system of breeding management will be dependent on the type of farm. For example, stud farms will do hand-mating or AI, while others will leave rams with groups of ewes for the duration of the mating season. Breeding camps must preferably be small and level and have multiple watering points. Grazing quality must be good when stimulating animals to come into oestrus, and must be maintained during breeding. Ewe selection is very important: bad mothers, infertile ewes or those with damaged udders and vulvas should be removed. Old ewes are culled at roughly six years of age depending on the state of their teeth.

The size of breeding flocks must be considered; smaller flocks are easier and better for mating, the maximum being 250 animals. The ideal ram to ewe ratio must be 2-3% and ewes should be bred for the first time at 14-18 months of age (2-4 tooth stage).

Before the breeding season rams should be forced to exercise by separating watering and feeding points, to prevent them becoming fat. The testes and semen of sheep rams should be examined to ensure freedom from epididymitis which affects their fertility.

The advantage of spring lambing in summer rainfall areas is a good food supply at weaning, and high fertility when they are bred in the autumn. Disadvantages are the occurrence of cold spells in spring and the prevalence of blue tongue (in certain areas) when the colostral immunity of lambs is low. Autumn lambing will avoid the danger period of blue tongue in sheep, but ewes are less fertile when bred in spring months. Lambs should be weaned on weight rather than age, at roughly 15-20 kg. They can be weaned earlier if given creep feed. The selection of genetic traits is based on the breed and its specific production requirement; for example, wool fineness or growth rate, and advice on selection can be obtained from breeders' associations or animal scientists. The composition of the flock should be maintained for optimum productivity; for example, a wool producing flock should contain 44% breeding ewes, 15% ewe lambs, 14% young ewes, 25% wethers and 3% breeding rams.

Extensive small stock farming is practised on natural grazing in semi-arid areas.

DISEASE PREVENTION STRATEGIES

Many livestock owners think of disease prevention in terms of buying vaccine, dip and dewormer at the local co-operative. However much of disease control and prevention involves planning: for new farmers, this process must start even before animals are purchased. Guidelines for avoiding disease introduction on a farm or exposure of non-immune animals is given below. The efficient use of veterinary services, and veterinary remedies is outlined, as well as health monitoring which is the livestock owner's early warning system for detecting problems. The selection of appropriate vaccines, and their effective and safe application is explained.

Buying in animals

Many animal health problems can be prevented by following specific precautionary guidelines before animals are bought and brought onto the farm.

The **origin** of animals is important to avoid introduction from areas where outbreaks of disease are prevalent such as foot-and-mouth disease; introducing animals from areas with no **tick or insect borne diseases** can expose them to severe life-threatening diseases: a rule of thumb is that susceptible animals should not be introduced into areas with tick borne diseases such as heartwater, babesiosis and anaplasma, without careful consideration. Vaccination against these diseases is a long, expensive, and risky procedure in adult animals. Pregnant animals cannot be vaccinated with these vaccines. Sheep from blue tongue free areas such as the Karoo must be vaccinated before introduction into endemic areas.

It is essential to purchase animals from **reputable owners** who are able to give a full history and proof of freedom from inapparent diseases such as brucellosis and bovine tuberculosis. Where possible obtain a statement from the owner detailing vaccination, dipping and dosing programs that were followed.

Animals should never be bought without physical **examination** by a knowledgeable person: this is necessary to prevent buying old animals (see ageing of species at end of chapters), to prevent the purchase of animals with genetic defects (skewface, poor pigmentation), anatomical problems of the genitalia (missing teats, testicular degeneration, epididymitis), hoof problems, contagious diseases such as caseous lymphadenitis and signs of parasite infestation (fleece problems in sheep). Ideally animals should be examined by a **veterinarian** who will look for defects and ensure that stock are tested for infectious diseases. The Animal Disease Act 35/1984 requires that farmers do not buy or sell animals with diseases or parasites; this is not officiousness but a genuine attempt to prevent the spread of disease and resistant parasites. Even animals given a clean bill of health by a veterinarian should be placed in **quarantine** when newly introduced onto a farm. This is to prevent the introduction of parasites (e.g. worms, sheep scab, ticks or lice), since this is the most common

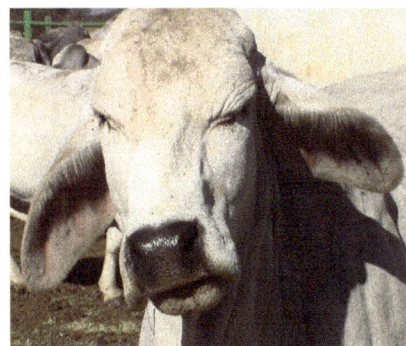

Skewface is a genetic problem of cattle which will cause difficulty with eating and subsequent poor weight gain.

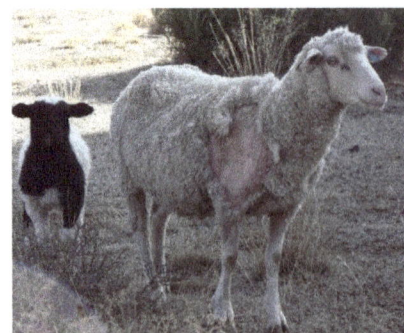

Small stock with visible fleece problems should not introduced into clean flocks.

Avoid buying cattle with lack of pigmentation.

means of introducing **resistant parasites** onto a farm. Quarantine is especially important when buying animals from auctions or farms where the history of parasite control is uncertain. Newly introduced sheep should be dosed twice and given two macrocyclic lactone injections with a 2-3 week interval to ensure that they are free from sheep scab. Cattle should be dipped twice with two different remedy groups, at two-week intervals, to ensure that resistant parasites are not introduced onto the farm.

Making enquiries about the **diet** of animals being brought onto a farm will prevent troublesome dietary adaptations such as acidosis or urea poisoning. Newly purchased stock should be **identified** by some means, e.g. by ear tags, tattooing or branding. Accurate **record keeping** of all management procedures such as vaccination, dosing, dipping etc, ensures good disease prevention and parasite control.

Disease monitoring

Primary Animal Health or disease monitoring

Veterinarians are trained to diagnose the cause of disease in animals. They do this by examining live animals, examining dead animals (post mortems) and performing or submitting laboratory investigations. However, learning to monitor the primary health of livestock is a basic skill which farmers can develop in order to manage disease problems before they become serious. This is done by observing animals daily and familiarising oneself with normal behaviour for the species. A brief summary is given here but for further details the reader should consult the **Animal Training Services Manuals**

available from Afrivet. Primary Animal Health Training is available for

Animal Training Services Manuals

livestock assistants and new farmers.

Normal behaviour of animals includes eating, drinking, excretion of faeces and urine, being able to walk normally, being attentive to surroundings, and holding the head and ears in a normal position. Examples of abnormal behaviour are refusing or being unable to eat or drink, being unable to rise when approached by humans, showing signs of depression such as drooping ears or straining to defecate. Common conditions can be diagnosed by doing a physical examination of the animal, while safely under restraint. All systems should be examined including the head-eyes, mouth, tongue, teeth, and ears; the chest is observed for abnormal breathing, the abdomen for asymmetry indicating digestive problems or pregnancy; the genitals must be examined for signs of discharges, inflammation or injury; the anus must also be examined for indication of diarrhoea or constipation. Taking the temperature of the animal will determine if there is a fever which usually indicates an infection. The information obtained on an examination is useful and can be relayed to a veterinarian or animal health technician who can then give advice on treatment or control. There are also cowside test kits which can be used where appropriate for example in determining the specific cause of mastitis in cows, or diarrhoea in calves. These tests enable farmers to discuss and plan treatment and

management of disease conditions. At present the range is fairly limited but this is a growing area of health technology which will expand in future.

A goat with drooping ears showing typical behaviour of a sick animal. Note also the discharge from the eyes.

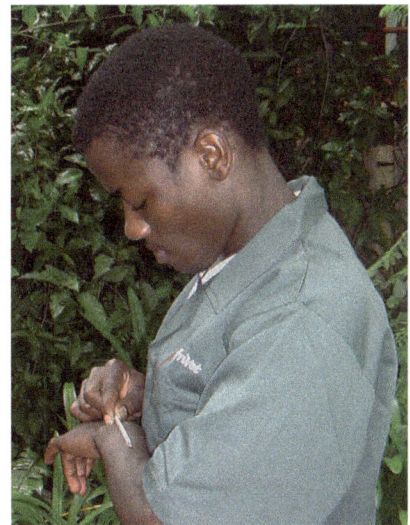

Taking the temperature of the animal will assist with making a diagnosis of the disease condition.

Veterinary assistance, stock remedies and first aid

The **veterinarian** is a highly qualified graduate who studies animal anatomy, physiology, reproduction, behaviour, medicine, surgery, parasitology, infectious diseases, nutrition, pathology and pharmacology – to name just a few subjects – over a period of 6 years. Veterinarians are therefore qualified to help the famer plan disease control and breeding programs on their farms; sadly many farmers only use veterinarians when they have an individual animal with a problem such as a difficult calving – the so-called "fire-engine" practice. Because of this, veterinarians find it difficult to make a living in country districts. Good farmers use veterinarians to prevent problems as well as solve them. The veterinarian should become a valued partner on the farm if one is serious about good management. Veterinary input costs of even the most progressive farms which use veterinarians frequently are below 4% of the operational costs of the farm, including stock remedies, vaccines and medicines. Nowadays many veterinarians are specialists in specific fields, for example feedlot management, nutrition, dairy, reproduction, etc. In areas where veterinarians are not readily accessible, Animal Heath Technicians may be able to assist livestock with simple diagnoses and procedures. All farms can benefit from keeping a small stock of **first-aid** remedies for minor animal health problems. The contents of the first-aid kit will naturally depend on the area, the type of farming and the type of animals involved, but the basics can be expanded to accommodate the specific problems of the region or the particular farm. Some suggestions are given below:

- Injectable oxytetracycline
- Injectable and/or oral sulpha remedy
- Wound oil or spray (containing insecticide if screwworm or blowflies are a problem)
- Tick grease for spot treatment
- Intra-uterine pessaries and plastic gloves
- Mastitis remedies for lactating and dry cows (type recommended by veterinarian or veterinary lab)
- Electrolytes (for calf raising units)

- Activated charcoal for plant poisonings (where necessary)
- Cotton wool or gauze dressing for bleeding wounds
- Sterile needles and syringes
- Thermometer
- Babesicide (redwater areas)

The sale of **stock remedies** is under the control of the National Department of Agriculture according to Act 36 of 1947, which requires that the manufacturers prove the product is effective, of good quality and safe for the animal, the handler, the consumer, and the environment before the product can be sold. Remedies which are deemed **safe and efficacious** by the authorities are registered and obtain a **"G" number** which identifies the product as officially acceptable. The product is identified by a label which clearly states the nature of the remedy (e.g. dip or dewormer), the animal species for which it is registered, the **claims** (which parasites/conditions it prevents/controls), the chemical group to which it belongs, and its potential toxicity. Most remedies have a **package insert** which gives more detailed information about the application (dosage and route), the precautions and side-effects.

It is essential before purchasing remedies to read the label and the package insert. The details should be read again before applying the remedy. The safety and efficacy of remedies are approved, based on the usage in a specific way and cannot be guaranteed by registration authorities and manufacturers if this is not adhered to. Some animal medicines are controlled by the Department of Health according to Act 101 of 1967; these medicines are only available to farmers on veterinary prescription.

When buying stock veterinary remedies, check that containers are

in good condition, with no broken seals, leakages, distortion or bloating of the container. Vaccines that have not been stored in the fridge must be avoided. No animal product should be purchased or used if it has expired or has a homemade label. Do not buy animal health products from auctions since these are often expired or damaged, or products that have been brought into the country illegally.

Always record dosing, dipping and vaccination, noting the date, the remedy and the batch number. In the event of problems with products, the batch number serves as an important and useful reference, since manufacturers keep archive material of all product batches for examination or testing in case of complaints.

From a scientific point of view, the use of home-made, herbal and homeopathic remedies is pointless and can even be harmful. Many plants contain substances which, while they may contain an effective active ingredient, may be toxic if the incorrect dose is given. This is why plants that contain pharmacologically active substances have been replaced by pharmaceutical products which are tested to ensure they contain a safe and effective dose. Home-made remedies were initially used by farmers in the absence of alternatives and have now become unnecessary. Many poisonings still occur due to the use of disinfectants, lamp paraffin and old motor oil, which are poisonous and cause suffering and deaths in animals. Home-made pour-ons for ectoparasites can cause severe burns and their use promotes parasite resistance. Equally dangerous are remedies containing plants extracts such as aloe or "khakibos" which claim to control external or internal parasites. They are totally ineffective for this purpose and their usage often results in the outbreak of tick-borne disease or losses due to worm infestations. Homeopathic remedies are those in which the active ingredients have been diluted millions of times – in other words, the active ingredient has been diluted out. The end product therefore contains only water or alcohol.

Although regulatory authorities control the **registration of stock remedies,** the manufacturers themselves have formed a body which regulates their industry by endorsing a code of conduct. Reputable veterinary companies are members of The South African Animal Health Association (SAAHA[1]) which has drawn up a code of conduct governing research and development standards, advertising standards, training of sales staff, warehousing standards, transport standards and after-sales service by staff. **SAAHA registered sales staff** are required to do an intensive training course in veterinary subjects which qualifies them for accreditation. Qualified sales staff receive an ID card which shows that they have sufficient background to sell stock remedies. Farmers should request these from sales staff to prevent buying from non-accredited sales people. Companies registered with SAAHA provide the client with back-up service, whether from salespeople or from company veterinarians. Problems encountered with remedies should be reported to sales staff who then contact technical support staff. In this the industry aims to prevent "sell and run" tactics by sales staff.

1 SAAHA is the animal health arm of the larger affiliation The Agricultural Veterinary Chemicals Association of South Africa (AVCASA), an organisation of manufacturers and distributors of agricultural chemicals. This is an industry organisation that, among other services, also provides training to farmers and farm workers on the handling of agricultural chemicals.

THE LAW AND LIVESTOCK FARMING

Apart from Acts 36/47 and 101/65 which govern veterinary remedies, the Animal Diseases Act 35/1984 specifies responsibilities of the Department of Agriculture and of farmers with regard to disease control. The full Act can be accessed on the Internet, but the main issue pertinent to farmers is their responsibility in preventing the spread of diseases not under government control and preventing the dissemination of resistant parasites.

Another law pertinent to farmers is the Animal Protection Act 71 of 1962 which makes it an offence to cause suffering to animals, either by failing to provide for their needs such as food, water, shade and ample space, or by active cruelty. The law makes provision for prosecution of farmers guilty of any contraventions. Farmers must also be aware of the Animal Slaughter, Meat and Animal Production Hygiene Act 87/1967, which governs the transport and handling of animals to be used for slaughter. This Act delineates clearly that animals must be transported and handled in a manner that will not cause them excessive stress, injuries or death.

VACCINATION

Vaccination is used to prevent infectious diseases i.e. those caused by bacteria, viruses and other micro-organisms. Many infectious diseases are untreatable, many are too acute for treatment and even if animals survive the disease there is still loss of production either through loss of weight, milk or a break in the wool. The use of vaccines to prevent infectious disease is a small investment with high returns, and as such can be considered an insurance policy. The cost of the vaccine is always low relative to the cost of the animal and since they are tax deductible, it is curious that farmers are often happier to buy antibiotics for treatment than vaccines for disease prevention. Vaccines must however be used correctly to give the best protection. Using vaccines at the incorrect time, or damaging them through poor storage and handling will be a wasted investment and put the lives of stock at risk. All vaccines have an accompanying package insert which details the storage directions, route of administration, the age, sex of animals to be inoculated, time of year, and any contra-indications or precautions for use. The package insert must be read carefully before the vaccine is used.

How to use vaccines

Vaccines are given by specific routes for particular reasons. It is essential to give them as recommended because the vaccine may not be effective or may cause severe irritation if given by another route. The most commonly used in cattle, sheep and goats are sub-cutaneous and intra-muscular routes. Heartwater blood vaccine is the only one currently given by intra-venous injection. The orf vaccine is administered by scarification, which involves scratching the skin with a sterile needle and dripping the vaccine organism onto the scratches. It is essential that all syringes and needles used for vaccination are sterile. If needles and syringes are re-used they must be **boiled** for at least 20 minutes directly before use. Failure to sterilise needles sufficiently will cause abscesses and possibly even death due to generalised infection. Sterilization of vaccine needles and syringes with alcohol or disinfectants is not acceptable as these chemicals may be detrimental to the vaccine.

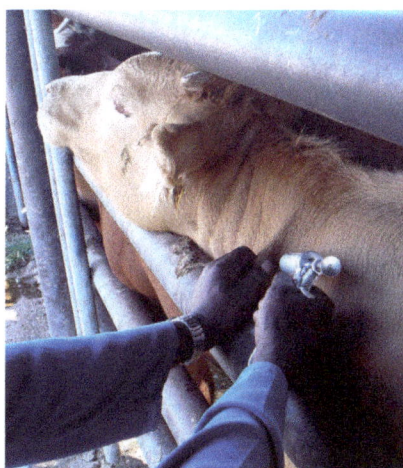

Vaccination is the method of choice for preventing infectious diseases in ruminants

When to use vaccines

To protect newborn animals against specific diseases, some vaccines are given to the mothers and immunity is transferred via the colostrum. This is called maternal or passive (colostral) immunity. Newborns must receive sufficient colostrum within 6 hours after birth for this to be successful e.g. against colibacillosis, tetanus and lamb dysentery.

Passive immunity prevents or suppresses the response to vaccination – this is called colostral interference. Therefore, in young animals whose dams were vaccinated, vaccination must be postponed until the age at which the colostral immunity is declining or has disappeared. There is a window period of susceptibility because of this change-over from colostral (passive) immunity to immunity produced by the young animal itself (active immunity) after their first vaccinations.

Depending on the time of occurrence of a specific disease, vaccination can be started at around weaning age when the colostral immunity is at a low level or it can be started from three months on if the disease occurred before weaning, as in the case of some clostridial diseases.

Because vaccination is a preventative measure, it is usually of little value to vaccinate during an outbreak of disease, because the incubation time of a disease is invariably shorter than the time taken to develop immunity after vaccination. Also, the vaccination of animals during outbreaks always carries the risk of the transmission of diseases from one animal to another, particularly in the case of lumpy skin disease, anaplasmosis and Rift Valley fever.

Insect-borne diseases are seasonal so vaccines used to prevent them must therefore be given in spring before the danger period. For diseases associated with management practices such as dipping (Corynebacterium ovis), shearing of sheep (quarter evil), castration and docking (tetanus), etc. vaccination must be done before these procedures are performed. In some cases, two or three vaccinations must be given so sufficient time must be allowed for the full course

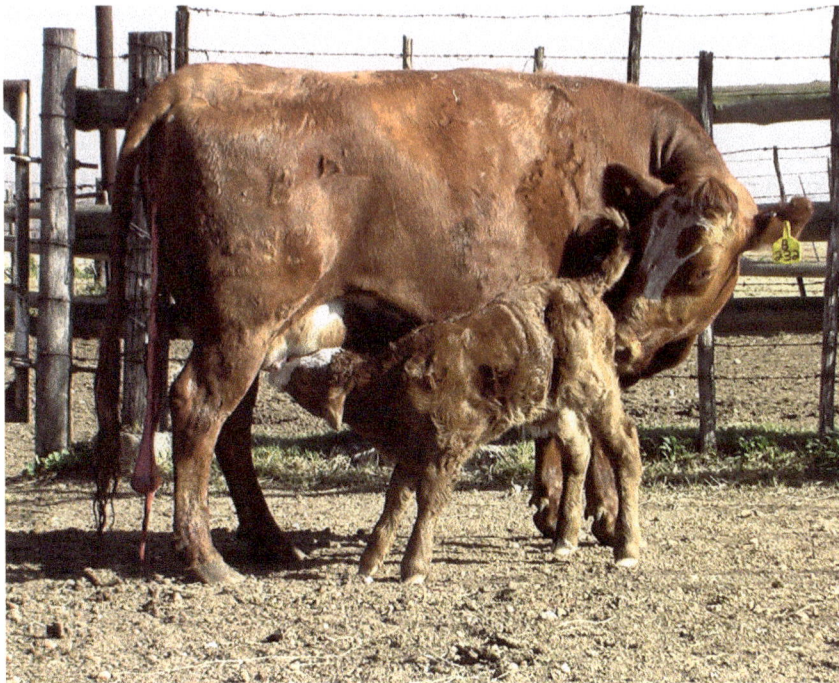

Passive immunity against some diseases is transferred through the colostrum

of immunization (for example bluetongue vaccination requires 9 weeks for completion of the full program).

Side-effects, adverse reactions and vaccine failure

Vaccination is generally a harmless procedure but occasionally there are side-effects. Anaphylactic shock is an immediate allergic reaction which may be triggered by any component in the vaccine. These responses occur in a small percentage of animals but can be fatal in some cases unless adrenalin is administered. Goats in particular are known to develop delayed hypersensitivity reactions after being injected with a vaccine or other stock remedy. These reactions are characterised by severe swelling at the injection site 3-4 days after injection. Try to avoid injecting a goat (Angora or Boer goat) in the neck region because should this reaction occur, the animals may suffocate. Rather inject over the triceps area or in the tail fold if the volume of the dose allows. Some live vaccines are contra-indicated for use in pregnant animals due to the possibility of abortion occurring. The package insert must therefore be carefully studied for contra-indications during pregnancy. Some vaccines may cause prominent swellings because they contain an adjuvant which stimulates the immunisation process; these vaccines must be given strictly according to recommendations to avoid severe reactions.

The reasons why vaccines may not protect under certain circumstances can be attributed to factors affecting the vaccine itself, the administration of the vaccine and the health of individual animals.

The vaccine: vaccine may be damaged by incorrect storage (heating or freezing) or exposure to direct sunlight, there may be a problem with a particular batch of vaccine or if the diagnosis is incorrect the wrong vaccine may be used.

Administration of the vaccine: failure to give boosters, using the wrong route, vaccinating while the animal is incubating disease, under-dosing vaccine either due to wrong dilution or faulty calibration of automatic syringes are all causes of vaccine failure. Note that overdosing vaccine is wasteful and may cause allergic reactions. Mixing vaccines with other products or vaccines may damage or inactivate them. Antibiotics given at the same time as live bacterial vaccines may inactivate them.

Animal-related factors: Chronic diseases, heavy parasite infestations, malnutrition or genetic factors in the individual may all cause a poor immune response.

Vaccination programmes

Following a set vaccination program ensures that vaccines are given timeously and boosters are not forgotten. The vaccination programmes given here are guidelines and should be adapted for local conditions with the help of a local veterinarian who knows the prevalence of local diseases. In the tables given below, essential vaccines are given in bold type while those given in normal type are optional or are only required in certain endemic areas. The term *multiclostridial* refers to vaccines which offer protection against a broad range of clostridial diseases (6-8 components). These are more convenient and cost effective to use than a combination of single component clostridial vaccines.

For more details about a specific vaccine, see the discussion under the disease chapters.

Table 1. Vaccination program for beef cattle on veld

AGE	VACCINE	ADMINISTRATION
Calves	**Anthrax**	Weaning age
	Botulism	Weaning age (booster 21 days later)
	Multiclostridial	3 months to weaning age (booster 21 days later)
	Lumpy skin disease	Weaning age
	Rift valley fever (live)	Weaning age
	Heartwater	1-21 days
	Redwater	3-9 months
	Anaplasma	3-9 months
	Rabies	3 months
Heifers	*Brucella abortus*	
	• S19	• 3-8 months before breeding
	• RB51	• 3-8 months before breeding 3 months before first breeding season
	Vibrio Reproductive combinations	2 months before first breeding
	(BVD, IBR, PI3)	
Cows	*Multiclostridial*	Annual booster 2 months before calving
	Lumpy skin disease	Annual booster in spring
	Anthrax	Annual booster (avoid late pregnancy)
	Vibrio	1-2 months before breeding
	Reproductive combinations	1-2 months before breeding
	Brucella abortus (RB51)	Repeat before breeding (S19 cannot be repeated)
	Rabies	Three yearly booster
Bulls	**Multiclostridial**	Annual booster
	Vibrio	1-2 months before breeding
	Botulism	Annual revaccination

Table 2. Vaccination program for dairy cattle

AGE	VACCINE	ADMINISTRATION
Calves	**Anthrax**	7 months
	Botulism	7 months (booster 21 days later)
	Multiclostridials	3-7 months (booster 21 days later)
	Lumpy skin disease	7 months
	Rift valley fever (live)	7 months
Heifers	***Brucella abortus*** • RB51 • S19	• 3-8 months before first breeding season • 3 months before first breeding season
	Reproductive combinations (BVD, IBR, PI3)	7 months and then 1-2 months before first breeding season
	Rota/Corona/ E coli combination	During the last trimester of pregnancy but not earlier than 3 weeks before calving
Cows	**Multiclostridials**	Booster in dry cows
	Botulism	Annual booster
	Lumpy skin disease	Annual booster in spring
	Anthrax	Annual booster (avoid late pregnancy)
	Reproductive combinations	Annual booster after calving
	Brucella abortus RB51	After calving before breeding (note that S19 cannot be repeated)
	Rota/Corona/ *E. coli* combination	During the dry period but not closer than 3 weeks before calving
	Rabies	Three yearly booster
Bulls	**Multiclostridials**	Annual booster
	Botulism	Annual booster

Table 3. Vaccination program for sheep

AGE	VACCINE	ADMINISTRATION
Lambs	**Multicomponent clostridials** including pulpy kidney.	Weaning – booster 21 days later
	Anthrax	Weaning
	Blue tongue	Weaning (all 3 vaccines)
	Rift valley fever (live)	Weaning
	Pasteurella haemolytica for pneumonia	Weaning or as directed on package insert
	Corynebacterium ovis abscesses	Before weaning and give booster
	Orf	From day old
	Botulism	Weaning
	Heartwater	1-7 days
	Brucella Rev.1	Vaccinate only ram lambs (stud) at weaning
Ewes	**Multiclostridial including pulpy kidney and tetanus.**	Last few weeks of pregnancy
	Anthrax	Annual –avoid late pregnancy
	Blue tongue	Annual booster in spring but avoid first third of pregnancy
	Enzootic abortion	Before breeding
	Chlamydia	
	Orf	When required
	C. ovis abscesses	Annual booster before shearing
	M. haemolytica pneumonia	Before danger period e.g. winter
	Botulism	Annual booster
Rams	**Multiclostridial with pulpy kidney.**	Annual revaccination
	Blue tongue	Annual revaccination
	P. haemolytica pneumonia	Before danger period for example winter

Table 4. Vaccination program for goats

AGE	VACCINE	ADMINISTRATION
Lambs	**Multiclostridial with** pulpy kidney.	Weaning (repeat 21 days later)
	Anthrax	Weaning
	Rift Valley fever (live)	Weaning
	Heartwater	1-7 days (monitor lambs for reactions)
	Pasteurella pneumonia (sheep vaccine)	Weaning or as directed on label
	Orf	From day old
Does	**Multiclostridial** with pulpy kidney.	Last few weeks of pregnancy
	Anthrax	Annual booster (avoid late pregnancy)
	Chlamydia	Before breeding
	M. haemolytica pneumonia	Before danger period such as winter
	Orf	When required
Rams	**Multiclostridial** with pulpy kidney.	Annual revaccination
	M. haemolytica	Before the danger period

PARASITE CONTROL

As with infectious diseases the prevention and control of internal and external parasites must be planned in conjunction with advice from a veterinarian or animal health technician. This is essential as the control measures must be based on the type of production system (intensive/extensive), the geographic area in the country (arid, grassland, bushveld, etc.) and the species involved. More details are provided in the separate chapters on Internal and External parasites.

Nutrition

RUMINANT NUTRITION

Nutrition is a specialist subject on which farmers should if possible, consult nutritionists or specialist veterinarians, particularly when feeding high-producing animals such as dairy and feedlot animals. This chapter discusses the basics of ruminant nutrition, as well as some nutritional considerations for different farming systems. The evaluation of body condition which is a vital management tool is also discussed.

The ruminant digestive system

Cattle, sheep and goats are ruminants which means they are able to utilise otherwise indigestible cellulose in plants due to the micro-organisms in their rumens which can digest this fibrous plant material. In this process volatile fatty acids are formed which can be taken up directly through the rumen wall. This is the main energy source for ruminants. The micro-organisms then use the rest of the digested material for food. As their numbers increase some of them will flow with the undigested plant material into the rest of the intestinal tract where they are digested in the abomasum and small intestine. The micro-organisms thus become the food and main protein source of ruminants.

Ruminants can eat a variety of fibrous foods such as forages (veld), planted pastures, crop residues such as silage and industrial by- products such as oil seed cake. Fibre is essential for the good health of the ruminal micro-organisms and for a high butterfat content of milk.

Digestion will be disturbed when the pH of the rumen is changed, becoming either very acidic (sudden increase in carbohydrate) or alkaline for example with excess urea intake. Under these conditions the micro-organisms may die off and lead to the condition called "indigestion" (for treatment and prevention see the chapter on gastro-intestinal diseases).

Certain drugs, toxins and folk remedies, such as old motor oil and disinfectants, can also cause damage to the rumen organisms and give rise to indigestion.

The most important components of the ruminant diet are:

- Energy, protein, phosphate and calcium (macro-nutrients)
- Vitamins and trace elements (micro-nutrients)

All of these elements are contained in the dry matter component of plants but because the nutritional components of plant matter vary with the time of year and the growing season, the diets of production animals are supplemented to optimise immunity, health, growth and production.

Energy: forage (veld) is essentially a low-energy feed and high producing animals such as dairy and feedlot cattle are given additional feed in the form of pastures, grain supplements such as maize products or sorghum residue and molasses. The energy supplements are usually combined with protein supplementation for maximal effect. The energy requirements of an animal are expressed in Mega Joule (MJ) which is the most convenient unit. The energy supplied by rations is expressed as metabolisable energy (ME) which is the amount of energy available to the animal after subtracting the energy lost through the indigestible component and expended by the digestion process.

Protein: supplementation is required when the quality of forage is low, for example in winter months (in summer rainfall areas) or at the end of the growth season. Supplementation is usually in the form of a protein-rich industrial by-product such as cottonseed oil cake, or can be a non-protein nitrogen (NPN) source such as urea, which can be utilised by the rumen micro-flora.

Macro-minerals: the minerals of greatest importance to ruminant livestock are calcium and phosphate, and the balance between these components is extremely important. Supplementing one may upset the balance of the other and one must ensure that the ratio between calcium and phosphate is maintained at a ratio of 2:1. Phosphate deficiency occurs widely in SA on forage and pastures, particularly at the end of the growing season, and should be supplemented to enhance production. Phosphate deficiency on the veld leads to grazing animals developing "pica" or bone-chewing which can lead to botulism outbreaks. Calcium-phosphate imbalance in the diet of dairy cattle may cause milk fever in high producing cattle. In sheep, calcium deficiency can arise when lambs are grazed on lush green pastures; these lambs develop a condition called "bowie", which causes the outward bending of the legs, due to poor bone formation. Supplementation of these minerals is usually given in the form of licks or additives.

Cow showing "pica" or bone chewing due to phosphorous deficiency.

Calcimax V3209

Vitamins: The ruminal microflora produce most of the vitamins required by ruminants and the only vitamin which has to be supplemented under normal farming circumstances is vitamin A. It is obtained in green feed, but as soon as the feed is cut for feeding, making hay or silage, the vitamin A content will fall. Vitamin A levels are low in veld grass late in the growth season as well as in nitrate-fertilised pastures. Since vitamin A deficiencies may cause reproduction and eye infection problems, cattle, sheep and goats should receive regular vitamin A supplementation using drenches or injectable preparations.

Vit-Aid G0678

Trace elements: these are minerals which are required in very small amounts but are essential for good health. Deficiencies seldom arise in animals on pastures or complete rations, but may occur on forage in certain areas of the country; deficiencies of iodine, copper, cobalt, manganese, selenium and molybdenum have been recorded. Zinc deficiency can lead to skin problems and may predispose to outbreaks of ringworm. Most of the trace element deficiencies however manifest as poor growth and reproduction. Supplements can be provided in licks, or as liquid or injectable forms.

Bovi-Min V24721

Dairy-Min V 24723

Ovi-Min V24722

Ovi-Min +CU V26349

The use of growth stimulants

Growth stimulants have been used for decades in animal production because they can improve weight gains by at least 10% and raise feed conversion by 15%. This is an important contribution since feed is the most expensive input in all types of farming. Feed additives are used most frequently in intensive production systems such as feedlots, piggeries and broiler production, but they can also benefit dairies and extensive beef cattle raising systems, to promote growth of calves and to facilitate feed utilisation during winter months.

The advantages of growth stimulants are that they improve growth and also the feed conversion on specific rations. This can be an advantage given the high cost of feed and the poor value of veld and pastures during the winter. The product (meat/milk) being produced therefore becomes cheaper and more cost effective. Antimicrobial growth stimulants promote animal health, improve feed safety and reduce losses due to deaths and production loss from disease. It also improves animal welfare, preventing disease rather than waiting for animals to get sick and treating them.

Developed countries are concerned about the use of antibiotics in animals as this is believed to cause the spread of resistant organisms to humans. It is important to note that most of the antimicrobial growth stimulants used in SA are not used for therapeutic use in humans (e.g. the ionophors or flavophospholipol). The use of antimicrobial growth stimulants is now banned in Europe in food animals so potential exporters should take note.

The banning of growth hormone use in the EU is based on perceptions and public opinions and not on scientific principles. The promotion of animal products as "hormone free" is a sales gimmick as all meat and milk contains hormones produced by the animals themselves, as do certain plants such as soya, peas and cabbage which contain phyto-oestrogen. Hormones are still used as growth stimulants in the USA as well as in other developed countries including

New Zealand, Australia and South America. BST is found in normal milk and since it is broken down in the intestine has no effect on humans at all. The banning of the use of BST in EU countries is based on milk politics, specifically overproduction.

Most growth stimulants are added either in a feed concentrate or added to the complete ration depending on the type of animals being fed. Thorough mixing is absolutely essential to ensure good distribution and intake. Poor mixing will result in some animals not receiving sufficient substance to affect a result. In some cases, like the ionophors, poor mixing can cause overdosing and toxicity. Mixing must therefore be entrusted to reputable companies. Remedies like zeranol and the hormones, are implanted under the skin and slowly released into the bloodstream. They are delivered with special applicators and good needle hygiene is essential for implantations.

Some of the stimulants have a withdrawal period before slaughter which must be observed.

Growth stimulants used in meat production are used to improve feed conversion which results in better carcass value.

TYPES OF GROWTH PROMOTORS

Antimicrobials

These compounds supress the growth of certain bacteria. They are used to prevent common diseases in in intensive systems (therapeutic effect) or to manipulate rumen organisms to ensure better utilisation of the feed.

Tetracyclines (oxytetracycline and chlortetracycline): In ruminants these antimicrobials are used in feedlots to medicate for certain problems like feedlot pneumonia and liver abscesses. The dosage used must recommended by the consulting veterinarian per prescription.

Oxytet FG 200 G1823

Chlortet 200G G3141

Macrolides: Tylosin and a newer molecule acetylisovaleryl tylosin tartrate is used to treat mycoplasma infections, mainly in poultry, pigs and ruminants.

Tyleco FG 100 G2152

Ionophores: Examples of these are monensin and salinomycin, which can be used as coccidiostats for the prevention of coccidiosis as well as the improvement of feed conversion. The ionophores change the bacterial flora of the rumen which enhances propionic acid production, increases available dietary protein and reduces methane production resulting in better food utilisation. This group is not used in human medicine and therefore does not contribute to the problem of resistant bacteria in humans, which is one of the concerns raised about antimicrobial growth promotants. Ionophores are widely used, especially in feedlots because of the improvement they provide in starch digestion and food utilisation.

Flavophospholipol: This antimicrobial is used as a growth stimulant and its use is confined to animals. It produces its effect by suppressing certain rumen microflora. Flavophospholipol will improve the growth of calves and lambs, and the performance of dairy cattle, beef animals, sheep and goats even on veld where it will improve the utilisation of poor quality of roughage. There is no withdrawal time for this product because it is not absorbed into the bloodstream.

Flaveco 80 G3149

Non-antibiotic growth stimulants

This group has a direct influence on the protein metabolism of the animal rather than on the micro-organisms.

Beta-agonists or repartitioning agents: zilpaterol is the only substance in this category. It causes an increase in weight due to muscle production rather than fat deposition. The effect disappears when the remedy is withdrawn, so it must be used right up to marketing and the withdrawal period must be borne in mind. The drug is especially suitable for feedlot animals.

Hormones: Hormones are natural substances produced by animals. The effects of the sexual hormones are to increase nitrogen retention, enhancing protein metabolism and feed conversion efficiency. Hormonal growth stimulants (male and female) are used chiefly in feedlot cattle in SA since they are not suitable for use in breeding animals. Bovine somatotropin (BST) is a bovine hormone which stimulates milk production. It raises milk production by 15% and therefore reduces the numbers of animals needed to produce a given amount of milk.

Hormone mimics: Zeranol is a synthetic molecule based on a substance initially isolated from a fungus of maize. The molecule mimics the effect of oestrogen and stimulates growth of animals by 10%. It is used mainly to round off beef cattle but is also suitable for use in sheep and ostriches. It can be used for fattening animals but also for replacement heifers before the age of 7 months. It is not suitable for use in animals at breeding age.

NUTRITION IN SPECIFIC PRODUCTION AND BREEDING SYSTEMS

Dairy cattle

Newborn ruminants have underdeveloped and non-functioning rumens: the milk they ingest bypasses the fore-stomachs via the oesophageal groove and reaches the abomasum where it is digested. As soon as the young ruminant begins to eat plant material the development of the rumen is stimulated and the animal begins to ruminate. It acquires the rumen micro-organisms from the mother and the environment. Dairy calves must be given plant fibre as soon as possible to stimulate the development of the rumen and promote growth. This can be done by giving a grain starter and a good quality, palatable hay, or a complete starter ration which contains plant fibre. The young heifer should begin to ruminate at 2-4 months – an indication that the rumen is developed. The feeding of starter rations to the dairy calf will allow early and smooth weaning at 5-8 weeks. Growth monitoring of the young heifer is a very important measure of correct feeding; because it is the weight of the heifer that determines sexual maturity rather than her age, correct feeding will avoid delays in sexual maturity and prevent calving problems due to underdevelopment of the heifer. Below is a guideline for the optimum growth and age targets:

Average daily gain g/day (ADG)
- before puberty ± 800
- after puberty ± 825

Age at first breeding > 15 months
Bodyweight at first breeding ± 66% of adult weight
Age at first calving < 24 months
Bodyweight after first calving ± 80% of adult weight

Dairy cows are best raised on fresh green pasture, but the ideal type must be selected according to the local climate, taking frost and rainfall into consideration. Cutting pasture as green chop has the advantage of not having to send animals to pasture and preventing prussic acid poisoning due to trampling. Other suitable feed sources are silage, hay, and concentrates. Nutrient requirements must be supplied to cows with consideration given to the stage of lactation or pregnancy, and must be carefully managed to prevent problems such as ketosis and milk fever. To ensure a regular supply of milk the dairy herd must have the correct ratio of pregnant and lactating cows, so regular veterinary visits must be scheduled. Dairy cows require a high level of feeding, both the quantity and quality, to ensure good milk production. For optimal milk production by high producers, the type and quality of the protein source become more and more important as this will also stimulate feed (and therefore energy) intake. The mineral and vitamin supplementation are also very important for production and optimal health as high milk production will deplete these stores.

During the dry period, the cow is fed a maintenance ration but in the last 3-6 weeks before calving, the energy component of the ration is increased by feeding concentrates because of the increased demand from the foetus. This regime will prevent the cow becoming too fat and developing ketosis. Dairy cows that are prone to milk fever will benefit from the inclusion in the ration of anionic salts such as ammonium chloride. Feeding of concentrate can be increased gradually as the cow becomes adapted and by the time she calves she will be ingesting 60% concentrate.

During lactation, protein, carbohydrates and roughage are important nutrients. If the cow is not achieving her expected milk production the problem is usually inadequate protein. If she achieves her peak but is unable to maintain the normal milk curve the problem is insufficient energy. High producers need roughly 17-19% protein in the diet. Good sources of protein for the dairy cow are soya or cotton oilcakes. As lactation progresses and the cow moves away from the peak (2-3 weeks into lactation), energy becomes more important and the protein can be dropped to 12% at the end of lactation. Excess protein is not beneficial as it requires more energy to excrete it. The dairy diet should contain a higher percentage of roughage than a fattening diet (40% and higher) because the butterfat percentage of the milk is dependent on the fibre content of the diet.

The heifer is still growing when she has her first calf and she should therefore be dried off a month earlier than cows, to allow her to build up reserves for her next lactation. See the insert on body condition for more information.

Feedlot animals

The main aim in a feedlot is to maximise growth and reduce costs. Maximal weight gain is achieved through maximal food intake and this is in turn influenced by palatability of feed and intake (trough access) to the feed. The average daily gain of animals in a feedlot will depend on the breed and sex of animal (heifer, steer or bull), and in cattle varies from 1-1,3kg per day.

Animals raised on zero grazing are fed complete rations, often with a high level of energy, which may cause problems if the animals are not given sufficient time for their rumen flora to adapt. As with dairy animals, the nutrition of these animals is a specialised area and it is best to consult a nutritionist for an optimal, economical production.

Problems specific to raising calves in feedlots are adaptation to concentrates, although they need less roughage in the ration (10%) to prevent acidosis than sheep in a feedlot situation. The use of growth stimulants to optimise production should be considered.

Nutrition for extensive farming systems

Livestock raised under extensive conditions unlike animals on zero grazing are dependent on range or veld. In most areas the nutritional level of veld grass varies with the season so feed supplementation must be given to compensate. The nutritional needs are also a function of the breeding cycle so this must be borne in mind when planning the annual feeding schedule or feed flow cycle for the year. In order to illustrate this the diagram below makes use of the example of the feed provisioning of beef cattle on veld in a summer rainfall area.

Feed planning diagram

(See diagram on the next page.)

Beef cattle

Beef cattle raised extensively on veld are mainly supplemented late in the growing season when the palatability and nutritional level of grass is low. In winter, the first limiting factor is protein, with energy as a secondary limiting factor to growth. The nitrogen level of plant material especially in the sourveld areas falls considerably so Non Protein Nitrogen (NPN) containing licks such as urea can be supplied when the nutritive value of veld grass is low; these licks can have an energy source such as maize meal added if the grass is really in bad condition. Urea feeding must be done gradually to prevent poisoning, so salt is added to limit the intake. Ensure that animals do not have a salt hunger before feeding such a lick.

Growth stimulants such as flavophospholipol can be used to maximise forage or late growth pastures. This induces better utilisation of poor roughage and increases the butterfat content of milk. Phosphate licks to supplement low levels of phosphate should include an energy source or the animal will lose weight. Vitamin A levels will be sufficient in fresh green pasture but animals fed on dried hay or winter grass may have deficiencies. Injectable supplements are useful in preventing reproductive and eye problems.

To be economical, extensive beef farming requires that a cow produces a calf every year. The cow must also produce sufficient milk to raise a strong, viable calf to weaning. As with dairying, the cow must be in good condition to be able to conceive and carry a calf. The cow should have a body condition score of 3 when she calves and should have a condition of 2,5 when she is to be bred. Underweight cows should be identified early so they can be supplemented before breeding, otherwise they should rather be culled. With veld grazing important concerns are good pasture management by preventing overstocking and overgrazing, which cause long-term damage like soil erosion, bush encroachment, plant invasion and the proliferation of poisonous plants.

Body condition determination

The determination of body condition is the evaluation of the fat reserves of adult cattle (cows and bulls) at a strategic time in the production cycle. In adult cattle body condition is the best available indicator of the nutritional status and is a more reliable measure than weight.

With replacement heifers the situation is the reverse. Her weight and her weight increase are of more practical importance than the overall body condition because the heifer does not yet have to use reserves for lactation and calf production.

Body condition is a good management and selection tool. As a management tool it reflects the general pasture conditions and the success of supplementary protein and energy feeding. If there is a shortage of either of these more than 10% of the herd will be under the target body condition. As a selection tool, body condition evaluation will identify animals that are unable to maintain condition. If less than 10% of the herd are below the target weight this will indicate that these are individuals which are unable to maintain condition while 90% are able to under the same conditions.

Condition determination is done at four strategic times in the production cycle because at these times the condition will have an effect on the reproductive performance; it can be used to make decisions about nutritional management:

1. At pregnancy diagnosis or weaning
2. Thirty days before the first cow calves.
3. At the beginning of the breeding season
4. At the end of the breeding season.

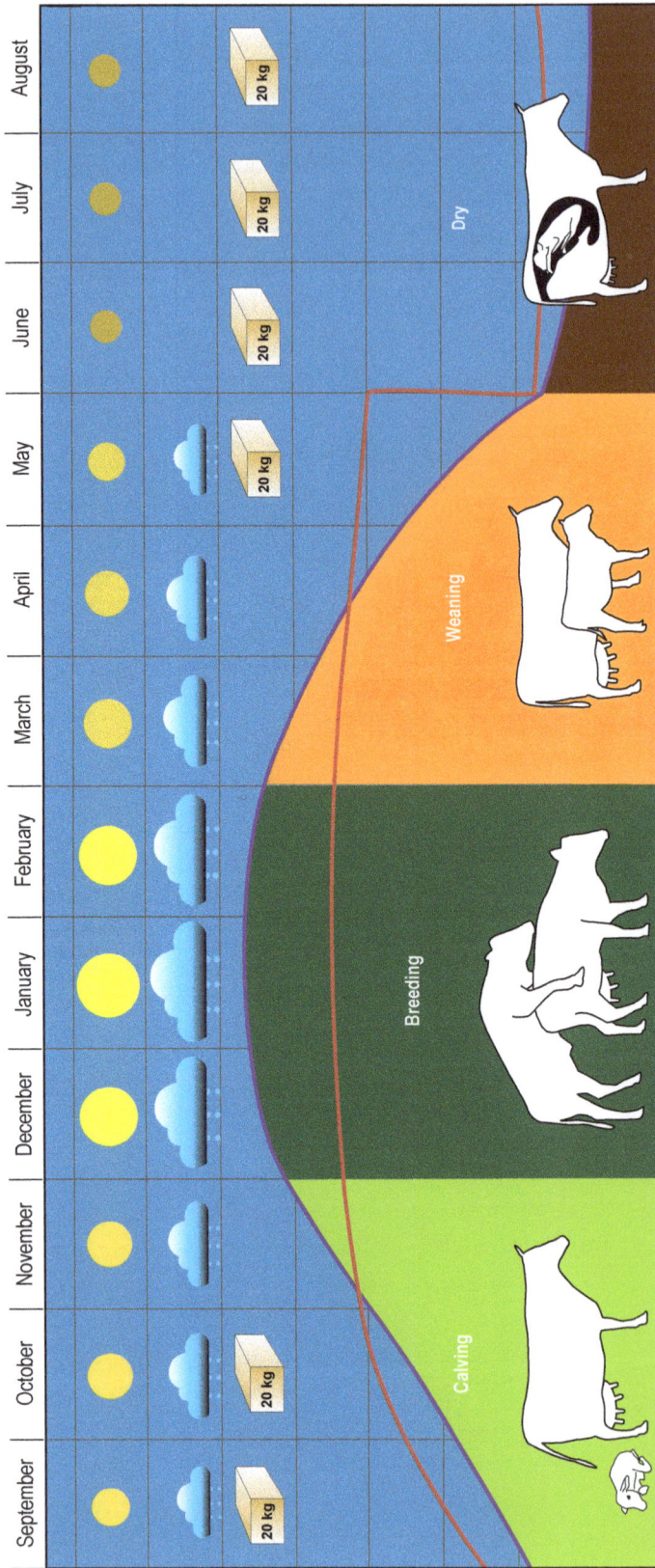

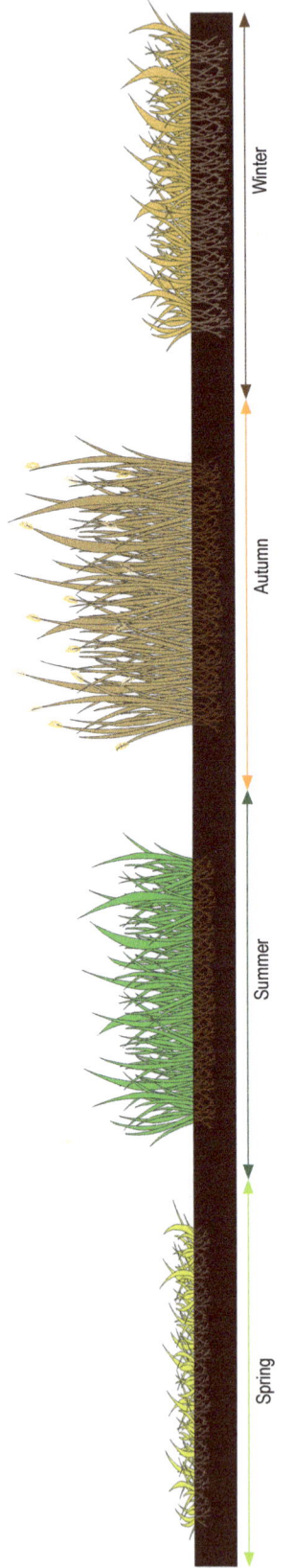

MONTHS	September	October	November	December	January	February	March	April	May	June	July	August

HEAT

PRECIPITATION (RAIN)

SUPPLEMENTARY FEEDING — 20 kg

Nutrition Available

Nutrition required

BREEDING CYCLE — Calving | Breeding | Weaning | Dry

GRASS

SOIL

SEASON — Spring | Summer | Autumn | Winter

Condition determination is done by determining the animal's fat and muscle reserves over the loins and around the pinbone (*see chart for explanatory details*).

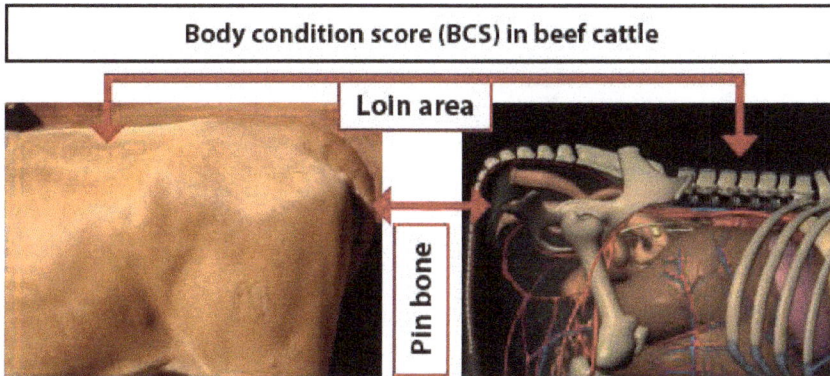

Body condition score (BCS) in beef cattle

Loin area

Pin bone

Determine the body fat and muscle reserves by observing as well as feeling (palpating) the loin area and pin bone.

Negative energy balance		Transition	Positive energy balance	
1	2	2.5	3	4
Loin area				
No eye muscle can be felt and the bone ends are sharp	Eye muscle very indented but the bone ends just feel rounded	The eye muscle is half full and the bone ends feel well rounded	The eye muscle is full and the bone ends can only be felt with pressure	The eye muscle is full and covered with fat and the bone ends can't be felt
Pin bone				
No fat between the skin and bone	1 mm fat can be felt under the skin	2-5 mm of fat can be felt under the skin	5-10 mm of fat under the skin	>10 mm of fat and can't feel the pin bone
1	2	2.5	3	4

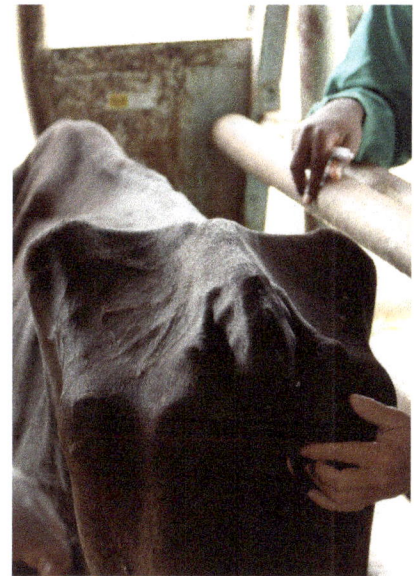

Body condition score 1. The cow is in very poor condition with almost no fat reserves and the hip bones are clearly visible.

Body condition score 2. The cow is in a reasonable condition but is not yet in optimal condition for breeding.

This cow is able to maintain good body condition while raising a calf to weaning age.

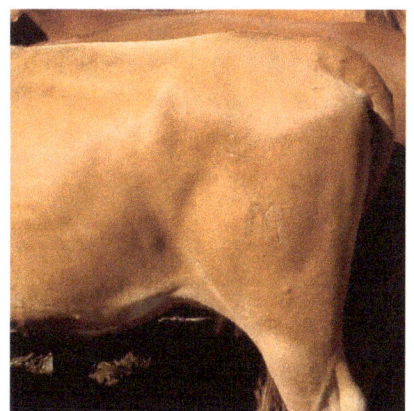

Body condition score 2,5. The cow is in the optimal condition for breeding, neither too thin nor too fat.

This cow has lost condition due to the drain of lactation on her body reserves.

Body condition as a management tool

Most of the cows in the herd (>90%) must have a body condition of 3 or more 30 days before the first cow calves. More than 90% of the herd must have body condition of 2,5 at the beginning of the breeding season and must improve in condition during this period.

Measuring body condition will allow adjustments of nutritional management to ensure high calving percentages. In many cases assessing the body condition of animals will identify the animals with unsuitable body frame or unsuitable breed for the environment. In these cases the breed or type of animal should be changed or the calving percentage will never improve.

Sheep and goats on extensive grazing

Since sheep and goats are mostly seasonal breeders, a good nutritional level is required just before the mating season (flushing), especially if the condition of the ewes is poor. Since most sheep and goats are raised on veld, their nutritional level will be determined by the quality of local grazing. This should be supplemented or at least improved late in pregnancy when the nutritional demands are high. Old land grazing is not suitable for pregnant ewes because of its low nutritional content and the presence of poisonous plants. Vitamin A supplementation should be done in animals on dry feeds, poor forage and pelleted rations.

"Flushing" of ewes is the additional feeding 2-3 weeks before breeding to stimulate ovulation. It is most effective in thin or poor condition ewes, but may not be necessary if ewes are in good condition as it can make them too fat. Flushing can be the feeding of concentrates, or moving them to better pastures. The feeding of "chocolate mealies" can be done but ensure that this is properly mixed and animals are given a period of adaptation or they will develop acidosis. For good milk production ewes must have adequate energy – if the grazing is inadequate this can be supplemented with a protein source such as soya bean oil cake which stimulates feed intake and increases energy intake. Planted pastures such as barley are ideal as an energy source, but only for a few hours a day.

Strip grazing is most economical and prevents trampling.

Creep feeding is strictly for lambs, so ewes should not have access to this feed. It supplies energy to supplement the protein supplied by the ewes' milk and can be given on demand to lambs from 3 weeks of age. Increasing the protein above 12% in creep will not improve performance. Do not add urea because an unweaned lamb does not yet have a functional rumen. If lambs are on veld or pasture roughage does not need to be added to the creep, but its addition at 15% or higher is recommended to limit acidosis.

Body condition assessment in small stock

The same basic principles around body condition apply assessment to small stock – ewes and does in poor condition will not conceive unless they have access to an increasing plane of nutrition before the seasonal breeding season. The diagram below shows how to monitor the body condition of small stock. Using this basic tool, the farmer will be able to decide whether supplementation is required. Supplementing ewes already in good condition before breeding can be wasteful and lead to overfat animals that may develop ketosis as a result.

Condition scoring in sheep, note the position of the hand with the thumb on the dorsal or vertical vertebrae process and the fingers on the transverse or horizontal process

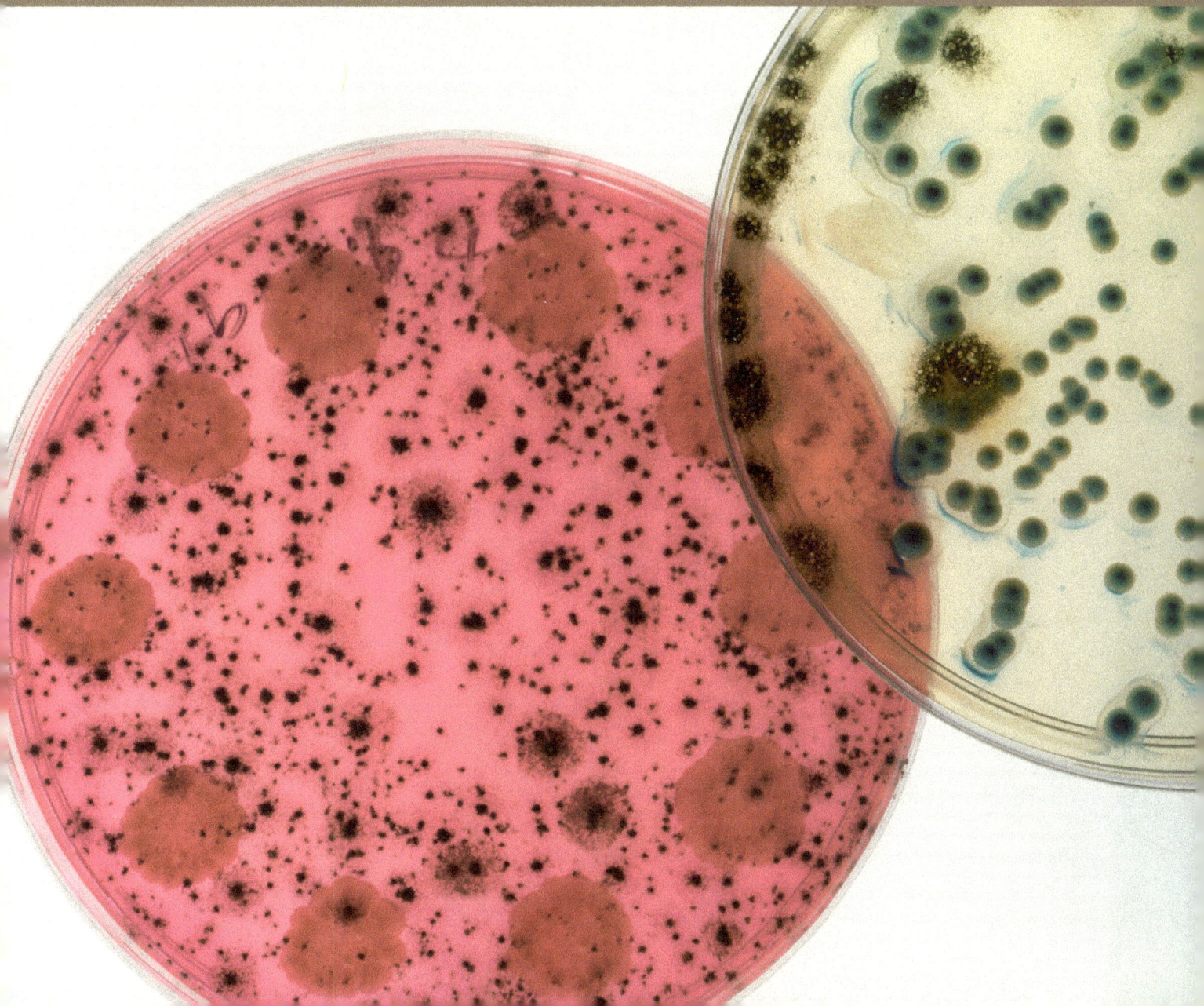

Diseases

ACUTE DEATHS

Some disease conditions show few if any specific symptoms so the stock owner will only notice that something is amiss when the animal is found dead. These are referred to as acute deaths. The most common causes of acute deaths in sheep are pasteurellosis, plant poisonings, anthrax, and the clostridial diseases which include pulpy kidney and gas gangrene infections. The major causes of acute deaths in cattle are the clostridia, various poisonings (including the plant poisoning "gousiekte") and anthrax.

Anthrax

Anthrax is caused by the bacterium Bacillus anthracis which forms spores and persists for very long periods in the soil. The spores are exposed when infected soil is grazed during dry seasons or when soil is disturbed by river courses or agricultural activities. Many livestock species are susceptible including cattle, sheep, goats, pigs and horses. Game animals are also susceptible and outbreaks occur from time to time in the Kruger National Park and Etosha Game Reserve.

Once the spores have been ingested or inhaled by the grazing animals, the bacteria multiply, invade the bloodstream and cause rapid death due to the production of potent toxins. During the incubation period animals have a fever but no typical symptoms are noticed by the stock owner. Occasionally animals may be seen showing convulsions in the terminal stages. The seepage of blood from the nose or the anus is typical of anthrax carcases but can be seen with other diseases too. If anthrax is suspected a specially stained blood smear should be made and examined by a veterinarian as the organism can be clearly seen under the microscope. The diagnosis can be confirmed on bacterial culture. Anthrax carcases should not be opened as this spreads the infection and can cause human infections during the process of cutting up the carcass. Anthrax is a controlled disease which means all confirmed cases must be reported to the State Veterinarian. Infected farms are quarantined until the outbreak is deemed to be over. The veterinarian will prescribe antibiotics to block the outbreak in an infected herd.

The anthrax vaccine which is currently used worldwide was developed by a South African, Max Sterne. The Sterne strain vaccine provides excellent immunity and should, by law, be applied annually to all ruminant livestock.

Animals usually die of anthrax before any symptoms are noticed.

Clostridial diseases

The clostridia are a broad group of bacteria which cause a wide range of diseases due to the toxins which they produce. Clostridial diseases of livestock can be divided into different groups based on the systems which they affect: those that affect the gastro-intestinal system **(enterotoxaemias)**, those that affect the muscles **(gas gangrene group)**, and those that affect the **nervous system**. The latter include tetanus and botulism which are discussed in the section on lameness. Clostridia are widespread in the environment and cannot be avoided or eradicated which is why vaccination is the most effective method of control.

Enterotoxaemias

C. perfringens A "Redgut" and wound infection

Whether this bacterium is the actual cause the condition known as "redgut" is still a controversial issue. In South Africa the condition occurs in sheep which are grazed entirely on lucerne or clover pastures, without receiving any source of roughage. Sheep die acutely and show blood-filled small intestines on post-mortem. The condition is thought by some to be caused by a large amount of gas production followed by displacement and strangulation of the intestines. Ensuring that animals on legume pastures receive some roughage every day has been shown to control the condition. *C. perfringens* A is included in multicomponent clostridial vaccines but manufacturers at present make no claim for the prevention of redgut syndrome. *C. perfringens* A can also occasionally cause wound infections which may be fatal.

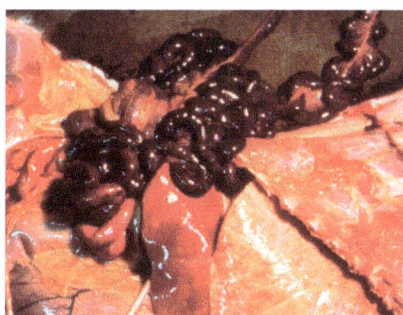

The typical appearance of "redgut" on post mortem

C. perfringens B (Lamb dysentery)

There are focal areas in SA where *C. perfringens* B causes problems in lambs. Lamb dysentery is a gastrointestinal condition that occurs within the first week of life, characterised by abdominal pain, bloody diarrhoea, and rapid death. On post-mortem examination the small intestine will show ulceration and haemorrhage. Treatment of affected lambs is seldom successful and therefore the only effective control measure is vaccination. The ewe must be vaccinated with a vaccine containing either type B or C organisms, since there is a cross-protection between the types. The ewes will then provide colostral immunity which will protect the lambs.

C. perfringens C (Necrotic enteritis)

Whether this condition occurs in ruminants in SA is unknown but the bacterium has been isolated from piglets, so it does occur in the country. In lambs the organism causes a syndrome very similar to that of lamb dysentery. If diagnosed, the condition can be prevented by vaccinating ewes with clostridial vaccines containing type B or C organisms.

C. perfringens D (Pulpy kidney)

Pulpy kidney is perhaps the single most important cause of deaths in small stock in SA. It is sometimes called overeating disease because it is precipitated by the increase of nutritional level of animals either by giving concentrated rations, moving animals to lush pastures or deworming of heavily parasitised sheep. The disease occurs most commonly in yearlings but is also seen in older sheep that have not been vaccinated. Lambs die acutely without showing symptoms a few days after an improvement in their nutrition. Post-mortal examinations are usually mainly negative with the exception of fluid accumulation in the heart sac (pericardium) and rapid breakdown of the kidneys. However, the latter change can be seen with some other conditions such as prussic acid poisoning (geilsiekte) and pasteurellosis, and it must be borne in mind that the kidneys of carcases in an advanced state of decomposition will also have "pulpy" kidneys.

Vaccination of sheep is the only method of control; lambs can be vaccinated from the age of 3 months, usually at weaning. As with all clostridial vaccines, pulpy kidney vaccination must be repeated within 3-4 weeks and annually thereafter.

Pulpy kidney causes acute deaths with no symptoms.

Clostridium perfringens intestinal infections in calves.
Calves on a high level of nutrition can develop gastro-intestinal conditions caused by *C. perfringens* bacteria.

It has been suggested that the "red gut" syndrome seen in feedlot cattle in South Africa is due to a proliferation of *C. perfringens* type A in the intestine. Similar conditions have been described in the USA as "jejunal haemorrhagic syndrome". The disease is acute, characterised by loss of appetite, bloat, haemorrhage in the gut and rapid deaths. Predisposing factors are possibly the high intake of concentrates and low roughage intake. There is no successful treatment for the condition. The use of vaccines for this condition is controversial although the organisms are included in certain vaccines. It is suggested that feed management can control the syndrome, namely consistent feeding especially with regard to the quantities, and restricting water intake after feeding. *C. perfringens* type A is included in some multicomponent vaccines because the organism causes wound infections, the so-called gas gangrene which also occurs in humans.

Newborn calves can develop necrotic enteritis as a result of C. perfringens type C. They show depression, weakness and may develop bloody diarrhoea. On post-mortem examination bleeding and necrosis of the gut may be seen.

C. perfringens type D, the cause of pulpy kidney in sheep, can cause an "overeating syndrome" in calves although it is fairly rare. On post-mortem the calves show kidney and brain damage. The syndromes caused by types C and D can be prevented by vaccination with multi-component clostridial vaccines.

Muscle gangrene group
Gas gangrene, quarter evil or black quarter

The syndrome known as black quarter or quarter evil is a gangrenous infection of the muscles of the body. There are a number of different clostridia which can cause the syndrome, but *C. chauvoei* is the most common cause. Other clostridia which cause a similar condition are *C. septicum*, *C. novyi*, and *C. sordelli*.

In **cattle** the disease occurs mostly in young cattle after weaning until roughly 3 years, but cases can also be seen in older animals. The organisms penetrate the muscles of cattle in the form of spores and remain dormant until the conditions in the muscle become suitable for their germination. It is still unknown what the precipitating factor is for the development of the disease. The bacteria germinate and produce a toxin which kills off the muscle tissue, and then spreads throughout the body causing death of the animal. The large muscles of the hindquarter are usually affected but occasionally it affects the muscles of the heart, diaphragm and tongue.

Cattle with quarter evil show stiffness and discomfort but the disease is seldom diagnosed at this stage and animals die acutely. Characteristically animals that have died of quarter evil have swollen carcases due to gas formation and rapid decomposition. On post-mortem the affected muscles are dark red to black when cut, may contain gas bubbles, and have a rancid smell in cases of *C. chauvoei* infection.

The diagnosis of quarter evil is confirmed by taking smears of muscle tissue at post-mortem.

Acute deaths caused by clostridial gas gangrene can be confused with anthrax cases. If anthrax is suspected, a blood smear must be examined by a vet before the carcass can be opened up.

In **sheep**, black quarter occurs after shearing, when the cuts from shears allow the invasion of *C. chauvoei* bacteria which are present in soil and manure. Some days after shearing sheep develop a fever, show depression and lameness, and die rapidly soon after the appearance of symptoms. On post mortem the affected muscles will be swollen, show gas accumulation and a black discolouration. The diagnosis of the condition can be confirmed on examining muscle smears in the lab or performing bacterial isolations. There are other clostridia such as *C. novyi*, *C. septicum* and occasionally *C. sordelli* which can also cause black quarter in sheep.

Gas gangrene infections in sheep and cattle is controlled by the use of a multiclostridial vaccine containing all the causative strains. The vaccine is generally given at weaning age, repeated 3-4 weeks later followed by annual revaccination.

The muscle lesions seen with black quarter.

C. novyi Big head ("Dikkop")

This condition occurs when rams fight and bruise the skin around the base of the horns. The *C. novyi* bacteria invade through small wounds in the skin and grow in the bruised tissue, causing massive swelling of the head. The rams may survive if treated with antibiotics but most commonly they die of the toxins produced by the infection. The condition can be confused with "bottle jaw" (parasite infestation), blue tongue, plant poisoning with "dubbeltjies" and snakebite. "Big head" can be controlled with vaccination with a clostridial vaccine containing either *C. novyi* type B or D as there is cross-immunity between the two types.

A case of "big head" in a ram

C. septicum Post-lambing gangrene and braxy

Ewes that have difficult births, particularly when lambs are very big, can develop gangrene of the uterus after lambing. The *C. septicum* organisms invade the uterus through small wounds which then multiply in the bruised tissue of the uterus. The ewes die very rapidly after lambing due to the toxin produced by the bacteria. The carcass shows swelling and blue discoloration around the vulva and perineum. On post-mortem the uterus shows typical signs of gas gangrene.

Another condition caused by this bacterium is braxy: this the bacterial invasion of the abomasum or stomach with *C. septicum*, after the animal has consumed frozen grass or ice water. This causes damage to the muscle of the stomach which provides suitable conditions for the invasion and multiplication by *C. septicum* organisms. The condition causes acute death and the cause is usually only identified on post-mortem.

Both conditions can be prevented using a clostridial vaccine which includes *C. septicum*.

Other *Clostridia* spp.

There are other less common clostridia such as *C. sordelli* which are included in vaccines because they can occasionally cause gangrenous infections. *Clostridium haemolyticum* is an organism which secondarily infects livers with primary liver fluke damage. The bacteria produce a toxin which causes haemolysis or destruction of red blood cells resulting in red discoloration of the urine, anaemia and death. The condition has never been diagnosed in RSA but the organism is included in some imported vaccines.

A note on clostridial vaccines

Multi-component clostridial vaccines are available for cattle and sheep. They contain the clostridia which cause enterotoxaemia and the most common causes of gas gangrene, as well as tetanus. They provide broad coverage against the clostridial diseases, which eliminates the need for identifying causative organisms when animals die, which is very often a difficult and time-consuming undertaking. All clostridial vaccines must given twice initially with a 3-4 week interval and thereafter annually. Failure to give booster vaccinations within the specified period will not give adequate results.

Pasteurella trehalosi septicaemia

Pasteurella trehalosi can cause rapid death in lambs due to septicaemia. This usually occurs in feedlot lambs and yearlings during stress periods such as weaning, dietary stress and bad weather. The lambs affected are usually in good condition and will die acutely without any noticeable symptoms, but close examination may reveal sheep in the incubation phase, typically looking depressed and separating themselves from the flock.

The bacteria multiply in lungs and liver and invade bloodstream. Typically, the carcass shows signs of septicaemia and isolation of organism from liver, lung and spleen will confirm the disease. The disease can be confused with other acute diseases such as pulpy kidney and pneumonia.

Sick animals may be treated with a course of oxytetracycline injections, but vaccination is the most cost-effective method of prevention. *P. trehalosi* vaccines for sheep contain the strains which are most likely to cause septicaemia and pneumonia. Vaccination should be done before the danger periods when animals are most likely to develop septicaemia. Initially the vaccine must be boosted 3-4 weeks later and thereafter annual revaccination is sufficient.

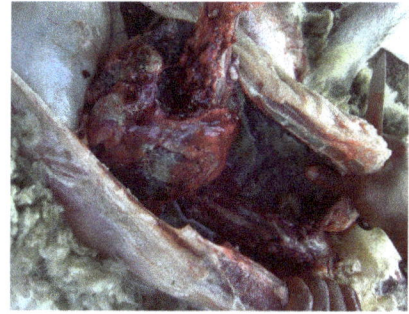

Septicaemia caused by Pasteurella trehalosi

Ultratet G0296

Ultratet LA G2857

Ultratet LA 200 G3559

SUMMARY OF CLOSTRIDIAL DISEASES

Clostridium species	Cattle	Sheep
C. chauvoei	most common cause of quarter evil	post-shearing quarter evil
C. septicum	quarter evil	post-lambing gangrene, braxy
C. novyi	quarter evil	"Big head"
C. sordelli	quarter evil	quarter evil
C. haemolyticum	"redwater" – not in RSA	N/A
C. tetani	tetanus	tetanus
C. botulinum C	botulism in feed	botulism
C. botulinum D	botulism in veld animals	botulism
C. perfringens A	wound infection, redgut (?)	redgut (?)
C. perfringens B	necrotic enteritis	lamb dysentery
C. perfringens type C	necrotic enteritis of calves	necrotic enteritis in lambs
C. perfringens type D	enterotoxaemia in feedlot animals (pulpy kidney)	pulpy kidney

Plant poisonings

Various plant poisonings can cause acute death notably those containing cardiac glycosides (various types of tulp, "slangkop" and "plakkies") and "gousiekte"-plants. These conditions are discussed under the section on plant poisoning. Prussic acid poisoning occurs due to the presence of prussic acid which occurs in a wide range of plants in various chemical forms. The details are discussed under the section on plant poisons.

DAIRY

The modern dairy cow is an astonishing animal: in one lactation she produces 10 to 20 times the amount of milk required to raise a calf; within 3 months of calving, she falls pregnant again, which means that she can have one lactation a year. Her metabolic rate is 30% higher than that of a beef cow. Given these statistics it is clear that the dairy cow is under tremendous stress and it is therefore no surprise to find that she is prone to metabolic and other diseases.

Heat stress

European dairy breeds, which are most commonly used for milk production in SA, suffer heat stress when the temperature is higher than 20-22°C. Heat stress has an effect on the conception rate as well as on milk production; cows that are heat stressed do not show external signs of being on heat (called "silent heat") and are therefore not mated or inseminated. After nutrition, failure to detect heat is the most important cause of prolonged inter-calving periods. Oestrus monitors can be used to help detect heat in cattle. To reduce the effect of heat stress it is important to provide dairy cows with sufficient shade, water and ventilation. Bear in mind that the water intake of a dairy animal is much higher than that of a beef animal and in summer months, it may be as high as 150 litres per cow per day.

Infectious diseases

Dairy cattle are susceptible to infectious diseases as are all other cattle but conditions which affect milk production are of specific importance, namely lumpy skin disease (see chapter on Wounds and skin) and three-day stiff sickness (see chapter on Lameness).

Ketosis (Domsiekte)

The condition called ketosis or "domsiekte" occurs in dairy cattle a few days to a few weeks after calving. Lactation exerts a huge glucose demand on the cow and if she has insufficient liver reserves of glycogen (stored glucose), her body will begin to break down fat, resulting in the release of ketones which are toxic in high concentrations. The primary cause of ketosis is usually insufficient energy in the ration, either in late pregnancy or during early lactation, or due to individual cows not eating because of an underlying disease like pneumonia or metritis. Cows that are grossly overweight are more susceptible to the disease because the intra-abdominal fat prevents adequate dry matter intake and worsens the energy deficiency cycle. Even cows receiving adequate nutrition during early lactation are in a negative energy balance because of the high energy demand of milk production and any situation that may exacerbate this negative energy balance, increases the chance of developing ketosis significantly.

Farmers should be aware that there are two main types of ketosis based on the causes:

Type 1 Reduced energy intake:

This type of ketosis is a result of a sudden drop in energy intake due to underfeeding, adverse weather events or heat stress which will prevent the cows from eating sufficient amounts of dry matter. It can be prevented by ensuring adequate dry matter intake cows or by ensuring any feed restriction (if needed) is imposed gradually (e.g. over a week). "Silage ketosis" occurs when cows are fed poor quality silage, that has not been properly fermented. To prevent this only good quality silage should be fed.

Type 2 - Post calving ketosis

Ketosis generally occurs post-calving when the cow is already in a negative energy balance and is mobilising excess body fat to meet the demands of milk production. Cows that are too fat at calving (BCS > 4 on a scale of 1-5) or cows that have been overfed pre-calving are particularly at risk. The risk of Type 2 ketosis doubles when calving BCS increases from 4 to 4.5 or 5. Cows that have been in milk for a long time before conceiving again tend to be particularly at risk because they had a lot of time to build body reserves.

The symptoms of ketosis are depression and a typical staring expression. The cow also shows constipation, a loss of weight and reduction in milk production. The diagnosis of ketosis is based on the history as well as the detection of ketones in the urine.

Veterinarians treat ketosis by supplementing glucose intravenously, administering an energy substrate such as propylene glycol orally and sometimes cortisone injections. Prevention is the proper management of the energy intake and body condition of the pregnant and lactating cow. Nutritional management is important to prevent ketosis: cows must not be allowed to get too fat and must have a daily intake of good quality roughage during the dry period.

Ketosis Diagnostic Kit

Megamilk V21623

Milk fever

Milk fever is caused by an imbalance in blood levels of calcium and phosphorous. The condition is seen in high-producing cows shortly after calving, as a result of a rapid drop of calcium in the blood caused by milk production. It is particularly common in Jersey cattle. Roughly 72 hours after calving, the cow will show signs of being unsteady on her feet, will finally lie down and be unable to rise. In the advanced stages of milk fever, the cow lies with her head held against the body. She refuses to eat, her eyes are dull and the ears are cold. From this stage the cow progresses into a coma and death follows if the condition is untreated.

Milk fever must be treated as soon as possible with injections of calcium to prevent the complications which can arise once these cows go down. "Downer cows" seldom recover because they develop complications such as mastitis and muscle damage Such cows often have to be slaughtered.

Veterinarians treat milk fever by intravenous administration of calcium salts while monitoring the heart function during the process because rapid calcium infusion can cause cardiac arrest. Sub-cutaneous administration of the calcium takes longer to reverse the condition but will prevent cardiac arrest. A dose of 200-500 ml of a 25% calcium borogluconate can be given subcutaneously. When cows are milked again some may show a relapse so the treatment will need to be repeated.

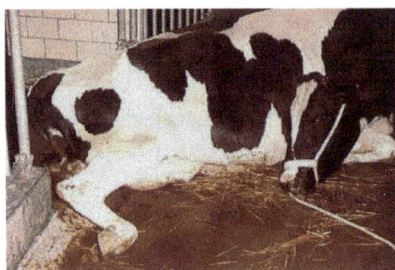

A case of milk fever in a dairy cow showing the typical sign of the head held against the body.

Calcimax Oral V3209

Mastitis

Mastitis is the single most important cause of reduced milk production in dairies. It is an occupational hazard of high producing dairy cattle because of the mechanisation of the milking process as well as the environment in which dairy cows are kept. Selection of good udder conformation is important but correct milking machine management, hygienic practices and supervision will contribute to reducing mastitis problems.

Mastitis is most commonly caused when bacteria gain entrance, via the teat canal, into the udder. The body reacts by mobilising white blood cells into the udder in an attempt to destroy the invading bacteria. This brings about changes in the milk which in mild cases are not visible but which in severe cases will be obvious to the stockman. The symptoms and severity of mastitis depend on the causative organism and the extent of the infection.

Sub-clinical mastitis (non-visible mastitis) is a low-grade infection in which the somatic cell count (white blood cell count) is raised but this is not visible to the naked eye. It is one of the most common causes of high somatic cell count in milk and is an insidious cause of low milk production, but because bacteria are present in the udder there is also the constant danger of acute and sub-acute mastitis flaring up. Because sub-clinical mastitis cannot be detected visually, somatic cell counts reported by the milk depot of >250 000 in the bulk milk sample is usually the first indicator of a problem. Cowside tests such as conductivity meters or the California Mastitis Test will enable detection of sub-clinically infected animals, and problem animals can be treated with intra-mammary therapy (see later).

Note that there is another type of sub-clinical mastitis (aseptic mastitis) in which the cell count is raised but no bacteria are present in the milk. It occurs due to rough handling, prolonged milking or defective milking equipment such as milking lines employing vacuum suction which is too severe. Ideal vacuum at peak milk flow for average milkers should be around 40 kPa. Using high vacuum pressure may damage the teat canals (sometimes permanently) which facilitates the entry of mastitis-causing organisms. A vacuum that is too low will cause liner slip with resulting vacuum fluctuation. Vacuum fluctuations > 10 kPa at peak milk flow warrant further investigation.

Clinical mastitis (visible mastitis) is classified into 4 main types:

- Sub-acute mastitis: The cow appears normal but the milk is abnormal when examined in a strip cup.
- Acute mastitis: The cow has a fever, the udder is red and sensitive. The milk is abnormal, showing clots and may be bloodstained.
- Peracute mastitis or blue udder: The udder shows clear signs of mastitis and in addition the cow is very ill. This form is usually caused by Gram-negative bacteria such as *E. coli*, *Pseudomonas* and *Klebsiella*. This form of mastitis usually requires immediate veterinary treatment to prevent save the animal's life.
- Chronic mastitis: This term is used to refer to cows with repeated episodes of acute or sub-acute mastitis, due to ineffective treatment or a deep-seated infection, which occurs most commonly with *Staph. aureus* infections.

Diagnosing the cause of mastitis

The most important basic step in solving mastitis problems is the identification of the causative agent. This must be done quickly and efficiently by allowing a veterinarian to take sterile samples of the affected milk for bacterial isolation before treating with an antibiotic. Once the causative agent has been identified the correct antibiotic can be selected and contributing factors can be sought and eliminated.

The most commonly encountered mastitis-causing organisms are discussed below:

Streptococcus agalactiae

This bacterium is specifically adapted to the cow's udder and is introduced into the herd by infected cows. It is very contagious, and is spread from one cow to another during milking, either on the hands of milkers, by rubber teat liners or by the milking machine itself (known as "cow-to-cow" infection). *Strep. agalactiae* is susceptible to economical remedies like penicillin G/streptomycin combinations and can be cleared up easily with proper treatment and good hygiene. This organism may exist in a herd as a low-grade infection, and will flare up should there be a breakdown in management pertaining to proper teat-dipping and dry cow therapy. It can affect 50% of the herd.

Staphylococcus aureus

Staph. aureus is an environmental pathogen, but once one cow is infected it turns into a cow-to-cow pathogen and spreads throughout the herd during the milking process. It is widely distributed in the cow's environment since it occurs on the skin of animals and humans. Once the infection has established itself in a herd, chronic or persistent infections develop, and this will serve as a constant source of infection for other cows. *Staph. aureus* mastitis can be difficult to treat because of its tendency to form micro-abscesses in the udder which cannot easily be penetrated by antibiotics. Although some strains are still susceptible to treatment with penicillin G/streptomycin combinations, numerous strains are penicillin resistant and may need treatment with cloxacillin/ampilcillin combinations or prescription remedies available through veterinarians. Successful *Staph. aureus* treatment can be achieved by drying the cow off and giving appropriate dry-cow remedies. Cows with chronic Staph. aureus cases must be culled as they have repeated flare-ups, and they serve as a source of infection for other animals.

Coagulase Negative Staphylococci (CNS)

This group of pathogens has become increasingly important causes of mastitis in recent years. These pathogens include *Staphylococcus epidermidis*, *S.hyicus* and *S. simulans*. The mastitis caused does not seem to be quite as severe as *Staphylococcus aureus* for example, but it is important to note that infection by CNS organisms predisposes the cow to infections by more serious pathogens.

Streptococcus uberis

This bacterium differs from other streptococci by being an opportunistic environmental pathogen which occurs on the skin of the udder and in bedding. In recent years *Strep. uberis* has become an increasingly prominent mastitis-causing pathogen probably due to the control of other mastitis organisms.

Gram-negative mastitis

The main causes of Gram-negative mastitis are coliforms (*E. coli* and *Klebsiella*) which are faecal bacteria and *Pseudomonas* which is an organism associated with water and soil. These organisms occur in the environment and flourish in dairies under wet conditions. *Pseudomonas* outbreaks are often associated with cows being allowed to drink at muddy dams. Gram-negative mastitis often occurs in high producing cows when environmental, milk machine or other hygiene factors are compromised.

These gram-negative bacteria cause peracute or acute cases which can kill the cow as a result of the bacterial toxins secreted in the udder. Rapid systemic treatment is needed with specific antibiotics as these organisms are not generally susceptible to remedies sold over the counter.

Treatment of mastitis

The correct treatment for a mastitis

case can be selected once the causative organism/s have been identified, and in the case of *Staph. aureus*, will also depend on whether the strain involved is susceptible to natural or synthetic penicillins. The administration of intramammary preparations must be done correctly to get the best results. First the affected quarter/s must be milked out to prevent the remedy being diluted. The teat tip must be disinfected with surgical spirits or 70% alcohol, and then the plastic cap of the syringe can be removed. The remedy must be injected into the teat canal and then the quarter is massaged to aid dispersal of the product within the udder tissue. The treatment must be repeated at subsequent milkings as recommended by the manufacturer. Failure to treat adequately will result in repeated flare-ups of mastitis. The golden rule is not to stop treating as soon as the milk seems visually normal again. Complete the course according to the manufacturer's recommendation.

Prevention of mastitis

Correct use of milking machine: under normal circumstances the teat canal is effective in keeping invading organism out, but these protective measures break down under certain circumstances including ageing of the cow. However, milking practices such as over-milking are very frequently the culprits. Other factors relating to the milk machine are cracked teat liners which serve as places for bacterial contamination and cause slippage of the milking cluster. Other predisposing factors are fluctuation of milk machine vacuum and failing to backwash the machines correctly.

Teat dipping: In general, teat dipping should be done after milking, when the milking cluster has been removed. The teat dip used must be registered for this purpose and must be made up to the correct dilution unless it is a ready-to-use product. This protects the outside of the teat canal when it is most vulnerable. Pre-milking teat dipping can be done if the herd is experiencing problems with environmental types of mastitis or viral infections such as herpes mammillitis or pseudo-cowpox. The practice of udder washing is not recommended as it causes pooling of dirty water at the teat tip. If muddy teats need to be cleaned, they can be briefly squirted with clean water and then dried off with a disposable paper towel.

Good general hygiene: Regular and effective cleaning and disinfection of buildings, of milking equipment, and storage tanks, as well as fly control will contribute to the prevention of mastitis.

Foremilk examination: The use of a strip cup to examine milk from the four quarters can identify sub-acute cases of mastitis and prevent the spread to the entire milking herd.

A note on antibiotic residues: It should be noted that all intra-mammary preparations have a withdrawal period which indicates how long the milk of treated animals must be withheld from the bulk tank. This is based on the residues which are acceptable for human consumption. Even at these low levels, the milk may not be suitable for use in products such as yoghurt or cheese where micro-organisms are used to "cultivate" the product.

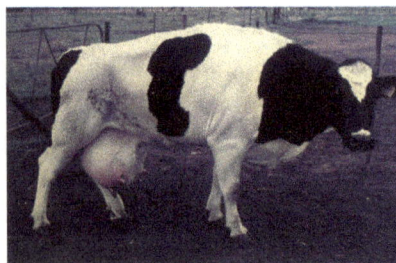
The Californian mastitis test kit used to detect sub-clinical mastitis.

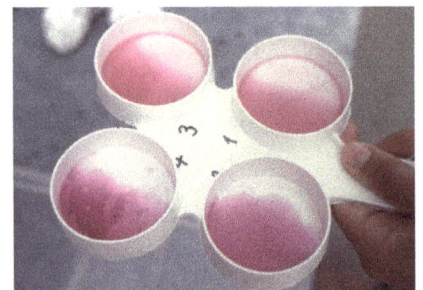

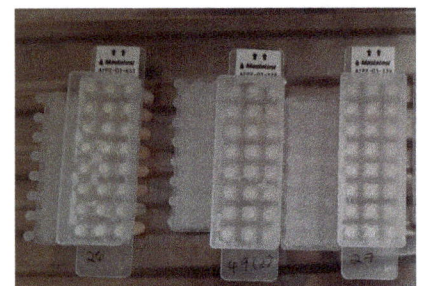
Afrivet mastitis diagnosis kit

Reproductive problems *(see separate section)*

Teat conditions of dairy cows

Lumpy skin disease: This condition involves the skin, and other organs including the teats and udders. It is a disease that has serious consequences for dairy cattle and preventative immunisation is essential (see chapter on Skin and wounds).

Allerton virus (Pseudo lumpy skin disease/ Herpes mammillitis):

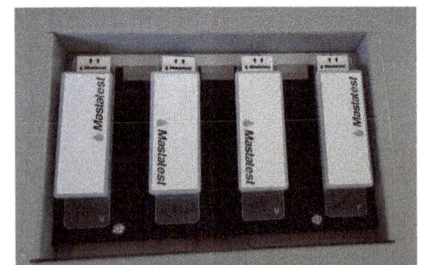
A severe case of clinical mastitis

This is usually a mild virus infection affecting the skin but can involve the teats and udders.

Other virus infections: Virus infections like warts (papillomatosis virus), herpes, pseudocowpox, cowpox and vaccinia virus cause specific infections of the teats. These conditions are usually introduced into the herd by infected animals. They are infectious, painful and can cause entrance of mastitis-producing bacteria. When outbreaks of local viral infections of the teats occur, veterinary help must be sought for diagnosis and treatment.

Non-infectious conditions of teats: Chemical irritation or chapping of teats can be caused by incorrect dilution of teat dips, using irritant or unregistered teat products. These conditions can predispose cows to mastitis. The cause of dry or chapped teats must be identified with the help of a veterinarian.

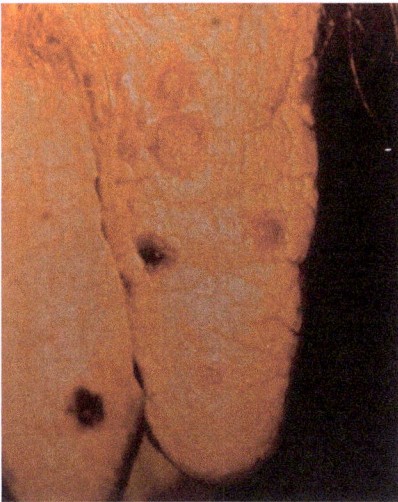

Pseudopox infection of the teats can pre-dispose to mastitis

Ticks and tick-borne diseases

Tick control in dairies is important for many reasons: firstly, ticks can severely damage the udders and teat but in addition heavy infestations can reduce production and transmit diseases such as anaplasmosis, redwater and in some areas, heartwater. Because dairy cattle are under enormous stress, they are very susceptible to tick-borne diseases (TBD); in addition to this problem immunisation against TBD is also stressful and may affect milk production. Intensive tick control without vaccination against tick borne diseases is therefore the most practical approach but this requires excellent management since any relaxation of tick control will cause an outbreak of TBD. Only dips/pour-ons that have no milk withdrawal requirements are suitable for dairy cattle (formamidines amitraz and cymiazol, pyrethroids not exceeding 0,5%). Dips/pour-ons containing amitraz will give good tick control but additional fly control remedies will be needed (combinations of are also available). Pyrethroid containing dips (flumethin, deltamethrin, cypermetrin) will give control of flies as well as ticks. When regular chemical control is practiced the farmer must be alert to the emergence of tick resistance. For more details on tick control, tick-borne diseases and management of resistance see the section on Ectoparasites.

Recommended tick and fly products for dairy animals

Afrivet Redline Pour-On G4245

Deltapor 5 Pour-On G4252

Eraditick Plus Pour On G4251

Ecobash Plunge and Spray G3382

Eraditick 125 Plunge and Spray G3585

Eraditick 250 Plunge and Spray G4047

Mistifly Green

Flybuster Fly Trap Kit

Eradifly Granular

EYE AND EAR

Bleeding ears

The adults of the brown ear tick (*Rhipicephalus appendiculatus*) cluster in the ears of cattle causing blood to leak from the tick wounds or the so-called "bleeding ears". These ticks are found in the more easterly parts of the country and the adults become problematic from December to March. For descriptions of these ticks and their control see the chapter on ticks.

Cancer of eye

Cattle, especially Herefords and Simmentalers, and even indigenous breeds such as Nguni, may develop a cancer called squamous cell carcinoma on the skin adjacent to the eye. These appear as small, raised areas initially but then develop into larger wart-like growths. Many of these regress, but a small proportion become malignant and invade the eye tissue as well as spreading to other parts of the body. The cause is thought to be the action of sunlight on the unpigmented areas around the eyes.

If this condition is suspected a veterinarian must be consulted. Early surgical removal can prevent problems developing further. Breeders are usually encouraged to breed animals with pigmentation around the eyes and not to use affected animals as breeding material.

Deafness

The spinose ear tick *Otobius megnini* occurs in the arid areas of the country and inhabits kraals and stables. The ticks infest the ear canal of a variety of animals including cattle, sheep and goats. This causes severe irritation and can lead to the rupture of the ear drum resulting in deafness. For description and control measures see the section on ticks.

Ear loss

Animals may lose ears as a sequel to the infestation of tick wounds being secondarily infested by the cattle screwworm *Chrysomyia bezziana*. For control measures, see the sections on ticks and flies.

Gedoelstia Popeye ("Uitpeuloog")

The invasion of the eyes of sheep and goats by the larval stages of *Gedoelstia* flies causes "popeye", the protrusion of the eye due to severe tissue inflammation and damage. For more details see the section on flies.

Genetic conditions

Genetic problems of eyes are seen at birth, and range from cataracts, squinting and conformational problems of the eye, particularly inverted eyelids (entropion) in lambs. Such animals should be removed from breeding herds as the defects are usually genetic and corrective surgery is not economical.

Infectious blindness or "Pinkeye"

Various infectious agents can colonise the eye and cause infectious blindness, for example *Moraxella sp* and *Chlamydia*. Certain primary factors are thought to predispose to these infections, namely high levels of ultra-violet radiation and vitamin A deficiency.

Infection is introduced into herds or flocks by infected carrier animals, often with no observable signs. The first cases seen are usually in young animals which are the most susceptible; the condition can spread explosively throughout the herd or flock, to in-contact animals either by direct contact or aided by fly or possibly also moth transmission.

The first signs seen are watering eyes, sensitivity to light, reddening and swelling of the eyelids. The watery discharge later becomes yellow and thick. The surface of the eye becomes blue and later white (so-called "pearl" formation) and may eventually ulcerate. The scarring of the surface of the eye may resolve or remain permanently causing partial blindness.

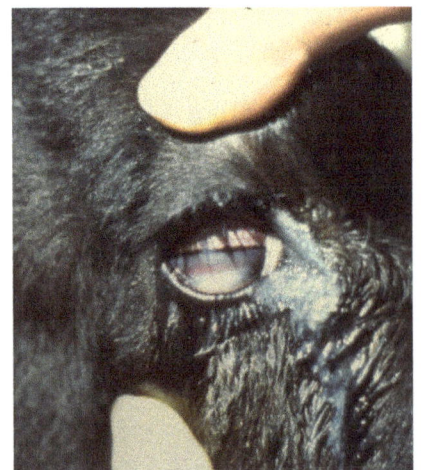

A case of infectious blindness caused by Moraxella bovis

Diagnosis is based on the clinical symptoms but a veterinarian can take swabs for bacterial culture to determine the specific causative organisms. Affected animals must be separated from the herd and placed in shady, dust-free conditions. Intramuscular injection with long acting tetracyclines is the most effective treatment and is preferable to using eye ointments which is painful for the animal and needs regular application. Insect control may be needed to prevent transmission to uninfected animals. Vitamin A injections may enhance the immunity to eye conditions. Moraxella vaccines are available for the prevention of outbreaks in cattle.

Ultratet LA
G2857

Ultratet LA 200
G3559

Ketosis (Domsiekte)

Ketosis is a metabolic disease of ewes which occurs shortly before lambing. Fat is broken down for energy and ketones are produced as by-product. These ketones are toxic, causing docile behaviour and apparent blindness. For more details, see chapter on reproductive problems.

Poisonings

Certain stock remedies can cause blindness in stock when the recommended dose is exceeded. Examples of such remedies are rafoxanide and closantel. Poisonous plants such as chinkerinchee (Ornithogalum sp) are a known cause of blindness in sheep. See the section on poisonings for more details.

Trauma

Lacerations of the cornea, the tough outer layer of the eye, if small and superficial may heal uneventfully or may become infected with resultant blindness or loss of the eye. Irritation of the eyes due to plants with sharp seeds such as *Hibiscus cannabinus* (wild stock rose) found on old lands, may cause infections and resultant blindness. Since eye surgery is a delicate and expensive procedure, it is seldom done on livestock. Animals blind in one eye will cope well, while totally blind animals will have to be euthanased.

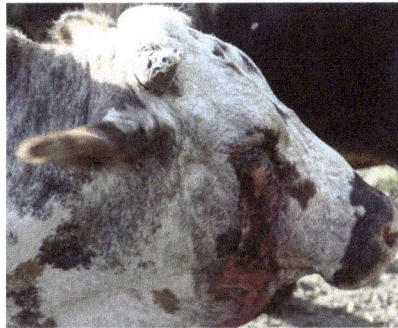

Wounds inflicted by horns can severely damage the eye causing infection and blindness.

Viral causes of blindness

Animals may develop keratitis (inflammation of the cornea) as a sequel to infection with some viral diseases such as bovine malignant catarrh, bovine viral diarrhoea and lumpy skin disease. Since these conditions are of viral origin there is no cure except for antibiotic therapy to prevent secondary infection.

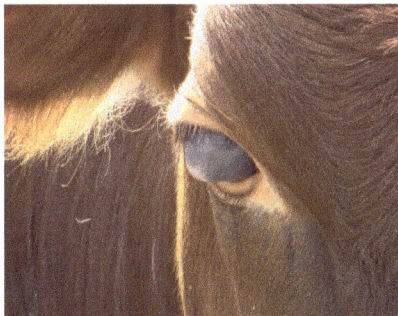

Keratitis caused by the Bovine Malignant Catarrh virus or "snotsiekte".

Vitamin A deficiency (Night blindness)

Vitamin A is supplied in sufficient quantities by green feed, but deficiencies may arise in animals fed dried or pelleted rations. Severe deficiencies can cause "night blindness" in cattle, which results in vision impairment in low light. Vitamin A deficiencies also causes reduced fertility, retained afterbirths and rough hair coats. For details on supplementation, see the chapter on Nutrition.

Vit-Aid Injectable
G0678

GASTROINTESTINAL

The gastrointestinal (GIT) system in ruminants includes in order of progression the mouth, pharynx (throat), oesophagus, the forestomachs (rumen, reticulum, and omasum), the abomasum or true stomach, the small intestine, and the colon or large intestine which terminates in the rectum. GIT disorders can be caused by trauma, incorrect feeding, poisoning, infections or parasite infestations. In addition, various infectious diseases can cause lesions in the mouth or tongue and need to be differentiated from each other.

Acidosis (Grain overload)

This results with the sudden intake of a large quantity of carbohydrate-rich feed such as grain. This can either be accidental or due to feedlot managers failing to allow sufficient time for animals to adapt to a high carbohydrate diet. The feeding of carbohydrates to ruminants causes an increase in the gram-positive bacteria, specifically *Streptococcus bovis*. These bacteria break down the carbohydrates into large amounts of lactic acid. This sudden increase in lactic acid levels causes the inflammation of the rumen and a drop in the pH of the blood (acidosis). The latter is a serious condition which will cause a circulatory collapse with renal failure, collapse and death.

Diagnosis of the condition is usually obvious since there will be a history of accidental gorging on grain or a sudden introduction of a high concentration of grain into the diet. Depending on the amount eaten, animals will show a variety of symptoms from temporary loss of appetite and mild, greyish and sour-smelling diarrhoea to more serious cases which show staggering and collapse. Examination of the animals by a veterinarian will show a rumen pH below 5.

Mildly affected animals will resume eating again within 3-4 days, and their condition will be improved by administering antacids and supplying good quality hay. Mortality is high in severe cases and emergency slaughter should be considered, as animals need intensive veterinary treatment. They will need intravenous bicarbonate fluid administration, and even removal of the rumen content.

Animals that survive severe attacks may have complications like fungal or bacterial rumenitis and laminitis.

Prevent the condition by ensuring accidental overeating of grain does not occur. Feedlot animals should be allowed 3 weeks to adapt to a gradual increase of carbohydrate in the ration.

Damage to the rumen after a bout of acidosis.

Lacticon Production Enhancers V21624

Megamilk Production Enhancer V211623

Blue tongue

This virus disease which occurs in summer causes ulcers in the mouth and swelling of the head and tongue, as well as other symptoms. See the chapter on lameness for a more detailed account of the disease.

Bloat

This is the massive distention of the abdomen due to the accumulation of gases of fermentation in the reticulum. Under normal circumstances the gas produced by the fermentation process in the rumen is eructated (burped) out through the oesophagus, but with cases of bloat this cannot occur.

The most common type is **frothy bloat** which occurs when animals graze on leguminous pastures such as lucerne and clover. The high level of proteins in these pastures causes carbon dioxide to form frothy gas bubbles which accumulate in the rumen causing severe pressure on the abdomen and later on in the lungs. **Free gas bloat** does occasionally occur as a result of some obstruction to the oesophagus.

Symptoms of bloat are the massive distention of the abdomen, difficulty with breathing, regurgitation of rumen contents and finally collapse and death.

Frothy bloat must be treated by administering antifoaming agents directly into the rumen through

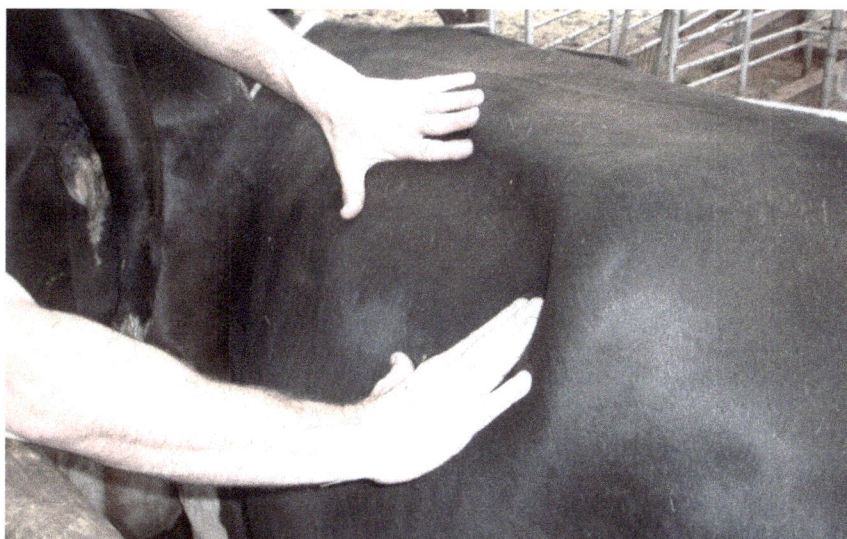
The paralumbar fossa allows access to the rumen for the relief of free gas bloat.

the passing of a stomach tube or insertion of a trocar directly into the rumen through the paralumbar fossa, a triangle on the animal's left side formed between the ribs, vertebrae and the hind leg (see the photo). If the condition is very serious, the rumen will have to be opened and emptied.

Frothy bloat must be prevented by dosing animals preventatively with anti-foaming agents before placing them on grazing, feeding hay before allowing them on pastures or limiting the time spent grazing on leguminous pastures.

Free gas bloat is caused usually by an obstruction in the oesophagus, which can be a lymph node, tumour or a foreign body. This type of bloat can be relieved by inserting a trocar through the rumen wall via the paralumbar fossa.

Braxy *(see acute diseases)*

Bovine Malignant Catarrh
(see respiratory conditions)

Coccidiosis
Coccidiosis occurs mostly in animals under a year of age. See diseases of young animals for more details about the disease.

Dental attrition
In ruminants as in other animals the teeth begin to show wear as the animals age. However, animals on the veld in sandy and semi-arid areas show greater wear to the teeth than animals on pastures. Animals with worn teeth or missing teeth are unable to eat or ruminate properly and will show a progressive weight loss. Cattle with worn teeth are often heavily infested with ticks because they cannot groom themselves. It is important to inspect the teeth when purchasing animals, to determine age and check overall condition. See the diagrams for tooth ageing in the appendix.

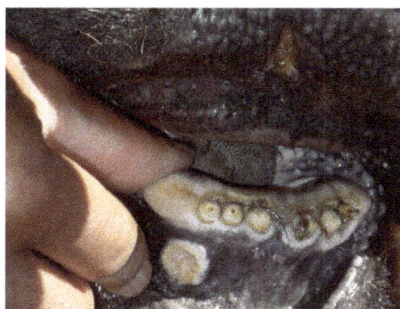
Severe dental attrition in a cow

Diarrhoea

Diarrhoea is the production of

liquid faeces which arises from the rapid passage of the contents of the GIT. One of the primary causes can be physical due to overloading, or overfeeding. This is commonly a cause of diarrhoea in dairy calves that are fed the total daily ration in one meal. Irritation of the gut mucosa as a result of parasites or plant poisons may also cause diarrhoea. Osmotic factors, for example high levels of magnesium ions in salt fed as a lick, can cause diarrhoea because it draws water into the cavity of the gut. Certain bacteria cause diarrhoea because they have toxins which interfere with the water flow dynamics of the intestine. Viruses generally cause diarrhoea because of primary damage which prevents proper digestion. (See section on young animals.)

In older animals, common causes of diarrhoea are intestinal parasites such as roundworms, conical fluke or much more rarely bilharzia, plant poisons, and infectious diseases like BVD and Johne's disease.

E. coli and *Cryptosporidium*
(see section on young animals)

Endoparasites
Most of the endoparasites of livestock occur in the gastro-intestinal tract and cause various syndromes from anaemia, weight loss, diarrhoea and death. See the chapter on Endoparasites for the worms affecting the various species.

Enterotoxaemias *(see acute deaths)*

Gall bladder enlargement ("Grootgal")
Many farmers believe that animals that show an enlarged gall bladder on post-mortem have died from a specific disease. In fact, this sign is merely an indicator that animals have not eaten

for a few days. Bile which is a black fluid produced by the liver is shed into the digestive system to help the digestive process. When the animal does not eat for a protracted period, the bile builds up in the gall bladder causing noticeable enlargement. An enlarged gall bladder is therefore seen when animals are hungry, or have not eaten because of some chronic disease such as anaplasmosis (galsiekte) and botulism (lamsiekte). It is therefore not a specific disease entity but rather a sign of lack of food intake.

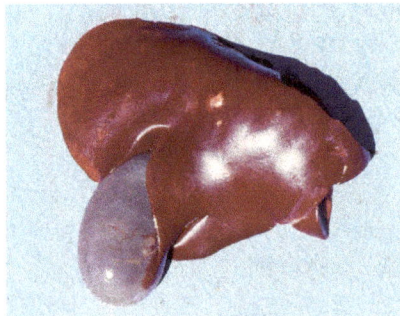

Gall bladder enlargement seen on post-mortem is not a disease entity, but merely a sign of an animal not eating for a few days.

Traumatic reticuloperitonitis ("Hardware disease")

Cattle have tendency to eat foreign objects so sometimes ingest hard, sharp foreign objects e.g. baling or fencing wires which has been passed into the chopped hay feed by feed choppers or forage harvesters. These sharp objects can sometimes lodge in the oesophagus and cause obstructions but most often pass into the forestomach where they lodge in the reticulum. This can cause penetration and leakage of stomach content into abdominal cavity. This will cause an inflammation called peritonitis or occasionally the sharp object can penetrate through the

diaphragm into the pleura, lungs or heart resulting in pneumonia or pericarditis.

Typical symptoms following these events will appear suddenly: an affected animal will show a fever, loss of appetite, severe drop in milk yield and painful movement, with arching of the back being the most prominent. These animals are reluctant to lie down, usually groaning due to the pain, so do this carefully. A consulting veterinarian will recommend antibiotic treatment but if this does not relieve the symptoms in 3 days, the only treatment then is a surgical procedure (rumenotomy) to remove the penetrating object.

For prevention of the condition on farms where this is a problem, caged magnets can be dosed to all animals. Using twine instead of wire to bale hay will prevent this condition but it should be noted that twine can also be the cause of obstructions if not properly removed and discarded.

Herniation of the abdominal wall

Hernias are openings in the abdominal wall through which intestines or other organs can protrude, causing swellings, pain or more severe symptoms. The breaks in the abdominal wall can be caused by a variety of factors such as injury due to rough handling, rupture of the muscles in heavily pregnant cows or may be an inherited abnormality as in the case of umbilical hernias. The appearance of the hernia will depend on where the break is in the abdominal wall – umbilicus, groin or in the pubic area, but in general a swelling appears under the intact skin due to the protrusion of the intestines or other organs. If this is suspected veterinary assistance will be required to confirm the diagnosis and advise whether treatment is possible.

A hernia or break in the abdominal wall showing swelling, most probably due to the protrusion of the small intestines.

"Indigestion" (rumen stasis)

This occurs mainly in cattle when the rumen function is reduced due to change in the quality of feed or in response to diseases such as anaplasmosis. Animals with indigestion will show a reduced appetite, drop in milk production and may be constipated. Examination of the rumen through the paralumbar fossa will show that the rumen has reduced movement, and no rumen sounds can be heard. If the rumen movement has stopped completely a veterinarian will need to dose the animal with fresh rumen content taken from abattoir or donor animals. An alternative treatment is to perform a rumenotomy. The use of rumen stimulants or rumenotorics is currently believed to be of limited value.

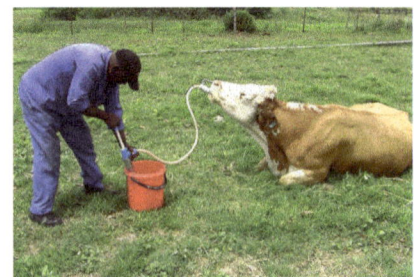

Cow being treated through a stomach tube for rumen stasis or indigestion.

Johne's disease (Paratuberculosis)

This is a bacterial infection of cattle, sheep and goats caused by

Mycobacterium avium paratuberculosis. It is now a notifiable disease in SA. Infection is spread from carrier animals but the organism can survive in the environment particularly in areas where the soil is acid and promotes survival (Western Cape). The bacteria infect newborn animals but the disease only becomes apparent at roughly 2 years of age. Animals can shed the organisms without showing any symptoms.

In cattle the symptoms are weight loss, constant diarrhoea, bottle-jaw and a rough hair coat. Eventually the animals become severely emaciated, dehydrated, and die. Sheep show weight loss and the faeces are soft but diarrhoea is seldom seen. They may shed their wool and show "bottlejaw". The condition can be confused with poor nutrition or a cobalt deficiency which causes gradual wasting.

The diagnosis must be made by laboratory culture of the organism or demonstration of the organism in the faeces. Cattle show typical severe thickening of the intestine. There is no economically viable treatment for the condition and detection of infected animals is difficult, and must be done using various laboratory tests. A vaccine is available on prescription for sheep. It will not eliminate infections but will reduce the number of clinical cases. It must be used in conjunction with eliminating infected animals and can only be used under state veterinary supervision.

A sheep with Johne's disease showing swelling under the jaw.

Liver abscesses

Liver abscessation is commonly seen in feedlot cattle because it is a sequel to the inflammation of the rumen that occurs with acidosis. *Fusobacterium necrophorum* bacteria which are always present in the gut, form small abscesses in the wall of the rumen. The bacteria then invade the blood vessels of the liver and lodge in the liver tissue, where they form round yellow foci of dead tissue which develop into abscesses.

The condition is seldom diagnosed in the live animal can be suspected in feedlot animals when they are doing poorly and showing 5-15% reduction in weight gain. The abscesses are seen as 4-6 cm yellow necrotic areas which can be low in number or as many as 100 in a single animal. Prevention of this condition is done by the feeding of chlortetracycline in the feed under veterinary prescription, but prevention can also be achieved by increasing the roughage component of the rations and giving multiple feedings rather than one large meal per day.

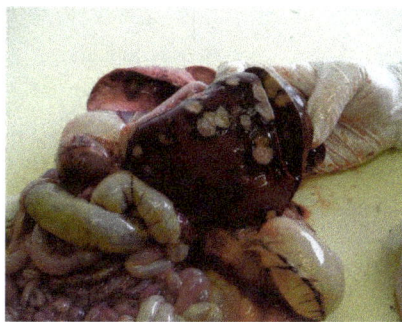

Liver abscesses are usually a sequel to acidosis.

Lumpy jaw

This is a chronic disease of the bony tissue of the jaw in cattle. It usually affects the upper or lower jaws and this gives rise to the common name "lumpy jaw". The condition is caused by the invasion of the bony tissue by the bacterium *Actinomyces bovis* as a result of wounding to the gums of the mouth by coarse feed such as silage or foreign bodies in the feed. The first signs are swelling of the skin around the jaws, with gradual bony knob-like development which may interfere with the teeth. The infection eats away at the bony tissue but can also affect the soft tissues and pus may be discharged through the skin. Animals will be unable to chew their food properly and will lose weight. The diagnosis is made based on the typical symptoms, and culture of the pus oozing from the lesions. Veterinarians treat early cases with specific antibiotics but animals with advanced cases can usually not be salvaged. Further cases must be prevented by milling coarse feed and eliminating foreign bodies from rations.

A severe case of lumpy jaw in a live animal showing extensive swelling of the tissue around the mandible.

Mouth ulcers

Various conditions cause erosions in the mouth. It is important to be aware of the various possible causes, as the presence of mouth lesions in cattle always raises suspicion of foot-and-mouth disease. Other causes of erosions in the mouth are bovine malignant catarrah (BMC/snotsiekte), lumpy skin disease, Bovine viral diarrhoea and IBR; in sheep mouth and tongue ulcers are characteristic of blue tongue infections. These diseases are discussed more fully in other chapters.

Oesophageal paralysis

Rabies in cattle and a plant poisoning which occurs in sheep ("vermeersiekte") can cause paralysis of the oesophagus. See these conditions under their separate headings.

Obstructions

Since cattle are non-selective feeders, they tend to ingest foreign objects such as plastic bags, and even the cocoons of insects which can cause obstructions. They may also take in pieces of wire which tend to lodge in the forestomachs and may cause a variety of conditions known as "hardware disease". This is either a peritonitis (infection of the abdominal cavity) or pericarditis (heart sac infection) – see under Traumatic pericarditis. The diagnosis of these conditions in the live animal is a specialised science but farmers may well see these conditions on post mortem.

Sheep are less inclined to eat foreign objects but do in semi-arid areas suffer from obstructions in the stomach due to plant fibre balls. These are formed from eating bushes and grass with fleecy flowers, namely *Stipagrostis obtusa* ("boesmansgras"), *Eriocephalus* ("kapokbos"), *Chrysocoma* ("bitterbos") and *Gnidia* ("januariebos"). Goats are particularly fond of eating these flowers and often suffer from plant ball impaction. If these balls are large, animals will show signs of emaciation and bloating. The fibrous plant balls are easily seen on post-mortem when the abomasum is opened up.

Prevention of the condition involves avoidance of the problem plants when they are in flower. In some areas, vegetables or fruit (e.g. potatoes or oranges) are utilised as cattle feed, but if these are not chopped up properly by feed choppers, large pieces can cause obstruction of the oesophagus and cause free gas bloat (see section on bloat). Vegetables such as potatoes are very high in carbohydrates and may also be the cause of acidosis (see section on acidosis).

Fibrous balls caused by the intake of certain plants can cause obstruction in the GIT.

Plant poisonings

Most plant poisons that affect the GIT cause diarrhoea (chinkerinchee, castor oil plants, Sesbania), but these poisonings are accompanied by other symptoms. Exceptions are "vermeersiekte" in sheep, which causes damage to the muscles of the oesophagus causing the muscular walls to thin and dilate. The affected animals are unable to swallow most of the time and regurgitate feed. With kikuyu poisoning in cattle there is severe damage to the lining of the forestomachs but diarrhoea is seldom seen. See the plant poisoning section for more details.

Rectal prolapse

This condition occurs mostly in mutton sheep breeds. The cause is most probably genetic but there are factors that may predispose to its occurrence. The condition is breed-related, seen particularly in Dorpers; it is speculated that cutting tails too short causes some muscle damage which predisposes to this condition. Feeding high energy rations and lack of exercise cause obesity which is another predisposing factor for rectal prolapse. The symptoms of rectal prolapse are the protrusion from the anus of a fold of the rectum. Initially it can be returned inside the body, but the protruding fold gradually becomes swollen, damaged and infected and cannot be returned inside the body cavity. At this stage the animal shows signs of pain, straining and may develop a fever. Ewes may develop a uterine prolapse simultaneously.

Veterinary help must be obtained as soon as possible as resolving the condition requires surgery. In early stages the protruding rectal fold can be returned and contained by loosely stitching the rectum closed. Damaged rectal folds must be amputated by a veterinarian. Preventative measures are avoiding the use of affected animals for breeding, and leaving longer tails. Animals prone to rectal prolapse must not be used in feedlots.

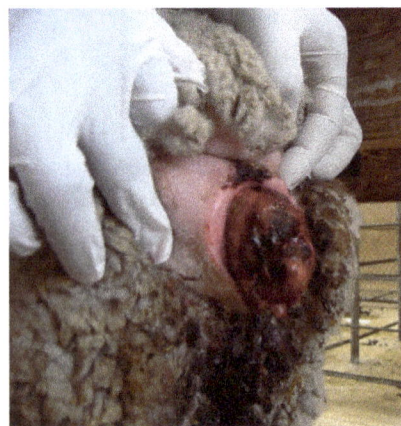

Rectal prolapse in a sheep.

Salmonella *(see diseases of young animals)*

Wooden tongue/Face abscesses

Both these conditions are caused by the bacterium *Actinobacillus lignieresi*. They occur in cattle, sheep and goats due to wounding which occurs during feeding. Coarse grass, grass awns, thorns and tick bites are usually responsible wounds that allow the penetration of bacteria. The site of the wounds differs within the species due to the different methods of feeding. Cattle use their tongues to feed and most commonly they develop inflammation, small abscesses and fibrosis of the tongue. This results in hardening of the tongue muscle which is then no longer efficient during the feeding process. Affected cattle will salivate and lose weight due to being unable to eat efficiently.

Sheep and goats make use of their lips and graze closer to the ground, so the condition often involves the lips and corners of the mouth. The small abscesses that arise spread

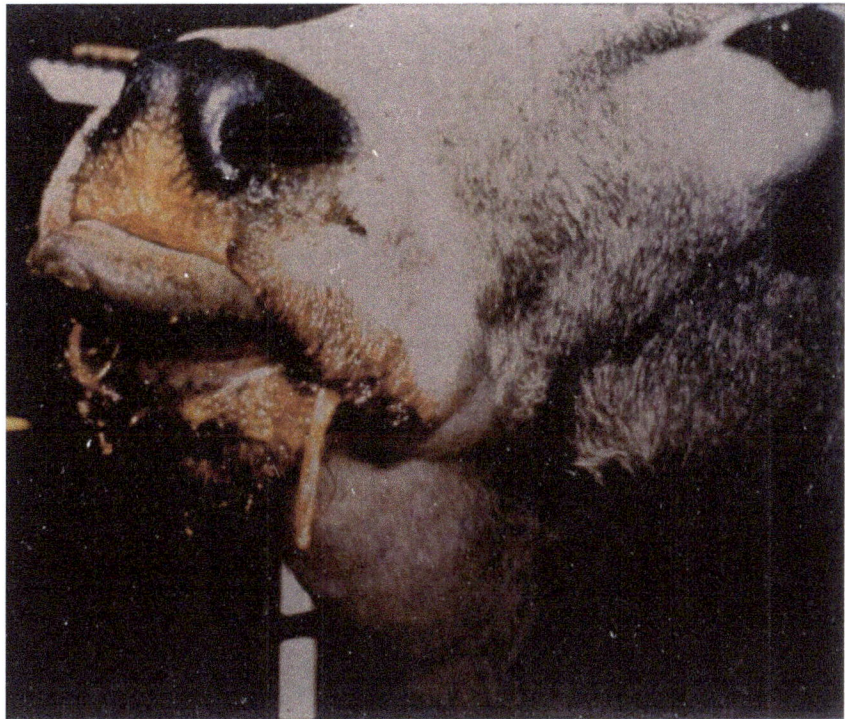

A case of wooden tongue in a bovine.

via the lymphatic system to cause extensive lesions all over the face (see image under Skin section). In small stock the feeding of prickly pears is often the cause of the problem. Small

external wounds can be treated with application of iodine; prevent the condition by removing the primary cause of the wounds. Severe cases are usually not worth treating.

LAMENESS

Lameness, a term which refers to any difficulty in walking, has a wide range of causes, from physical injury to various infectious diseases which affect the limbs or the brain. The primary cause can be hoof problems, or conditions affecting the muscles or spinal lesions which may cause paralysis. It is therefore important that a correct diagnosis is made. The most common causes are discussed below.

Abnormal hoof growth

The abnormal outgrowth of hooves can result when animals are raised in sandy areas of the country (Kalahari and some areas of the Waterberg) where less than normal wear on the hoof material causes the formation of long slipper like claws. These abnormally long claws make walking difficult, so the hooves have to be trimmed. This cause of hoof overgrowth must be differentiated from other causes discussed below (e.g. laminitis, plant poisoning, infectious causes of hoof distortion).

Botulism

Clostridium botulinum bacteria occur widely in the environment and grow in rotting material like carcasses. The bacteria produce a powerful toxin which is responsible for the clinical symptoms of botulism. Livestock can contract botulism when grazing on the veld or when kraaled and fed hay or silage containing the toxin. The veld form involves *C. botulinum* type D which is found on the carcasses of dead animals or old tortoise shells. When the phosphate levels of veld grass begin to drop, animals develop a phosphate hunger which causes them to eat old bones or tortoise shells (a condition called "pica"). These bones often contain botulism toxin. Under kraal conditions the source of contamination is the carcasses of small animals like rats, birds and cats. This type of botulism usually involves

C. botulinum type C. Broiler manure is very commonly contaminated because it almost always contains chicken carcasses. Once animals have ingested botulism toxin the symptoms will be seen 2-3 days later.

The first signs of the disease in cattle are weakness in the hind limbs, and then paralysis of the throat and jaw; this makes it difficult for animals to swallow their saliva which streams from the mouth. Attempts to dose such animals will cause gangrenous pneumonia as the remedies will land in the lungs. As the condition progresses, these animals are eventually unable to stand and lie down with their heads held against their bodies. Eventually the breathing muscles are affected and the animal suffocates. In sheep the early signs of botulism are standing aside from the flock, with the neck bent to one side, and some may show a spasm of the tail. As the disease progresses the animal walks stiffly and then becomes

recumbent. The tongue may protrude from the mouth due to paralysis. Later the animal is unable to rise and will die from suffocation as in cattle. A post-mortem will reveal nothing specific and confirmation can only be done by taking intestinal content for isolation of the toxin from the gut.

Treatment with botulism antiserum can be attempted but it is seldom successful except in very early cases. The most economical control measure is vaccination which must be given before or at weaning; a booster must be given 3-4 weeks later and this must then be repeated annually. Supplementation with phosphate licks in late summer and winter will reduce eating of bones and will improve the condition of animals.

The symptoms of botulism can be confused with fungal poisoning by *Stenocarpella maydis*, which grows on maize, "krimpsiekte," a plant poisoning of sheep, rabies, and three-day-stiff-sickness.

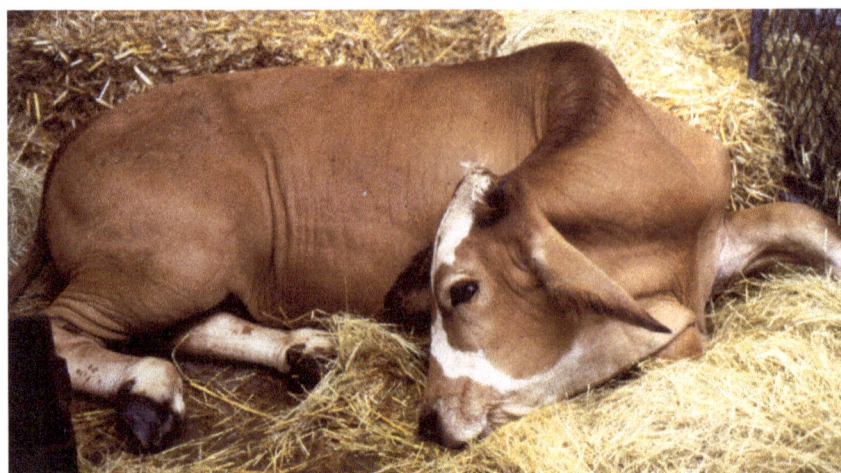

Botulism in bovine showing the typical signs of head held to the flanks.

Blue tongue

Blue tongue is a viral disease transmitted by *Culicoides* midges. It occurs virtually all over South Africa except for certain mountainous areas. To date there are 21 different types of blue tongue virus that can cause disease in sheep and there is no cross-immunity between these types, which all have to be included in the vaccine. The disease is seen in summer and autumn when the *Culicoides* midges are numerous. Because the midges need moist areas to breed they occur especially in vleis and around dams. They are active after sundown until sunrise.

In the early stages of infection with blue tongue virus, sheep have a fever and lose their appetite. They develop reddening of the nose and mouth, and a while later they show erosions on the nose and inside the mouth. Occasionally severe swelling of the tongue (blue tongue) and the head may occur. Affected animals may become lame due to inflammation of the coronet of the hoof and may be so severe that sheep may be seen walking on their knees.

Blue tongue infections cause severe economic losses as the disease causes a break in the wool due to the fever reaction, weight loss due to the sheep not eating and there may be permanent damage to the muscles of the neck causing it to be held skew (torticollis). The hooves grow out unevenly and have to be trimmed to allow normal locomotion. Young lambs affected may die of starvation and secondary infections.

There is no specific treatment for blue tongue because it is a viral disease, but severely affected animals can be treated with a broad-spectrum antibiotic such as an oxytetracycline, to prevent secondary infections such as pneumonia. The focus of blue tongue control must be prevention by vaccination. The vaccine which comprises three separate inoculations must be given 3 weeks apart and this must be repeated annually. Vaccination should preferably be done in spring before the height of the blue tongue season, but the schedule can be adapted to accommodate the lambing season. Lambs of vaccinated ewes should be immunised at weaning age when colostral immunity is waning.

Other control measures that can be used are to limit exposure to the midges by avoiding of low-lying vlei areas during sundown to sunrise, and to graze cattle together with sheep as the midges prefer to feed on cattle.

Although goats may also become infected with the blue tongue virus, they do not become ill and vaccination is therefore unnecessary in this species.

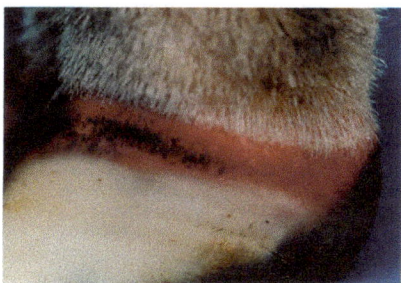

Lesions on muzzle in a case of bluetongue.

Coronitis or inflammation of the crown of the hoof is seen in acute cases of bluetongue.

Calving paralysis

Damage to the large nerves of the hind leg can occur during difficult calving especially when there is human intervention. In such cases the cow shows lameness or paralysis of the hind limbs after calving; she is unable to stand and may lie with her hindlegs spread-eagled, or sometimes drag herself with her front-legs. Cows with calving paralysis will appear alert, unlike those affected by milk fever or other post-calving disorders like metritis or acute mastitis.

The complications that arise from a cow being unable to rise (downer cow) are bedsores, mastitis and a progressive loss in condition. Most importantly, muscle necrosis may occur if the cow is not turned regularly. Once muscle necrosis sets in, the animal will never be able to rise, so the sooner one can get the cow on her hooves, the better. Because of the dangers of calving paralysis, interventions in difficult calvings are best left to veterinarians. The use of tractors or pulleys should never be attempted as this will always cause serious damage. See also Dystocia in the Reproduction section.

Cow with splayleg or calving paralysis.

Fluorosis

Underground water in some districts in RSA such as Limpopo Province contains high concentrations of fluorine. If this is the only source of drinking water for animals, a condition called fluorosis may develop: this causes abnormal growth of the long bones of animals leading to stiffness or lameness. In young animals, the growth of the teeth are severely affected causing problems with digestion. See the section on Poisoning for more details.

Foot abscess

🐖 🐐

Foot abscess in small stock must be differentiated from a condition called footrot (see below) which has a different cause and epidemiology. Foot abscess develops as a result of wounding of the skin around the claw. The primary cause is wounding by tick bites or particularly in goats, predominantly by thorny bushes or stony ground. These wounds become infected with the bacterium *Trueperella pyogene* (formerly *Corynebacterium/Arcanobacterium*) causing the formation of an abscess which eventually affects the joint. Affected animals become lame in one or more legs. The foot is red, swollen and painful and will later swell up above the claws and may burst open. Animals lose condition rapidly and may even die of septicaemia. Because antibiotics penetrate abscesses poorly, treatment is not very successful. However, if combined with proper care, valuable animals may be saved with a 2-3 week course of oxytetracycline injections. Because of the poor rate of recovery with treatment, prevention should be implemented by removing the cause of the condition or if this is not possible, making use of footbaths containing 5% formalin. This will reduce the level of bacterial contamination. If ticks are the primary cause, use of a footbath containing a tick remedy or apply a pour-on tick remedy on the feet at regular intervals.

The use of the *Actinomyces pyogenes* vaccine has been advocated to control this condition but there is no scientific proof of its efficacy.

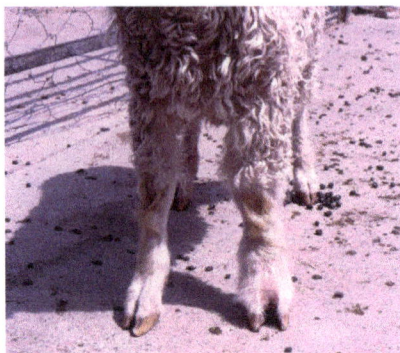

Foot abscess in Angora goat

 Ultratet G0296

 Ultratet LA G2857

 Ultratet 200 LA G3559

Footrot in sheep

🐖

Footrot in sheep is caused by two specific gram negative bacteria (*Dichelobacter nodosus* and *Fusobacterium necrophorum*). *Fusobacterium necrophorum* is a normal inhabitant of the skin but when breaks occur due to wounding or tick bites, it penetrates into the underlying tissues. This facilitates the entry of *Dichelobacter nodosus* which produces a toxin which dissolves flesh and horn. *Dichelobacter* is a contagious organism which is easily spread by infected animals as it can survive in muddy soil for two weeks or even more. Some breeds such as

Merinos are more susceptible than mutton breeds to the condition. An outbreak begins with a few animals becoming lame, with one or more foot being involved. Early examination will show reddening, swelling of the skin between the claws and later an exudation of pus. The condition progresses further to affect the sole and the tissue around the claw.

A veterinarian should be consulted to distinguish this from foot abscess (see above). The treatment of sheep with footrot involves early isolation of cases in dry camps or sheds, to limit the spread. Daily foot bathing in 10% zinc sulphate will heal the affected claws.

Sheep with hoof involvement must have the claws trimmed and disinfected. Injectable antibiotics such as oxytetracycline and sulphas will help clear up the infections. Infected animals should be removed from the flock if possible as they act as a source of infection. The bacteria may survive in muddy conditions for two weeks or even more.

Prevent outbreaks at the beginning of the problem season, by using formalin (5%) or zinc sulphate (10%) footbaths. Poorly drained, muddy camps must be improved with the use of gravel. Footrot vaccines are available but the usage is too small in SA to warrant their importation by distributors.

 Ultratet G0296

 Ultratet LA G2857

Ultratet 200 LA G3559

Ecosulf LA G3037

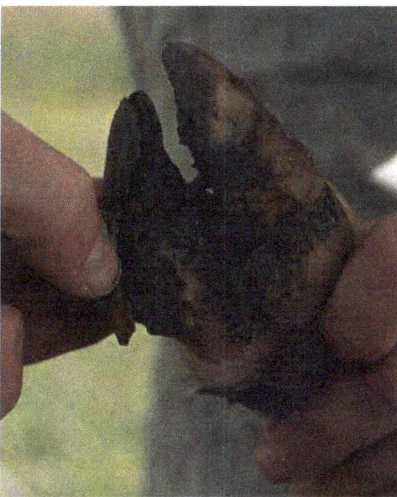

A case of footrot in a sheep

Footrot in cattle

Footrot in cattle is primarily an infection with *Fusobacterium necrophorum*, although other bacteria may also be involved. The bacterium thrives in faeces and wet muddy ground. The causes include trauma of the feet (sharp gravel, thorns), wet conditions, breed (*B. taurus* cattle are more susceptible) and possibly zinc deficiency in dairy cattle.

The condition affects usually the hind legs and usually only one foot. Animals show lameness and examination of the affected foot will show reddening and swelling between the claws, which can spread around to the heels.

Treatment in many cases requires surgical trimming away of the infected hoof material by a veterinarian and simultaneous antibiotic therapy. Control in affected herds will require regular hoof trimming and the use of footbaths containing formalin, Zn S04 or CuSO4. Footbaths must not be administered too frequently or made too strong as this can predispose to footrot. Advice must be obtained from feed consultants if additional zinc is added to rations.

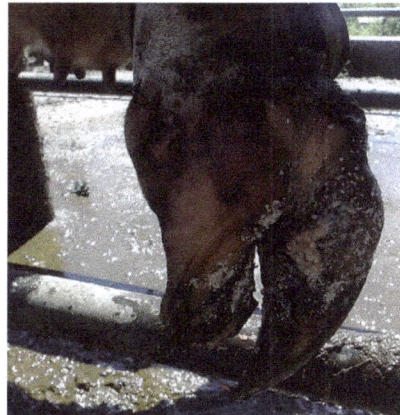

A case of footrot in a bovine

Foot-and-mouth disease (FMD)

FMD is a highly contagious virus disease of cloven-hoofed animals which is spread by direct contact between infected and susceptible animals. In South Africa the main source of infection used to be the infected buffalo in the Kruger National Park, but the breakdown of border controls has resulted in numerous outbreaks occurring due to cross border movement of cattle. Recent findings show that the SAT serotypes which occur in Southern Africa at present are mainly cattle- adapted (rather than buffalo – adapted). As a result, they cause little or no clinical symptoms especially in indigenous or crossbred cattle. This makes it difficult for owners and even veterinarians to detect the disease on physical examination alone. While the disease itself does not cause high mortalities, it is catastrophic when it occurs in the traditionally "FMD free zone" because it affects high-producers such as dairy and feedlot cattle and prevents the export of any agricultural product to developed countries. The most recent outbreaks in the Limpopo Province at the end of 2019/beginning 2020, once again highlighted the disastrous economic effect the disease can have on the agricultural sector. Over and above the quarantine of infected and in-contact farms, all auctions were suspended indefinitely across South Africa.

Cattle, sheep, goat (as well as pigs and wild antelope) can develop clinical signs of FMD. Early in the disease, blisters form on the mucosa of the mouth and on the tongue. When the blisters rupture, they leave raw and painful erosions causing the animals to salivate profusely; this is usually the only symptom noticed by stock owners. If blisters occur between the claws of the hoof, the animals may show signs of lameness. Dairy cattle are more severely affected than beef animals as they develop blisters on the teats which leads to mastitis with subsequent loss of milk production.

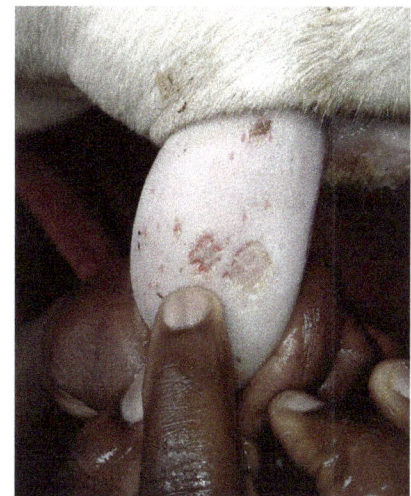

Tongue lesions caused by foot-and-mouth disease.

The foot lesions caused by FMD can be confused with other conditions such as Senkobo disease, laminitis or footrot. The mouth lesions can be confused with those caused by lumpy skin disease and bovine malignant catarrh. Any stock owner suspecting the presence of FMD on their property must immediately contact the local state veterinarian. All FMD vaccination is done by animal health authorities and may not be done by private stock owners.

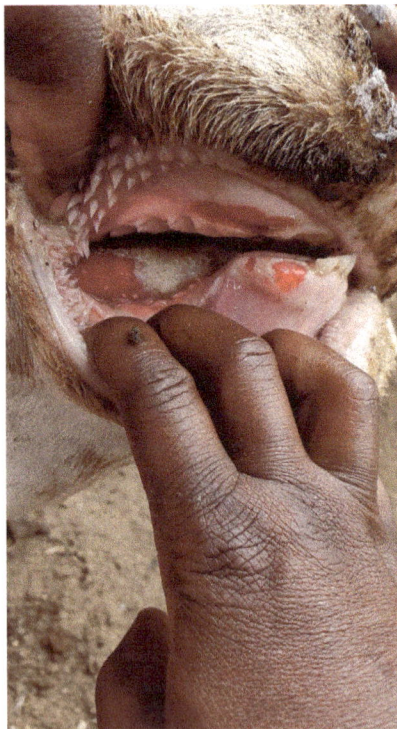

Mouth ulcers in a case of foot-and-mouth disease.

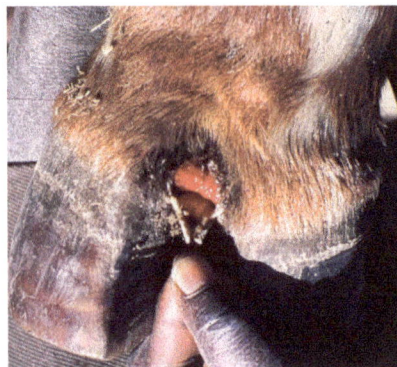

Hoof lesions are seen in some cases of foot and mouth diseases causing lameness in the affected animal.

Laminitis

Laminitis in cattle is the non-infectious inflammation of the hooves of cattle which results mainly after conditions such as rumen acidosis, caused by overfeeding with carbohydrates. A history of overeating and occurrence of the condition in large numbers of animals is an indicator of nutritional laminitis. After the acidosis episode, the animals become lame and walk on their heels as a result of the pain. Later the hooves grow out and turn up at the toes. Such animals should have their hooves trimmed to enable the animals to walk comfortably. Acidosis should be prevented by the correct feeding of high-carbohydrate feeds.

A toxic plant *Crotalaria burkeana*, also known as "rattle-bush" or "stywesiektebos" which occurs in Mpumalanga, Limpopo, NW Province and Namibia can cause laminitis and should be suspected as a possible cause if the affected animals have not been fed concentrates.

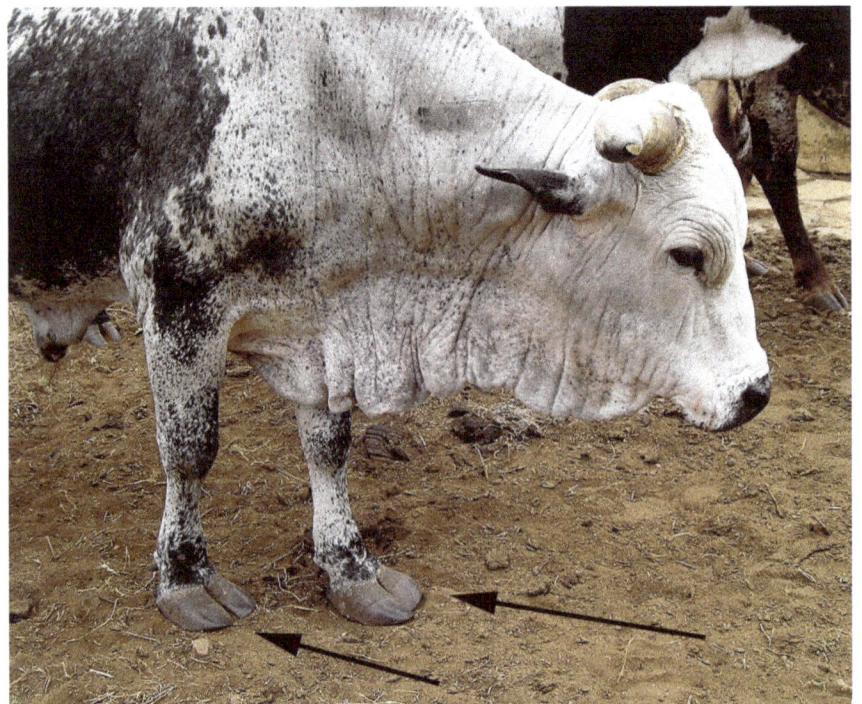

Chronic laminitis in bovine.

Nutritional causes

Various nutrient deficiencies or excesses can cause defective bone metabolism resulting in abnormalities of the skeleton and general health. Deficiencies of both calcium or phosphorous can cause skeletal problems: calcium deficiency tends to manifest in young animals with swollen joints and tendency to fractures, while phosphorus deficiency will present with bone abnormalities and pica. An excess intake of fluorine will interfere with bone development in young animals (see under Poisonings). These conditions are beyond the scope of the farmer to diagnose accurately, so veterinary help will be required.

Polyarthritis

Polyarthritis is a bacterial infection of one or more joint on the limbs. It occurs mainly in lambs and calves as a sequel to navel ill, which is an infection of the umbilicus with

Trueperella pyogenes. This occurs when animals calve or lamb in unhygienic camps or pens. Animals with polyarthritis will show lameness and swelling of the knee joints which may make walking very difficult. These cases must be treated promptly with injectable oxytetracyclines. Prevention is based on allowing animals to calve in clean camps or on the veld. Disinfection of the umbilicus can be done with an iodine suspension or any other disinfectant suitable for the purpose. Polyarthritis can also occur due to post-dipping lameness (see below).

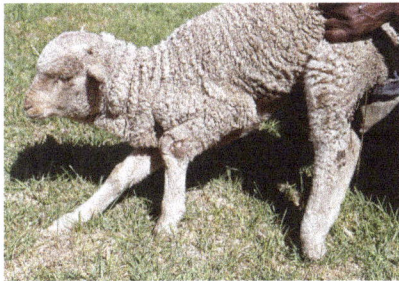

Polyarthritis in a lamb

 Ultratet G0296

 Ultratet LA G2857

 Ultratet 200 LA G3559

Post-dipping lameness

The bacterium _Erysipelothix rhusiopathiae_ which occurs in the faeces of sheep and goats is able to survive and grow in dip tanks. It penetrates the wounds caused by shearing and other management practices and causes a condition called post-dipping lameness.

On entering the small wounds, the bacteria cause local inflammation of the skin. The infection may spread to the joints, causing lameness and eventually chronic arthritis which leads to rapid loss of condition.

Animals with suspected post-dipping lameness must be treated with oxytetracycline before the condition becomes chronic. Prevention is simple and efficient: any dip which is used over more than a day should have 10% Zn SO4 added to prevent bacterial growth.

 Ultratet G0296

 Ultratet LA G2857

 Ultratet 200 LA G3559

Spinal abscess "Sitsiekte"

This condition occurs often in lambs as a result of poor hygiene during tail docking. In these cases the wound becomes infected with abscess-forming bacteria such as _Corynebacterium ovis_ or _Trueperella pyogenes_, which is spread by the bloodstream to the spinal cord area. Here the abscess grows and eventually becomes so large that it begins to affect the spinal nerves causing the so-called "sitsiekte". These lambs are unable to move their hindlegs so will drag their hindquarters along the ground. They lose weight rapidly because they are unable to feed and usually die. Treatment with high doses of antibiotic such as oxytetracycline can be attempted to salvage them but as with other abscesses this is most often unsuccessful and animals will most likely have to be slaughtered. The abscess can be demonstrated on post-mortem by opening up the spine. Prevention must be done by disinfecting docking wounds with iodine spray or other suitable preparations. Knives used for docking must be thoroughly cleaned and washed in disinfectant.

Tail docking has been banned in some European countries for years because there is no evidence that it prevents fly-strike or that it promotes successful mating by rams. This is supported by the fact that indigenous fat-tailed breeds as Pedis, whose tails are not traditionally docked, are able to mate quite successfully.

Spinal abscess is also seen in cattle but the source is usually the bites of ticks with long mouth parts that attach around the tail and the anus. This creates entry wounds for abscess-forming bacteria which then spread and lodge in the spinal canal. Control in this case is adequate tick control. Hand dressing in addition to dipping or spraying may be required to reach areas under the tail. See the tick control section for additional information.

Spinal abscess in a bovine.

Swollen joints in cattle

Swollen joints are commonly seen in cattle in various types of farming. The causes are varied and numerous, including inherited defects of the joints, trauma (injury), or infection. Severe swelling of the joints is usually painful, causing lameness, and loss of weight. Veterinary assistance will be needed to make a diagnosis and recommend treatment if at all possible.

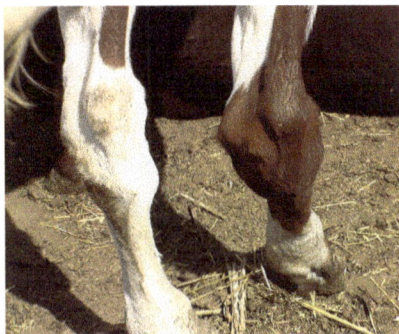
Severely swollen joints indicate inflammation and possible infection which can impact on the future of the animal.

Tetanus

The *Clostridium tetani* bacteria which cause tetanus to occur widely in soil, and when the spores contaminate deep wounds they will germinate and secrete a powerful toxin. Ideal conditions for tetanus occur in small stock when castration and docking are done using elastrators., which creates the ideal conditions for the growth of the tetanus bacteria. The powerful tetanus toxin causes spastic paralysis which is almost always irreversible. Lambs die soon after showing symptoms, due to paralysis of the respiratory muscles (see also disease of young animals). Vaccination of ewes with clostridial vaccines which include tetanus will provide lambs with optimal colostral immunity at 3 weeks of age when it will be safe to castrate and dock them.

Cattle are not very susceptible to *Clostridium tetani* bacteria, but cases do occur after surgical procedures such as dehorning, castration or hoof trimming. Initially, affected animals show stiffness of the legs, which they hold far from their bodies as if trying to balance. The third eyelid may collapse across the eye, and the animals are constipated and depressed. In the terminal stages they develop spastic (jerky) paralysis. Eventually they die when the respiratory muscles become paralysed.

Treatment of affected animals with antibiotics is usually too late as the toxin has already been produced when the symptoms appear. The use of tetanus antiserum is also usually not very effective unless given early in the course of the disease. Since cattle are less susceptible than sheep or horses, they are usually not vaccinated against tetanus but control measures such as stringent wound hygiene must be practiced when doing dehorning, hoof paring and any other surgical interventions. Sterile instruments and wound disinfection must be used. Tetanus in cattle can be confused with laminitis, certain plant poisonings, and in the late stages with heartwater.

Tick paralysis (see tick-borne diseases).

Three-Day stiff-sickness/ Ephemeral fever

This is a viral disease of cattle thought to be transmitted by insects, probably *Culicoides* midges. The disease occurs in summer to late summer when the insect vectors are numerous. Roughly five days after animals become infected they develop a fever, depression and stiffness. The condition usually clears up after 3 days as the name implies. However in severe cases, there is pronounced stiffness, nasal discharge and lacrimation (increased tear flow). Muscle tremors may be seen. Seriously affected animals may lie down and be unable to rise again. They become bloated, and salivate due to paralysis of the oesophagus. Later the animals will slip into a coma and die. Beef cattle are usually not severely affected with the exception of very heavy animals like bulls. The most serious problems occur in dairies, where the disease causes a drop in milk production and abortions. Dairies near vleis or dams which are breeding sites for midges or other insects have a high risk of the disease.

Cases of three day stiffsickness that do not clear up after 3 days will need supportive treatment from a veterinarian: animals that do not rise despite intensive treatment and nursing, usually have to be euthanased as they suffer complications such as mastitis, muscle necrosis and the development of bedsores.

The vaccines available locally and overseas, are live attenuated

A "downer" case of three day stiff-sickness in cow, resulting in the animal being unable to stand.

products which have to be emulsified just before use in an oil adjuvant. Although some improvements have been made to the local vaccine to make emulsification easier, the virus may still be too attenuated to give sustained immunity. Insect control must be done in conjunction with vaccination in high risk farming set-ups such as dairies. If possible cattle must be kept away from vleis, dams or rivers during summer months.

White muscle disease

Selenium is necessary for the function of the enzyme glutathione peroxidase which is an essential anti-oxidant produced by the body. A deficiency in selenium may occur in animals grazing on deficient soils in high rainfall areas, those grazing lush, rapidly growing pastures or grazed solely on legumes. A high soil content of molybdenum will also potentiate a deficiency of selenium. Selenium deficiency causes free radicals to attack the skeletal and heart muscles, resulting in lameness, muscular weakness and heart failure. The symptoms are unsteady gait, stumbling, or acute death due to heart failure. On post-mortem whitish streaks can be seen in the large muscles of the body such as the gluteus and in the heart muscle.

NERVOUS SYSTEM

Diseases which affect the nervous system can cause a wide range of symptoms including blindness, lameness, and partial or total paralysis. Some of the conditions have therefore been discussed in other sections. The most common causes of nervous symptoms in sheep are gid ("draaisiekte"), heartwater, botulism, tetanus, ketosis, milk fever, rabies, and various plant poisonings. In cattle, common causes are botulism, rabies, heartwater, Asiatic redwater and many plant poisonings.

Gid ("Draaisiekte")

Gid is the name given to the condition seen mainly in sheep and goats. It is caused by the intermediate or larval stages of the tapeworm of dogs *Taenia muticeps* lodging in the brain. The eggs of this tapeworm are picked up from the faeces of carnivores (domestic or wild dogs) by grazing sheep. On reaching the intestine, the eggs hatch and give rise to a cyst which eventually finds its way to the brain of the sheep. The life cycle is completed when a dog (wild or domestic species) eats the brain of an infected sheep and the cyst then develops into a tapeworm in the intestine of the dog. Humans are incidental hosts and can become infected with cysts if they pick up the eggs from the faeces of infected dogs.

The presence of the cyst in the brain causes varying symptoms depending on the size and location. Affected sheep are seen walking around in circles or standing with their heads pressed against an object. The animal may behave as if it is blind, bumping into things and the head may be held to one side. Sometimes sheep may show a high-stepping gait, a symptom which is also seen with heartwater. The animals may be completely paralysed if the brain is extensively affected and the cysts can be so large that they cause the bones of the skull to be worn away. There is no treatment for this condition.

The presence of the cyst can be demonstrated on sectioning the skull on post-mortem examination. The cyst has the appearance of a large fluid-filled bladder, and often the brain has shrunken to a fraction of its size.

Gid is prevented by regular dosing of domestic dogs on the farm with tapeworm remedies containing praziquantel. Since the condition is also dangerous for humans, this prevention measure is of immense importance. Under no circumstances must infected sheep tissues be fed to dogs as this will infect them and re-establish the worm lifecycle once more.

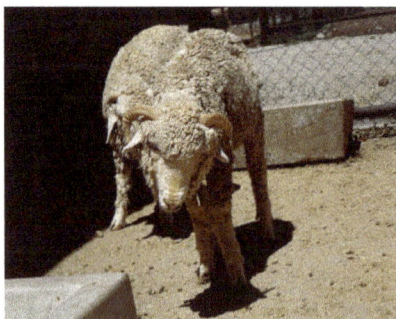

Case of "gid" in a sheep

Rabies

Rabies is a fatal virus disease which can affect a wide number of mammalian species including cattle, kudu, cats and dogs, occasionally sheep and goats, and of course humans. Depending on the area in SA the source of infection could be rabid bat-eared foxes, jackals, yellow mongoose or domestic dogs (see map). Animals such as cattle and sheep probably become infected when investigating the strange behaviour of rabies-infected wild animals, which lose their fear and display either docility or aggression. They may enter farmyards or even buildings. The most common method of transmission of the disease is through a bite from a rabid animal, but contact with infected saliva can also transmit the infection.

After transmission, the incubation period can be long, as the virus moves along the nerve tracts until it finally reaches the brain tissue. Once it reaches the brain the animal will start to show symptoms. Although rabies symptoms are notoriously variable in cattle, in the early stages the animal typically separates from the herd, does not eat and is either irritable or docile. Tooth grinding and eating strange objects may be seen. Rabid cattle have a lean look because they stop eating and they show tenesmus (straining to defecate). Later the animal shows paralysis of the tongue, salivation and bellowing. Farmers often confuse the symptoms with those of an animal with something stuck in the oesophagus and try to remove the "obstruction" by hand. Aggression is a common symptom which manifests as head butting or sometimes vicious attacks on humans. In the final stages the animal drags its limbs and then paralysis becomes more pronounced, terminating in recumbence, coma and death.

Sheep rams show heightened sexual excitability, goats bleat excessively and are even more aggressive than cattle. In outbreaks of kudu rabies, the animals become docile and even enter buildings, before the paralytic stage sets in.

Rabies is a controlled disease and if suspected the local state or a private veterinarian must be contacted. The presumptive diagnosis is based on the history, namely incidence of the disease in the areas and the presence of wild animals acting strangely, as well as the symptoms of the domestic animal infected. There is no economically viable treatment for rabid animals and as they pose a threat to humans and other animals they should be destroyed. The diagnosis of rabies must be confirmed by a veterinarian taking a brain sample for laboratory examination.

Vaccination is done in areas where rabies is prevalent in a particular species, most commonly cattle, dogs and cats. Initially animals are vaccinated at 12 weeks of age, boosted a month later, and repeated every 3 years. Wild animals such as meerkats or jackals may not be vaccinated according to animal health laws.

IMPORTANT NOTES:
- Never handle animals suspected of having rabies.
- If human contact has occurred wash the contact area with soap and running water for at least 10 minutes, and report this immediately to the district surgeon who will arrange for treatment.

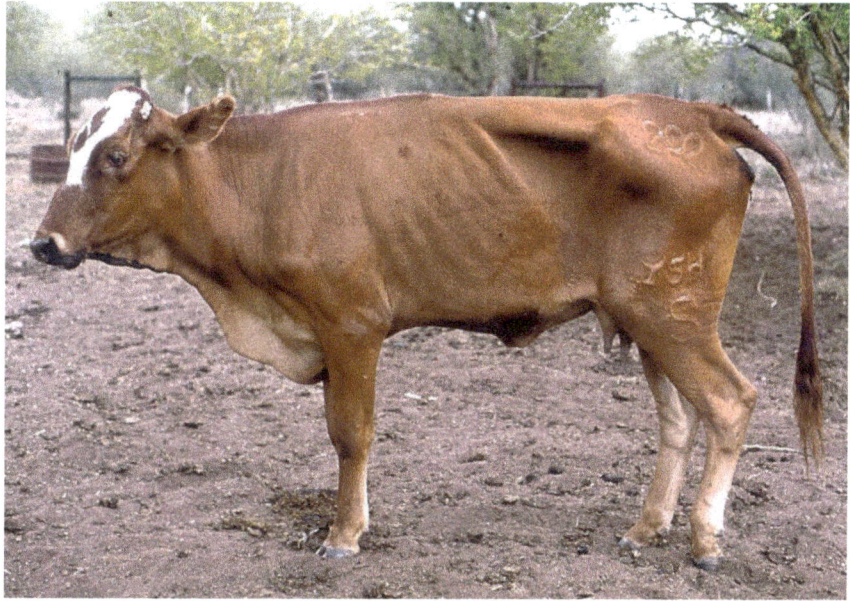

In this early case of bovine rabies the animal has stopped eating and is showing signs of stiffness in the hind legs.

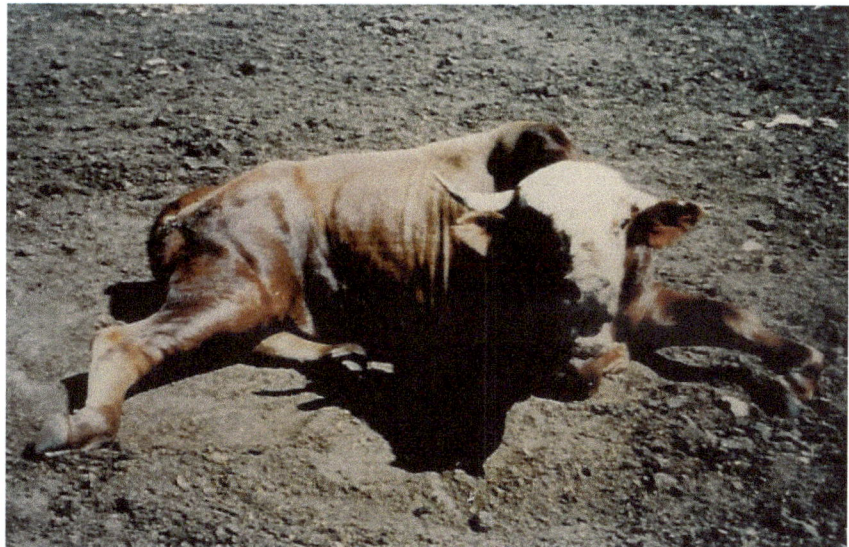

An advanced cases of rabies showing recumbency due to paralysis and continual bellowing.

Plant poisonings

There are currently 20 different plants and fungi that can potentially cause nervous symptoms in livestock. Many do not cause any pathological lesions and the diagnosis often has to be made based on circumstantial evidence or the presence of recognisable plant parts in the gastro-intestinal tract or the presence of fungal growth on grazing or feed. See the plant poisons section for discussion of the main plants involved.

REPRODUCTIVE SYSTEM

In **cattle** the most common reproductive problems are typically a return to oestrus without conception, low calving percentages, the birth of deformed or stillborn calves or abortions. Depending on the cause, one or more of these syndromes can be seen.

Infertility is seen when there is early damage to the embryo or foetus before 42 days before the skeleton develops, resulting in resorption so there are no external signs. Cows that appeared to be pregnant will come on heat again or may develop endometritis.

Abortion is the rejection of the foetus at a stage between 42 and 260 days, at which stage the foetus is fairly well developed and will usually be seen by the stock owner when it is expelled. Abortions in a herd may be sporadic or can occur in "storms" which means that a substantial number of animals abort. Stillborn foetuses are those which die after 260 days usually as a result of a difficult birth process. The importance of reproductive problems is not only the loss of the calf but the lengthening of the intercalving period and the shortened lactation period in dairy animals.

In **sheep and goats**, reproductive failure is typically abortion, the birth of weak young, and low lambing percentages due to resorptions, early abortions or failure to conceive. Infectious diseases involving both ewes and rams must be considered, so both sexes must be examined for possible problems. Diseases which affect the health of small stock the animals must also be eliminated as a cause of problems. Non-infectious factors such as appropriate breeding season, adequate nutrition, correct ram- to- ewe ratio can also affect the lambing percentage.

The investigation of reproductive problems in livestock must be undertaken thoroughly with the help of a veterinarian. It requires taking a full history of the symptoms, the number of animals involved, the stage of abortions, use of AI or bulls, history of introduction of new animals, vaccination programmes etc. Aborted foetuses, weak or misformed newborns can be valuable material on which to do post-mortems and microbiological isolations. This material should be submitted as soon as possible to veterinarians or veterinary laboratories. Never freeze this material and use gloves or plastic bags when handling it. Blood samples from the herd may also aid in a diagnosis. Although it can sometimes be difficult to ascertain the cause of reproductive problems in the long term a successful diagnosis will justify the trouble taken.

Abortions

Abortions in **cattle** can be caused by a wide range of factors including genetic, environmental, toxins, nutritional imbalances, handling or infectious factors. It is therefore essential that the specific causes be sought on a particular farm if the abortion rate is outside normal parameters (3-5%). The most common infectious causes are discussed here but the farmer must be aware that there are less common causes which may sporadically cause abortions such as *Salmonella*, *Streptococcus sp.* and various fungi.

There are various causes of abortions in **sheep and goats**, including genetic factors and some infectious agents such as *Chlamydia*, and more occasionally *Brucella melitensis* and *Coxiella burnetti*. For more details see below under these specific disease headings.

Abscesses of the testes

Abscesses of the testes of rams, usually caused by *Trueperella* (*Arcanobacterium*/ *Corynebacterium*) *pyogenes*, may occur as a result of tick bites or as a sequel to other infections. The feasibility of veterinary treatment of these abscesses will depend on whether they are localised under the skin or whether there is testicular involvement, in which case the prognosis for drainage and treatment is poor. Draining abscesses must be done carefully preferably by a veterinarian. See the section on skin and wounds for the treatment of abscesses.

Angora goat abortions

Although the infections that affect other species can also affect Angora goats, the breed is known to suffer from a syndrome called "Habitual Abortion". This is a heritable metabolic problem of certain individuals in the breed and its high prevalence is thought to be due to inbreeding since it occurs particularly in ewes which show fine hair quality. These ewes abort most commonly at 4 months, without showing any signs of illness or abnormalities such as retained placentas. Adverse weather conditions or other stress factors can precipitate these abortions. The only control measure is the elimination of habitual aborters from the flock.

Balanoposthitis and vulvitis ("Peestersiekte")

This venereally transmitted infectious

condition of the genitalia of ewes and rams is thought to be caused primarily by a *Mycoplasma sp*. It is seen in 2% of flocks in South Africa and is seen predominantly in Dorpers, Karakul and indigenous sheep although it is also seen in Merinos.

The problem appears when the mating season commences, as rams refuse to mate and show signs of severe pain. On examination they will show ulcerative lesions on the penis and sometimes the sheath. These can be so extensive that the penis adheres inside the sheath or is too swollen to be retracted into the sheath. Ewes show ulcerations of the vulva but can lamb without incident; however, they do experience discomfort which they show by constant tail-stump wagging.

Affected rams must be withdrawn from the breeding herd and their lesions must be treated with local application of acriflavine-glycerine obtained from a veterinarian. Injection of infected animals with oxytetracyclines will help recovery. These treatments do not however eliminate the infection and the symptoms will reappear as soon as rams engage in sexual activity again. The condition seems to disappear after 2-3 years, but experts advise culling of infected rams.

Non-infected farms must prevent introduction of infected animals by examining both ewes and rams for ulcers of the genitalia before purchase and again while they are in quarantine.

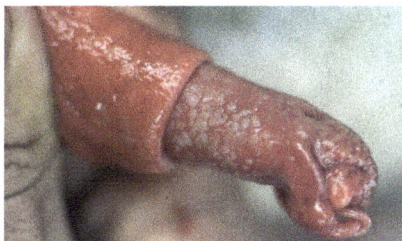

A ram with balanoposthitis showing ulcers on the penis.

Ultratet G0296

Ultratet LA G2857

Ultratet 200 LA G3559

Ecosulf LA G3037

"Big lamb disease"

This condition is a plant poisoning caused by a Karoo bush *Salsola tuberculatiformis* (the cauliflower saltwort) found in the arid areas of the country and therefore the problem has a limited geographic location. Big lamb disease occurs primarily during drought periods when sheep are forced to eat this shrub. The toxin is thought to interfere with the hormonal balance required for normal pregnancy, resulting in a prolonged pregnancy period of up to 213 days. Typically, ewes will be seen with enormously distended abdomens but no signs of udder development. If seen early enough birth can be induced by giving oxytocin injections, but in advanced cases in which the lambs are too large, they have to be removed by caesarean section. These lambs can weigh up to 12 kg and will have with erupted teeth and long hooves. The condition can cause economic losses either due to the death of lambs, or damage to the skins in the case of Karakul sheep.

The plant only affects ewes in the last 50 days of pregnancy and therefore pastures containing this plant must be avoided in this specific period.

A ewe with big lamb disease.

Blue udder (mastitis)

There are a number of bacteria that can cause mastitis or "blue udder" in sheep and goats. Some cases occur shortly after lambing (*Staph. aureus*) while others are seen later in lactation, caused by trauma to the udder during suckling (*Mannheimia (Pasteurella) haemolytica*).

In the early stages the ewe separates from the flock and refuses to allow the lamb to suckle. Examination of the udder will show either one or both quarters to be hard, red and swollen and when milk is expressed it is blood stained and contains clots. If the ewe is not treated with injectable antibiotics at this stage, the condition may become gangrenous, the affected quarter turning blue. *Mannheimia* infections can be effectively treated with injectable tetracyclines. Taking a sterile milk sample before antibiotic therapy will allow identification of the organism involved.

Some types of mastitis can be prevented by allowing the ewes to lamb on the veld instead of in camps. If the causative organism has been identified, specific vaccines can be used for prevention. In chronic cases of the disease the bacteria cause small, encapsulated abscesses in the dry udder, and erupt again during the next lactation. On infected farms pre-breeding inspection with affected udders will help prevent the disease.

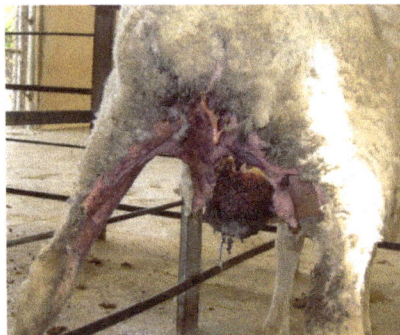

A gangrenous case of blue udder in a ewe

Ultratet G0296

Ultratet LA G2857

Ultratet 200 LA G3559

Bovine Viral Diarrhoea

Bovine Viral Diarrhoea (BVD) is a virus disease which is widespread in SA. This virus is spread by direct contact between animals and is generally introduced into clean herds by a permanently infected (PI) carrier animal, and is spread mainly by animal to animal contact. After introduction into the herd cows may show mild symptoms of diarrhoea, but these may go unnoticed. The next sign will be repeat breeding, abortions and some calves may be born with a range of brain, eye and skeletal defects. Apparently normal calves will be born but these can be persistently infected (PI) with the virus. These PI calves will be a constant source of infection for the rest of the herd and may later develop a serious disease syndrome called mucosal disease.

The primary goal in controlling the disease is the identification and eradication of PI calves. Several laboratory tests are available in order to identify PI calves, which then have to be removed from the herd. In addition, cows must be protected by vaccination to ensure that infected calves are not produced. Live vaccines give the best immunity but cannot be used in pregnant animals. The optimal application of vaccines is complicated and should be done with the advice of veterinarian, as must the testing and elimination of PI animals.

Brucella abortus (Bovine brucellosis)

Infection of cattle herds with *Brucella abortus* remains one of the most important causes of reproductive problems in SA. The bacterium causes abortions, loss of milk production, prolonged intercalving periods and reduces the value of animals. Humans can become infected by handling infected calves, foetuses or foetal membranes, or drinking unpasteurised infected milk. Human brucellosis is a highly unpleasant and debilitating disease which can be difficult to treat once it becomes chronic.

B. abortus is introduced into a clean herd by exposure to an infected cow. When this cow calves, the calf, foetus and placental membranes will be covered with millions of bacteria which will contaminate the environment for months and can also be transmitted to other animals by flies. In high rainfall areas or on irrigated lands Brucella organisms can survive for up to 8 months in the shade.

Clean herds that become infected initially show abortion rates of 30-70% at 5-7 months of pregnancy. Weak calves are sometimes born and often die soon after birth. Following abortions there is a high incidence of retained placentas, metritis and a 20% reduction in milk production. Once all cows have been infected and have aborted, only heifers or newly introduced susceptible cows will abort. In chronic cases swelling of the knee joints (hygroma) may be seen in some animals. Bulls may develop orchitis, with subsequent infertility, but they do not seem to play an important role in the transmission of the disease, except if infected semen is used for AI.

The eradication of brucellosis is most successful using a combination of vaccination and culling of infected animals. While the live attenuated vaccine S19 has been very effective in eradicating the disease, the recent development of RB51 commercial vaccine which can be given twice, resulting in more solid immunity. Eradication programmes should be implemented with the help of a veterinarian since serological testing and planned application of vaccine are involved. Cattle brought into clean herds should be tested and certified negative by a veterinarian to prevent introduction of infection.

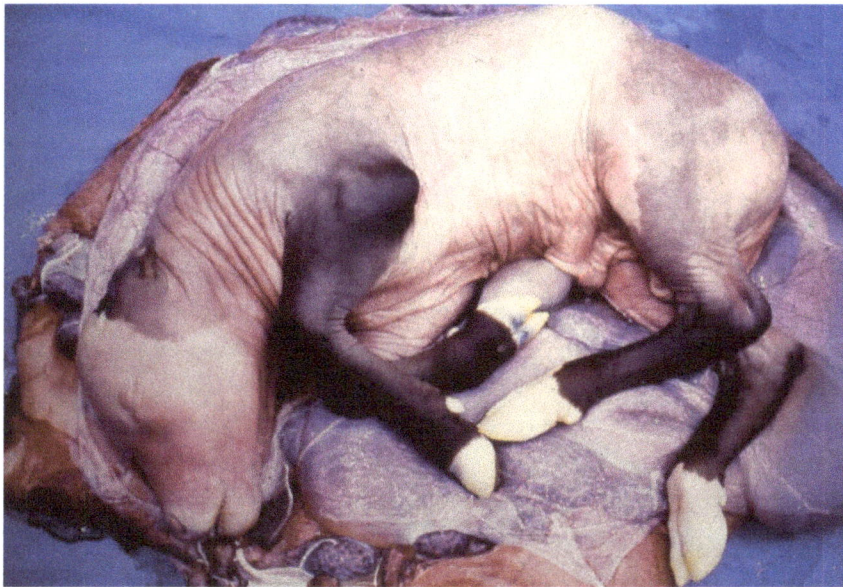
Abortion caused by Brucella abortus

Typical hygroma or swollen joint which is sometimes seen with chronic cases of brucellosis.

from the testes.

On examination, affected testes show a hardening of the epididymis of either one or both testes. The diagnosis is made by a veterinarian taking a semen sample which is examined in the laboratory. Confirmation of the presence of *B. ovis* by culture or staining is important because there are other non-contagious causes of epididymitis (see below).

All affected rams should be culled and young rams should be given a single inoculation at weaning age with the *B. meletensis* Rev 1 vaccine. Eradication will not be successful unless infected rams are removed from the flock. It is unnecessary and undesirable to vaccinate ewes as the vaccine can cause abortions. When introducing rams into clean herds the testes should be carefully examined and laboratory tests should be done to confirm their freedom from *B. ovis*.

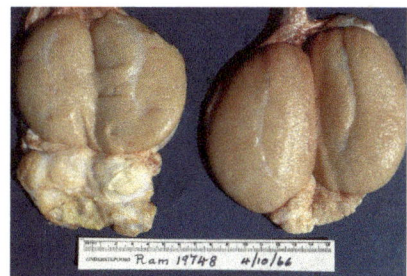
The testes of a ram with epididymitis caused by B. ovis. Note the shrinkage of the affected testicle.

Brucella ovis

This is a contagious cause of epididymitis in ovine rams which causes infertility and therefore a low lambing percentage. *B. ovis* bacteria are transmitted from adult carrier rams to young susceptible rams by direct contact, during "play mating", by fly transmission, or by licking of genitalia. The bacteria enter through the mucosal surfaces of the body (eyes, mouth, genitalia, rectum) and can migrate to the genital tract where they lodge in the epididymis. This is the system of tubules which transports semen from the testes. It lies on the outer surface of the testis and forms a tail at the lowest point of the testis. The bacteria cause inflammation of the epididymis, which becomes red and swollen in the acute stages but later hardens into a large fibrous lump. This can cause partial and eventually total blockage of the ducts or tubules which carry semen

Brucella melitensis

Brucella melitensis is a sporadic cause of abortions in sheep and goats, which has been seen in flocks in certain areas of SA namely Mpumalanga, Limpopo and Kwa Zulu Natal. Although not widespread the importance of these outbreaks is that apart from the losses suffered by stock owners, *B. melitensis* is a cause of "Malta Fever" in humans. In animals, the disease initially causes abortion storms in late pregnancy and retained placentas may be seen. It may cause reduced fertility in rams. As the disease progresses the incidence of abortion declines but infection persists and may become inapparent. Definitive diagnosis of this infection is best done by isolation of the organism from foetal or placental material, or even from milk samples of lactating nannies or ewes. Serology can also be used to detect the presence of infection in a herd. Control of the disease can be achieved by vaccination of ewes, but this must be done before the breeding season as the Rev 1 vaccine causes abortions in pregnant animals.

Campylobacter (Vibrio)

Campylobacteriosis or vibriosis is one of the most common reproductive diseases in cattle in SA. It is a venereal disease, caused by a bacterium Campylobacter fetus venerealis which is transmitted during mating. Bulls are the main carriers of the bacterium, but they show no clinical symptoms. In cows the infection causes embryonic death, aberrant oestrus cycles, delayed conceptions, reduced fertility and occasional abortions. These symptoms closely resemble those caused by trichomonosis from which the infection must be differentiated by diagnostic methods. Young bulls become infected during mating, but they can clear themselves of infection. Bulls infected for more than 3 years tend to become permanent carriers of the disease.

A diagnosis is made by taking sheath washes or scrapings from all bulls used for breeding and having these examined in a veterinary laboratory. Infected cows can be identified by examining vaginal mucous microscopically.

The introduction of Campylobacter fetus venerealis into clean herds can be prevented by using AI (source the semen from accredited AI centres only) or bulls certified to be free of the disease.

In infected herds, heifers, cows and bulls can be vaccinated to reduce the level of infection. Initially 2 vaccinations are given followed up by annual vaccination. This does not eliminate the disease but prevents embryonic infection. Some commercially available vaccines may be curative when given as a double dose, but bulls will have to be re-tested to confirm that the disease has been eliminated.

Some veterinarians advocate treatment of infected cows with antibiotics if this is deemed economically viable by the owner.

To establish a clean herd, virgin heifers must be mated to uninfected bulls or inseminated, and this herd must be effectively separated from infected herds. Artificial insemination should be used until all the cows in a herd have been through at least two pregnancies.

Coxiella burnetti (Q-fever)

This organism is widespread in livestock in SA and is transmitted primarily by ticks. It is an occasional cause of abortions in sheep (3% of abortions investigated by OVI) and even less common in cattle. Sporadic outbreaks of abortions and the birth of weak lambs occur in association with this organism. It is usually diagnosed on examination of the foetus in veterinary laboratories in conjunction with serology. Abortions are sporadic and there is no treatment or prevention that can be economically applied.

Abortion caused by Coxiella burnetti.

Dystocia

The term dystocia is used by veterinarians to describe a difficult birth process. The causes can be divided into maternal and foetal factors. **Maternal factors** include weakness of the mother because of malnutrition, malformations of the pelvic cavity presence or presence of tumours or growths or large amounts of intra-abdominal fat.

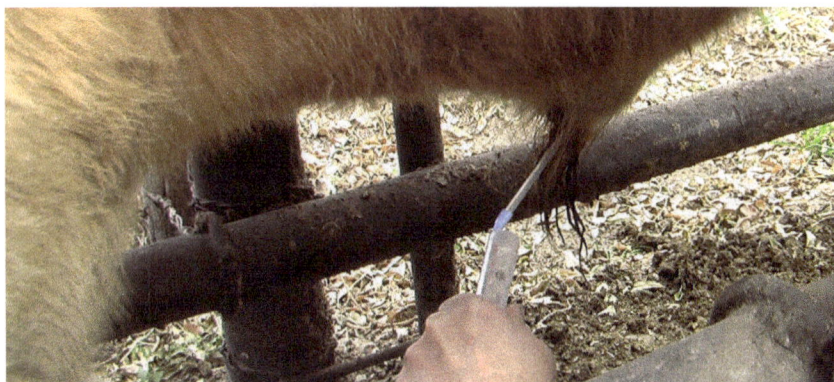

Sheath scraping can be used to sample bulls for campylobacter diagnosis.

Diseases

Foetal factors include oversized foetuses, deformation of the foetus due to infectious agents (see foetal malformations), or faulty position of the foetus.

The normal presentation of the foetus is anterior, in other words with the forelegs facing forward in the birth canal. Less common are posterior presentations with hind legs facing forward. Minor problems with presentation can be corrected by straightening of the limbs but more complicated ones must be left for veterinary intervention, often by caesarean section.

Dystocia in cattle is usually due to either faulty foetal position or some abnormality in the cow which makes the birth process difficult. Certain breeds are known to produce large calves. It has also been shown that the use of specific bulls in some cases causes prolonged gestation. Intervention in calving should not be done without consultation with a veterinarian; the use of excessive force (using tractors etc) will cause post-calving paralysis or death of the cow.

In this neglected case of dystocia in a cow, the calf has died of suffocation in the birth canal.

If an adult cow has not succeeded in delivering a calf within 2 hours from the start of contractions, veterinary help should be sought. In the case of heifers, allow for four hours, as they are still inexperienced and their birth canals are still "tight". Experienced farmers will attempt to deliver the calf themselves but if no progress is made within the first 5 minutes of traction, using 2 assistants only, veterinary help should be summoned, as the dystocia is probably due to serious malpresentation or oversize.

Endometritis

Endometritis is an infection of the uterus which manifests as a thick, yellow custard-like but odourless discharge. It usually results from untreated or insufficiently treated metritis.

It can be treated by a veterinarian with a prostaglandin injection or with an intra-uterine instillation.

Enzootic abortion

Enzootic abortion of Ewes (EAE) is a contagious condition caused by the rickettsial organism *Chlamydia abortus*. It causes abortions and the birth of weak offspring mainly in **sheep** and **goats**, but does occur occasionally in cattle. Ewes become infected when exposed to infected animals contaminating pastures during lambing; the first sign that these exposed ewes have become infected is an abortion storm will occur during the last month of pregnancy. They also have weak lambs, or show a low lambing percentages due to early abortions. Lambs that survive may be stunted and have joint infections or diarrhoea. Although the incidence of abortions drops as ewes become immune, weak lambs will still be seen. Enzootic abortion is suspected when there is a history of abortion storms and weak offspring. A definitive diagnosis can be made on veterinary examination of the foetus, placenta and using serology. The treatment of pregnant ewes with tetracyclines during abortions storms may limit the extent of infection but the best method of control is vaccination of the ewes before the breeding season.

Chlamydia infections in cattle can cause abortions, stillbirths or and the birth of weak calves.

Killed vaccines containing relevant strains are recommended for the control of EAE in small stock.

Ultratet G0296

Ultratet LA G2857

Ultratet 200 LA G3559

Fever

Any disease which causes a temperature reaction can cause abortion in late pregnancy. The most common culprits are the tick-borne diseases redwater, heartwater, and anaplasmosis. There are also certain live vaccines which must be avoided during pregnancy. The package inserts of vaccines must therefore be studied carefully before administration to pregnant animals and if in any doubt exists consult a veterinarian or the manufacturer.

Foetal malformation

Foetal malformation due to genetic defects occurs normally at low level but when the prevalence is high, the involvement of infectious agents must be suspected. The culprits are generally a group of insect-borne viruses which are predominant during summer. The Akabane virus group causes sporadic abortions and foetal malformations in ruminants, chiefly joint and brain deformities. However, the prevalence of problems caused by this virus does not justify the importation or production of a vaccine.

Certain live vaccines can cause foetal abnormalities if administered early in pregnancy, for example blue tongue, some RVF vaccines, and Wesselsbron vaccine (no longer available). History and post-mortem examination can usually establish the cause of these foetal malformations.

In cattle, abortions due to genetic causes are generally accepted to be 3-5% in any herd and this figure is accepted as normal. An increase in this rate is usually an indication of a reproductive problem for example due to the use of a specific bull or the involvement of infectious agents such as BVD and IBR. When this is suspected a thorough investigation must be conducted.

Infectious Bovine Rhinotracheitis (IBR)

The IBR virus is widespread in SA. It has the potential to cause respiratory infections in young animals or feedlot animals, but can also affect the reproductive system. It causes a syndrome called Infectious Pustular Vulvovaginitis (IPV) in cows and Infectious Pustular Balanoposthitis in bulls, which is a local inflammation and ulceration of the genitals. More commonly in SA the IBR virus causes abortions in pregnant animals at 4 months, or the formation of mummified foetuses.

Diagnosis of the disease is based on history and the isolation of the virus from aborted foetuses, examination of foetal organs or two blood samples from cows that have aborted.

Vaccination of cows and heifers before breeding will prevent losses due to the virus. It should be repeated before each breeding season to prevent abortions. Veterinary advice should be sought to select the correct vaccine.

Infertility

Fertility in livestock is influenced by a variety of factors as summarised briefly below:

Genetics: the ability to produce viable sperm and ova is a heritable genetic trait which must be selected by breeding.

Physiology: various factors that affect the physiology can interfere with fertility or libido: in females these may be excess heat, nutritional imbalance, high milk production and hormonal interference (oestrogen in pastures), while in males overwork can cause exhaustion and failure to mate.

Anatomical: any defect of the genitals or anatomical defect which interferes with mating can prevent breeding. In bulls especially those of the *Bos indicus* breeds conformational problems of the sheath mainly collapsing of the sheath lining (phallocampsis) can interfere with mating. This is a genetic tendency so must be prevented by selective breeding.

Management: in dairy cows in particular, incorrect management of young heifers can prevent conception and pregnancy.

Infectious diseases: there are a number of specific diseases that cause infertility which are discussed in this section. Diseases which primarily affect other systems such as lumpy skin disease and besnoitiosis in cattle may also affect the scrotum or testes, causing infertility in bulls (see these under Skin section).

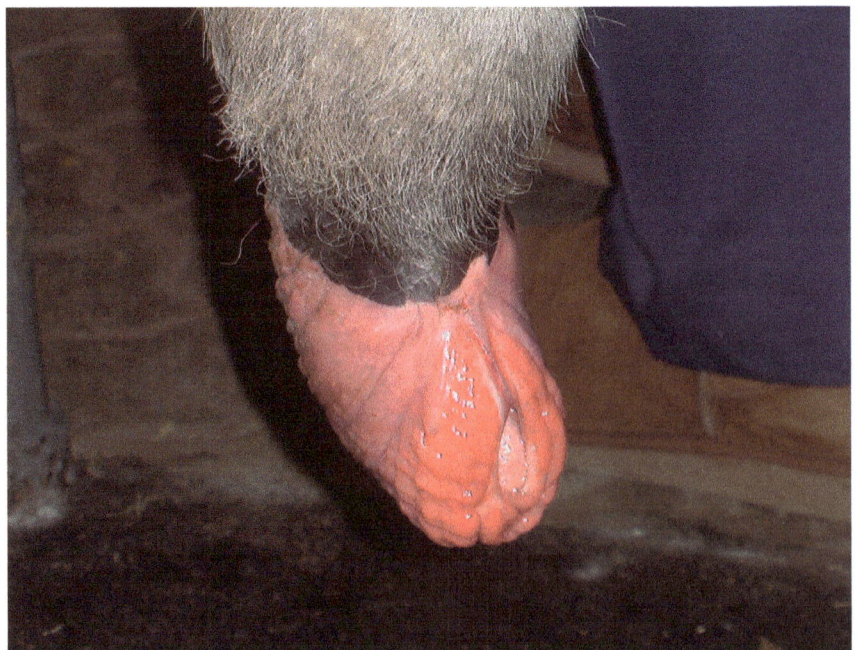

Sheath problems such as this fibrous lesion can interfere with mating.

Ketosis ("Domsiekte") in sheep

For a discussion on ketosis in cattle, see the section on diseases of dairy cattle.

Ketosis in sheep is a disease of pregnant ewes, usually those carrying more than one foetus. It occurs due to insufficient energy intake during the last 6 weeks of pregnancy and this is especially crucial in ewes carrying more than one foetus because it doubles the amount of energy required. Causative factors can be overfat ewes, poor grazing, long periods of handling of heavily pregnant ewes which prevents them from eating, inclement weather, heavy parasite infestations, and anatomical factors like worn teeth and lameness. When there is insufficient energy the body starts to break down fat, resulting in the production of ketones. These ketones cause acidosis, liver damage and affect the brain, causing a change in behaviour.

In the early stages ewes separate from the herd, will not eat and seem to be unusually tame or blind when approached. Later the ewe will lie down and refuse to rise. If she is not treated, she will progress into a coma. The whole process can last about 10 days before the animal finally dies.

The diagnosis of the condition is made on the symptoms and the history of multiple births in the flock. Injection with calcium borogluconate under the skin (roughly 50 ml) will eliminate milk fever as an alternative diagnosis. Veterinary intervention will be needed to treat affected sheep; glucose administration and caesarean sections can be attempted to save the ewes' lives, but if liver damage is too severe this may not be successful.

On post-mortem a typical sign is fatty degeneration of the liver which manifests as a yellowish colour and

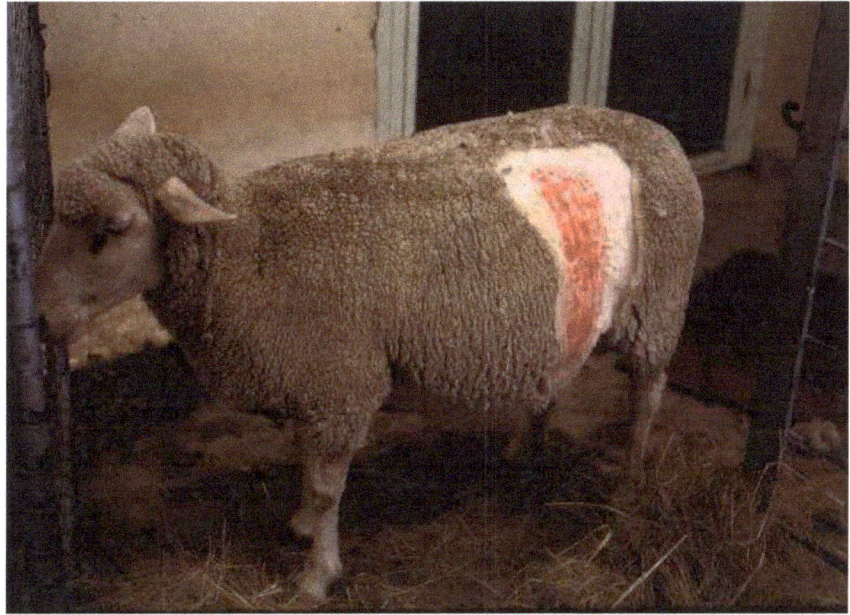

Ketosis in a ewe showing "head pressing" behaviour. Here flank has been shaved in preparation for a caesarean section.

a friable texture. The uterus will be very large, containing more than one foetus and ketones will be found in the urine.

To prevent ketosis ewes must not be allowed to get fat during pregnancy, but must be given a higher level of nutrition during the last 6 weeks. Avoid unnecessary handling of ewes during late pregnancy.

Leptospirosis

Leptospirosis is a bacterial disease which can cause abortions mainly in cattle. It is not very common in SA and is usually confined to herds in coastal and high rainfall areas. There are many varieties of *Leptospira* some of which are specifically adapted to cattle and will be brought into the herd by carrier animals. However, the types which occur in other species may also cause problems, especially the varieties which infect pigs. Infection is introduced by an infected animal which may be an infected bovine, pig, dog or rat.

Transmission occurs by means of infected foetuses or through the urine of infected animals and will cause abortions which may, depending on the type, be associated with mastitis (*L. hardjo*) or a haemolytic disease which may cause jaundice (*L.pomona*). The diagnosis is based on the isolation of the bacterium from the foetus or from the urine of the cow, positive serology can confirm the presence of infection. Infected animals can be treated by a veterinarian with specific antibiotics. The level of infection can be reduced by the use of vaccines containing the Leptospira strains which caused the outbreak.

Listeriosis

This is an occasional cause of abortion in cattle and even less frequently in sheep and goats. *Listeria* bacteria are widespread in the environment but have a particular affinity for plant material. The organism grows particularly well on poor quality silage which has become alkaline. Abortions of up to 15% may result and will be accompanied by retained placentas, clinical illness in the dams and fever.

The condition should be suspected when abortions occur in conjunction with the feeding of silage. The diagnosis can be confirmed if *Listeria* is isolated from the foetal and placental material. Animals may require supportive veterinary treatment if very ill. To prevent further outbreaks the source of the infection must be eliminated.

Metritis

Metritis is a uterine infection characterised by a red, smelly discharge from the vagina, which occurs roughly within the first 2 weeks after calving. It usually follows abortions or dystocias which are complicated by a retained afterbirth. In most cases there is a watery, foul smelling discharge from the uterus. The infection can be so severe that the milk production of the cow drops or the cow may even die from the toxins produced by the infecting bacteria. The condition must be treated with antibiotics under veterinary supervision. The use of pessaries as a routine immediately after calving will prevent the development of metritis. Always use a glove when inserting pessaries.

Eco Afterbirth Pessaries G3115

Mycotoxins

The presence of mycotoxins in feed can cause abortions. For more details see the section on poisonings.

Non-contagious epididymitis

Rams develop non-contagious epididymitis due to a variety of bacteria including *Actinobacillus seminis*. Young rams become infected with these bacteria when they are confined to camps with heavy faecal contamination. It is thought that these bacteria invade the genital tract through the sheath and lodge in the epididymis where they cause an inflammation.

The symptoms are inflammation and enlargement of testes, with eventual hardening of the epididymis and the testes. The condition must be distinguished from *Brucella ovis* infections with veterinary help, by the staining of semen smears, performing bacterial isolation and/or serology.

On infected farms all rams must be examined for lesions and semen samples should be taken. Rams with extensive fibrosis (hardening) of the testes must be culled because they will be infertile. Individuals that shed bacteria may clear the infection themselves by the 2-tooth stage. Treatment with a course of long-acting oxytetracyclines has been advocated but the results are variable. Rams that have been treated rams should be tested before the mating season and those still infected should be culled. The condition can be prevented by turning rams out onto the veld after weaning or frequently moving them to clean camps if kraaling them cannot be avoided.

A ram with swollen testes cause by A.seminis infection.

Ultratet LA G2857

Ultratet 200 LA G3559

Orchitis in bulls

Orchitis or inflammation of the testes in bulls is caused by trauma or infections with a variety of different microorganisms, including *Brucella abortus*, *Mycobacterium spp*, *Truperella pyogenes*, *Histophilus* and *Bovine Herpes Virus 1*. In bulls orchitis is usually one-sided (unilateral); the symptoms are a stiff gait and a reluctance to mate. On examination the testis will be swollen, painful and hot to the touch. The cause of the orchitis must be investigated by a veterinarian so that a decision can be made about the bull's reproductive future.

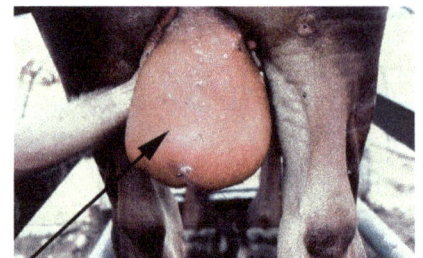

Orchitis of unknown origin in a bull.

Post-lambing gangrene (Malignant Edema)

Post-lambing gangrene is a clostridial infection which is common in goats although it also occurs in sheep with multiple lambs. The condition occurs after birth, usually when the ewe has had a difficult or multiple birth, or is confined in stables during the birth process. The trauma caused to the uterus during the birth process allows the invasion of *C. septicum* (or other clostridia) which causes a gangrenous infection of the muscle of the uterus. Affected ewes develop a fever, show straining, have a reddish discharge and a purple discoloration of the vulva. Prompt treatment with broad spectrum antibiotic like tetracycline may save the ewe's life. On post-mortem the red-purple discoloration of the uterine muscle will be clearly seen.

The condition is controlled by annual vaccination with a multicomponent clostridial vaccine before lambing.

Post lambing gangrene in a ewe showing a massively swollen vulva.

Prolapsed uterus

Prolapse of the uterus in **sheep** has been linked to two possible causes: high oestrogen levels in certain plants particularly clover pastures which also causes infertility, difficult births and even prolapses in non-pregnant ewes; another cause is excessively short tail docking which weakens the muscles of the perineum or after a difficult birth. If sheep on clover pastures are developing prolapses the animals must be moved to other fed sources and veterinary help must be sought to salvage the ewes, as neglect will cause them to be untreatable.

Prolapsed uterus in a ewe.

Prolapse of the uterus in **cattle** occurs sporadically, especially after difficult parturition, and should be treated as an emergency for veterinary treatment. The longer the uterus remains prolapsed, the worse the cow's chances of survival. Place clean hessian or plastic bags under the uterus, rinse with lukewarm water and pour sugar or glycerine over the organ to reduce the swelling while waiting for veterinary help.

Rift Valley fever

Rift Valley fever (RVF) is a viral disease primarily of cattle, sheep and goats which occurs as an epidemic in SA under certain conditions. The virus is transmitted by a mosquito species which feeds on livestock rather than humans. These mosquitoes breed to enormous numbers in certain years when there is heavy rainfall early in the summer, which allows massive numbers of vector mosquitoes to breed in shallow surface water or pans. Livestock become infected as a result of mosquito bites. RVF causes abortion storms as well as the deaths of newborn and young animals. It is estimated that millions of animals died during the outbreaks during the 1950s before vaccines were available. The infection is transmissible to man when infected animals are handled in the course of farm work, veterinary investigations and handling of samples in the laboratory. The infection in humans is unpleasant,

occasionally life-threatening and can cause blindness in some cases.

Annual vaccination with live attenuated vaccines such as Smithburn or Clone 13 is recommended. Vaccination during early pregnancy should be avoided if using the live Smithburn strain. Killed vaccines give poor immunity unless repeated 2-3 times which is usually impractical.

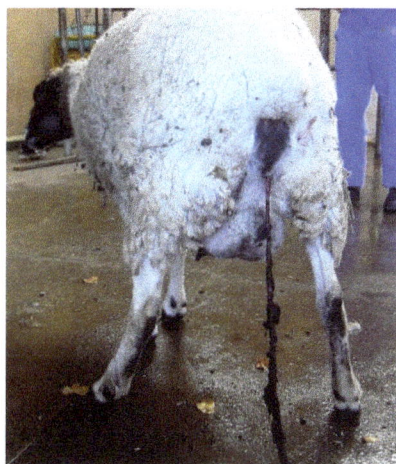

Ewe aborting due to Rift Valley fever.

Trichomonosis

This is a venereal infection caused by a protozoan called *Tritrichomonas foetus*. Before the advent of artificial insemination this condition was as common in dairy cattle as *Campylobacter* infections but now is seen mainly in extensive herds where infected bulls are used. Signs of trichomonosis are aberrant oestrus cycles, infertility, a low percentage of abortions and pyometra (endometritis). These symptoms are similar to the signs caused by *Campylobacter* infections and therefore a definitive diagnosis must be made by taking sheath washes or scrapings from all bulls and submitting these to a laboratory for microscopic examination.

Infected bulls should be culled as neither treatment or vaccination

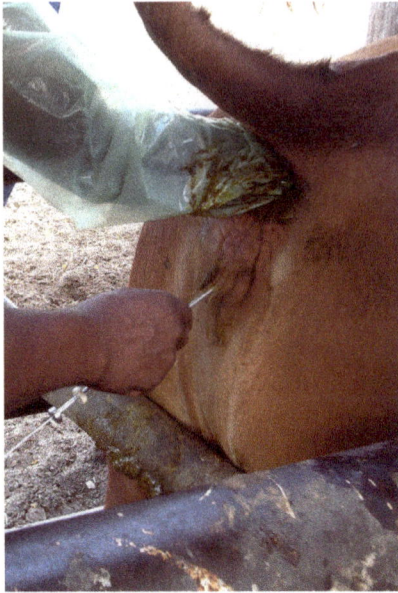

The use of Artificial Insemination will prevent venereal infections like trichomonosis and campylobacter.

is economically viable or effective. Heifers and cows can be vaccinated to reduce the level of infection. Initially 2 vaccinations are given and these are then repeated annually. Infected cows may need sexual rest to allow recovery of fertility. Clean herds can be established by using virgin heifers and bulls/or artificial insemination with certified clean semen.

Vitamin A deficiency

Vitamin A deficiencies cause low conception rates, an increased incidence of retained placentas, eye problems and a dry hair coat in cattle. Although the vitamin is plentiful in fresh green pastures, as soon as the pastures are made into hay, the level declines. Winter pastures and pelleted rations are also low in vitamin A. Since vitamin A is light sensitive, it breaks down when included in dry rations. Supplementation with injectable or oral vitamin A preparations will improve breeding performance and general health of livestock.

Vit-Aid Injectable
G0678

RESPIRATORY SYSTEM

The respiratory system comprises the nasal cavity and sinuses, the bronchi and the lungs themselves, which are enclosed in a thin membrane called the pleura. The nasal cavity is an important defence mechanism for the respiratory system as it warms incoming air and filters out large particles which could harm the lung. The lungs are separated from the rest of the body organs by the muscular diaphragm which maintains the negative pressure in the chest cavity and assists in breathing.

The process of breathing connects the respiratory system directly to the outside world and there is the potential danger of damage and infection. The upper respiratory system which comprises the nose, sinus cavities and the trachea serves a protective function, filtering out large particles and trapping them in the mucous of the nasal and sinus cavities. Small hairs on the mucosa of the trachea move the mucous upwards and, in this way, keep the particles and other contaminants clear of the lungs.

Environmental factors such as cold and dust, and infectious agents, especially viruses, damage this filtering system and in this way permit access to the lower respiratory system, which lead to infections of the lungs and bronchi. The result is bronchitis or pneumonia.

Abscessation

Lung abscesses in **sheep** and **goats** are chiefly caused by *Corynebacterium ovis* and more occasionally by *Trueperella (Arcanobacterium/Corynebacterium) pyogenes.*

These bacteria are shed by infected animals when abscesses rupture to the outside. Infection is transmitted from one sheep to another, especially during management practices which involve wounding such as ear-tagging, shearing, castration and docking. Infection can be spread more widely at dipping. *C. ovis* usually lodges in the lymph nodes of the head, the neck and the shoulder, causing severe enlargement of the affected node which may rupture to the outside. The abscesses when cut open have a dense, dry, cheese-like consistency which is often layered like an onion.

The bacteria can spread from the lymph nodes to the lungs via the blood, causing the development of a few or sometimes extensive abscesses. The signs of lung abscessation are initially gradual loss of weight and eventually difficulty in breathing due to the extensive invasion of the lung tissue. At this stage the condition can be confused with bacterial or viral pneumonia. These animals die soon after showing respiratory signs. Antibiotic therapy of affected animals is not effective because the drugs cannot penetrate the thick capsule layers of the abscess. C.ovis abscessation can be controlled with the use of a vaccine which helps to limit the spread and protect young uninfected animals. Various vaccines are available on the market. The vaccine should be given to lambs at the age of 3 months of age, repeated again after 4 weeks, and thereafter must be repeated annually.

In **cattle** lung abscesses are an occasional finding usually only diagnosed on post-mortem. Occasionally a lung abscess may rupture and blood will be seen flowing from one nostril. These lung abscesses are most commonly caused by *Trueperella pyogenes* and usually spread to the lungs from a primary focus of infection, either pericarditis (heart sac infection) or endometritis.

For further discussion of the control of abscesses in cattle, see the chapter on skin conditions and wounds.

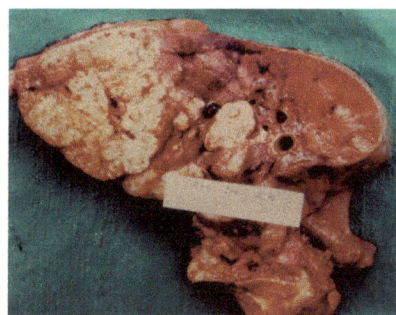

Lung abscesses in a sheep caused by C. ovis.

Bovine Viral Diarrhoea

Apart from the effects of this virus on the reproductive tract as a cause of abortions and foetal malformations, the virus causes a syndrome called mucosal disease in calves. This arises when calves infected as foetuses with non-cytopathic BVD become tolerant to the virus: when they are exposed to cytopathic BVD virus later in life the calves are unable to mount an immune response to the virus and develop a serious infection, characterised by severe respiratory infections which resemble calf pneumonia. They also develop gastrointestinal infections with severe diarrhoea. These calves do poorly and usually die eventually. Apart from the fact that these calves are runts they shed BVD virus and must be removed from the herd. See the section on reproductive problems for BVD control measures).

Bovine Malignant Catarrh ("Snotsiekte")

Bovine Malignant Catarrh (BMC) is a disease of cattle caused by a virus which in South Africa is mainly associated with wildebeest. Wildebeest are carriers of the virus, but they show no symptoms of infection. Wildebeest calves shed virus from birth until roughly 3 months of age and are a source of infection for cattle at this time. The transmission of the virus is airborne for over roughly one kilometre. The disease is mostly fatal, especially in young animals. Infected animals develop fever, depression, watery eyes due to light sensitivity, salivation due to mouth ulcers and typically a purulent nasal discharge (snotsiekte) which causes the crusting of the muzzle. Animals showing these symptoms die despite the use of antibiotics or other treatments.

The diagnosis of the disease is based on the symptoms and a history of contact with wildebeest in the last 9 months. A definitive diagnosis is made by a veterinarian by performing a post-mortem and submitting samples for histology. There is no specific treatment for the disease, but a vaccine has been developed by a Scottish research organisation which protects against artificial challenge; it has also been used experimentally in SA. The vaccine will hopefully become available in the near future. Currently the only control measure to prevent transmission, is to separate cattle and wildebeest by a distance of 1 km particularly around the wildebeest calving season when large amounts of virus are shed.

An early case of BMC showing watering eyes.

Calf pneumonia

Pneumonia is an important condition in calf-rearing units. As with feedlot animals it is a result of the interaction between stress factors and micro-organisms. The respiratory viruses (Infectious Bovine Rhinotracheitis, Bovine Viral Diarrhoea, Respiratory Syncytial Virus and Parainfluenza 3, are involved in causing primary damage followed by secondary infection with *Mannheimia (Pasteurella) haemolytica*. Some of the stress factors involved in calf pneumonia are listed below:

Housing: Poor ventilation and high humidity, as well as the build-up of ammonia due to faecal build-up contribute to lung irritation.

Management: Calves weaned before they are ingesting enough fibre or placed with calves of other age groups may be predisposed to pneumonia.

Feeding: Overfeeding calves with milk or milk replacer can cause problems as they produce high volumes of urine which then results in wet bedding.

Dairy calves develop pneumonia at 6-8 weeks, when colostral immunity to respiratory organisms is waning. They develop a fever, have a dry cough and show a mucous nasal discharge. Later they have difficulty in breathing and the nasal discharge becomes yellow due to secondary bacterial infection. If calves are treated early with antibiotics such as oxytetracyclines or sulphas, they may recover effectively, but calves that develop chronic infections do poorly and cannot be used as replacement heifers.

The vaccination of calves at 35 days of age with live combination vaccines containing the respiratory viruses will help prevent losses; however, it must be stressed that unless contributing management problems are rectified the effect of vaccination may be minimal.

Ultratet LA
G2857

Diseases 68

Ultratet 200 LA G3559

Ecosulf LA G3037

Dosing or gangrenous pneumonia

This condition occurs usually as a result of poor dosing techniques when administering stock remedies. In these cases, the remedies are delivered directly into the lungs instead of down the oesophagus. Gangrenous pneumonia can also result when ruminants regurgitate and then inhale rumen content; this usually happens when the animals are lying flat on their sides and are unable to rise.

The symptoms of gangrenous pneumonia are fever and difficulty in breathing 1-3 days after the dosing or inhalation incident. The mortality rate is usually high because of the extensive damage caused to the lung tissue. If dosing pneumonia is suspected, prompt treatment with a broad-spectrum antibiotic such as oxytetracycline must be done and supportive treatment by a veterinarian may be useful for valuable animals. Guidelines for correct dosing are:

- Do not dose faster than the animal can swallow.
- Do not lift the animal's head up as this prevents swallowing.
- Do not pull the tongue out as it is needed in the process of swallowing.

Feedlot pneumonia

Chronic respiratory disease (CRD) is seen in feedlots where young animals from various farms are brought together in camps with zero grazing. This results in stress due to the mixing of strange animals and transport and lack of shelter which expose them to wind and dust. This is thought to impair the protective mechanisms which usually function effectively in the upper respiratory tract. The animals are therefore susceptible to a range of respiratory viruses (IBR, PI3, BVD and RSV) which cause primary damage in the respiratory tract and therefore allow secondary infection chiefly with *Mannheimia haemolytica* type 1. This bacterium is a normal inhabitant of the upper respiratory system but when the viruses damage the lower respiratory tissues, the bacterium opportunistically enter these tissues. The combined effect of the viral and bacterial infection is a severe pneumonia which has a huge economic impact, not only in terms of deaths or poor subsequent growth but in the expenditure on treatment.

Cattle with CRD initially show a fever, rough hair coat, a clear nasal discharge (during the viral phase of the disease) and watery eyes. Animals may show difficulty in breathing, sometimes with open mouths. Later the animals become severely depressed and the nasal discharge is yellowish, indicating secondary infection. Although the mortality is low, the number of affected animals can be high and economic losses are due to the expense incurred by treatment and the poor weight gains/stunting of affected animals. Prevention by using respiratory vaccines is practised by some feedlot managers if justified by the cost-benefit ratio. The best time to

vaccinate feedlot calves is before they arrive at the feedlot, on the farm of origin. To encourage the supplier of these animals to spend money and labour on the vaccination of the calves, some feedlots will pay a premium for vaccinated calves. To help prevent the disease predisposing factors should be eliminated by providing shelter from wind, implementing dust control, limiting handling of animals to a minimum, and restricting herds to a maximum of 200 animals.

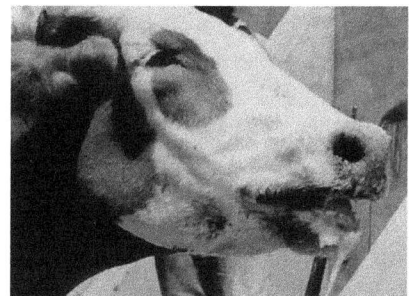

A severe case of feedlot pneumonia. Notice the "open-mouth" breathing.

Ultratet G0296

Ultratet LA G2857

Ultratet 200 LA G3559

Ecosulf LA G3037

"Jaagsiekte"

This is a cancer of the lungs which is induced by a retrovirus. The infection is introduced into a clean flock by an infected animal, which will spread the disease by coughing. Lambs less than 6 months old are the most susceptible to infection and they usually contract infection from infected mothers.

The disease has a long incubation period, and signs of infection can take as long as 8-24 months to appear after initial infection. The most prominent symptom of "jaagsiekte" is shortness of breath especially when the sheep are driven. Severely affected animals will lag behind in the flock and have a severe cough. They may have a watery discharge from the nose. The condition of the animal deteriorates gradually and they die 2-4 months after the initial symptoms appear. They may contract secondary bacterial infections which will cause acute death.

At post mortem the lungs can clearly be seen to be abnormal as they have a grey colouration and have a solid consistency instead of the normal spongy texture. There is usually an increase in volume of the affected lung lobes. The lung lesions for jaagsiekte are characteristic and histopathological examination by a veterinary pathologist will confirm the diagnosis. There is no treatment for this condition. Infected sheep must be identified by serological testing and must be eradicated from the flock as soon as possible.

Lungworm infestation

Lungworm infestation occurs in focal areas of the country which experience cool misty conditions, such as coastal areas of Natal and mountainous regions such as Lesotho. Animals become infested by taking in larvae on infested grazing. The worms migrate to the lungs and cause respiratory symptoms such as coughing and nasal discharge. Most roundworm remedies are effective against lungworm infestations. For more details on treatment and control of the condition see the roundworm section of the endoparasite chapter.

Lungsickness or Contagious Bovine Pleuropneumonia (CBPP)

This disease is caused by the bacterium *Mycoplasma mycoides*. It is a chronic and eventually fatal pneumonia which develops very slowly but is irreversible. Infection is spread from infected individuals to others by droplet infection (coughing). Infected animals lose condition, tire easily when driven and develop a dry cough. At post mortem the lungs show typical "chequerboard" lesions. The danger of this disease is that infected animals take a while to show clinical symptoms and can during this period spread the condition.

Lungsickness was eradicated in SA by veterinary authorities using a test and slaughter method, but it does occur in neighbouring countries such as Namibia, Angola and Zambia. The import of animals from these countries is therefore strictly controlled and smuggling of animals across borders presents a danger to animal health.

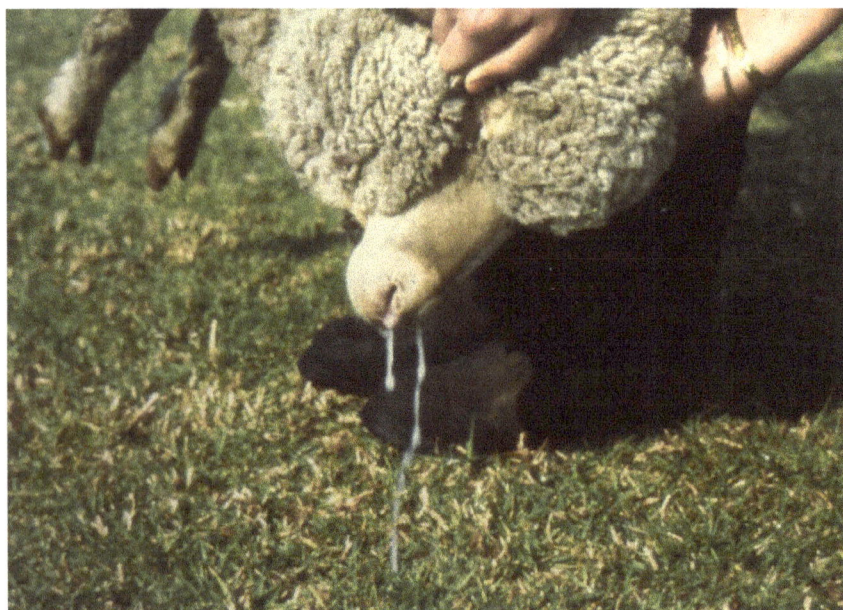

The typical "chequerboard" lesion seen with CBPP.

Nasal worm

This condition occurs in sheep and goats. It is the infestation of the sinus cavities with the larval stages of the sheep nasal fly *Oestrus ovis*. The fly is active during summer months when it seeks out animals and lays its larvae

A sheep with an advanced case of jaagsiekte, showing the massive accumulation of fluid in the lungs.

around the nostrils. The larvae enter the nasal cavity and climb up into the sinus cavity where they feed on the secretions. Here they moult a number of times to become fairly large, before they are sneezed out and the larvae then pupate in the ground. The nasal fly larvae cause severe irritation of the sinuses, resulting in a sometimes copious nasal discharge which can become thick and yellow. Infested animals sneeze and shake their heads and progressively lose weight due to the discomfort. Heavily infested rams may refuse to mate and ewes may refuse to suckle their lambs.

Nasal worm infestations are treated by dosing with remedies containing rafoxanide or closantel, or injections with macrocyclic lactones (ivermectin, moxidectin etc). For more details about control see the ectoparasite chapter.

Moxziben Drench G4040

Ecomectin 1% Injectable G2275

Ecomectin Sheep Drench G2630

Pasteurellosis ("Bontlong")

Lung infection with *Mannheimia (Pasteurella) haemolytica* serotypes typically occurs in sheep under certain conditions. The bacteria occur in the upper respiratory tract without causing problems but when the animals are stressed by transport, crowding (feedlots), during change in weather conditions or after driving over long distances, the organisms could begin to multiply and move down to the lungs.

The condition is most often seen in lambs although it can also occur in older sheep. Acute deaths may result or sheep may show symptoms of fever, lack of appetite, difficulty in breathing, coughing and nasal discharge. The condition can therefore be confused with nasal worm infection, blue tongue, "jaagsiekte" and photosensitivity. Death follows if the animals are not treated promptly with broad spectrum antibiotics such as oxytetracyclines.

On post mortem the lobes of the lung will show various degrees of thickening and darkening resembling liver tissue. The diagnosis is confirmed when *Mannheimia* organisms are isolated from the lung. However, it must be borne in mind that *Mannheimai* infections of the lung are sometimes secondary to conditions like dosing pneumonia and "jaagsiekte". Farms on which *Mannheimia* pneumonia is a problem can use vaccination for prevention. When using the vaccine for the first-time lambs can be vaccinated within the first few weeks of life. Lambs born to vaccinated ewes will have colostral protection one month after birth,

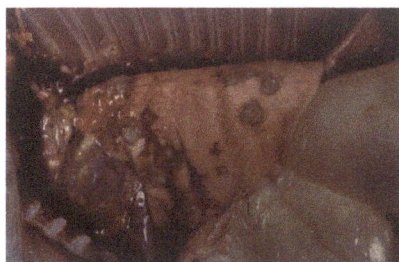

A lung affected by pasteurellosis

Ultratet G0296

Ultratet LA G2857

Ultratet 200 LA G3559

Ecosulf LA G3037

after which they can be vaccinated. Booster vaccinations must be given a month after the initial vaccination and annually thereafter.

Plant poisonings

Certain plant poisonings cause respiratory conditions in sheep, namely *Crotalaria sp* ("jaagsiektebossie"), *Gnidia* ("harpuisbos"), *Cucumis* (wild cucumber) and *Hertia pallens* ("springbokbos").

In cattle intoxication with *Crotalaria spartioides* can been described as a cause of "jaagsiekte" in cattle in the Kuruman district. "Fog fever" which is an acute respiratory distress seen on green pastures occurs occasionally in SA. For more information see the section on plant poisonings.

Tuberculosis (BTB)

Bovine tuberculosis is a slow progressive disease caused by the bacterium *Mycobacterium bovis*. It primarily affects the lung but can also lodge in the udder and other organs. Humans are as susceptible to M. bovis as they are to *M. tuberculosis*, which is the main cause of tuberculosis in humans. *Bovine tuberculosis* is therefore of enormous importance to public health and is the reason for the introduction of the pasteurisation of milk sold for human consumption.

Because BTB symptoms are slow to develop the condition is not detected in infected herds until the disease is advanced, when animals show non- specific signs of emaciation, rough hair coat and possibly enlarged lymph nodes. Infection in individual animals must be identified by a veterinarian performing diagnostic methods such as the intra-dermal test or submitting samples for various laboratory tests. On post-mortem the tuberculous lesions will be detected.

When TB has been diagnosed in a herd, a state veterinarian must be contacted and an eradication programme must be devised. This usually involves testing to identify infected animals which are then branded with a "T" to identify them. Hereafter the animals are slaughtered in specified abattoirs. Disinfection of the premises must be done regularly with 2,5% phenol or other recommended disinfectants.

Bovine tuberculosis is enjoying a resurgence since the collapse of the TB eradication scheme, so stock owners must be extremely careful not to introduce infection into the herd. All animals should be tested by a veterinarian prior to introduction into the herd or should be purchased from accredited disease-free herds.

A bovine with advanced tuberculosis showing emaciation.

The skin test for the diagnosis of bovine tuberculosis measures the increase in thickness in response to the injection of tuberculin.

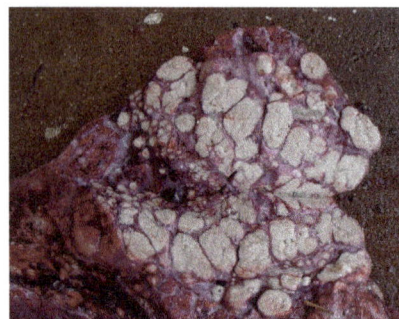

A lung affected by bovine tuberculosis.

SKIN AND WOUNDS

A wide variety of conditions can affect the skin of livestock. These conditions can be specific problems of the skin or can be part of other disease complexes. Since many skin conditions look similar it is essential to obtain a diagnosis by careful examination and the taking of samples for laboratory diagnosis. This will enable the correct treatment of the condition.

Abscesses

Abscesses in **sheep** and **goats** are most commonly caused by *Corynebacterium ovis* and Trueperella *(Arcanobacterium)* pyogenes. The bacteria causing these conditions are spread by infected animals and are picked up by susceptible animals through the wounds inflicted by management procedures such as ear-tagging, castration, and docking, but also through wounding by ticks, thorny plants, stony ground, ticks and grass seed awns and weeds. In sheep grass seeds penetrate soft skin around the throat causing *Trueperella* abscesses around the tongue and pharynx. When abscesses develop the lambs refuse to feed due to discomfort and lose weight. These abscesses are seldom detected in live animals but will be seen if a careful post-mortem is performed. The only useful control for *Trueperella* abscesses is good hygiene (see below under cattle). *C. ovis* which most often affects sheep and goats generally causes abscessation and massive enlargement of the lymph nodes around the head and neck. The abscesses may rupture to the outside and infection may spread to internal organs. *C. ovis* infections, also known as **caseous lymphadenitis**, are usually associated with wounds caused by shearing. Effective vaccines are available for preventing infection of young animals and limiting infections in adult animals.

Good hygiene practices such as the disinfection of shearing equipment are essential to prevent the spread of infection. Prevent introduction of infected sheep into a clean herd by requesting examination of sheep by a veterinarian who will examine the lymph nodes of sheep in quarantine.

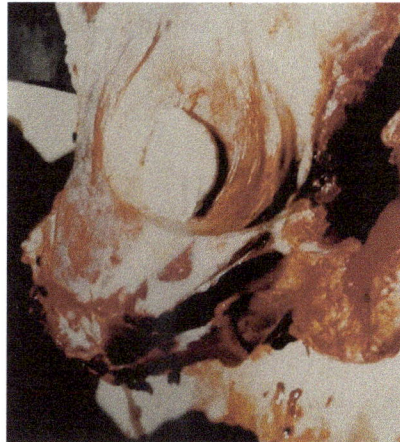

A Corynebacterium ovis abscess in the prescapular or shoulder lymph node of a sheep.

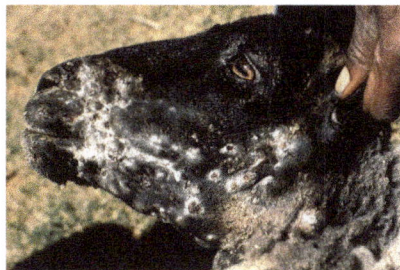

Face abscess in a sheep caused by A. lignieresi.

Face abscesses are seen in sheep forced to graze on thorny forage such as prickly pears or grass with sharp seeds. These wounds become infected with *Actinobacillus lignieresi* organism which occur in faeces and soil. Infection can spread extensively all along the skin of the head and can metastasize to various other parts of the body. Veterinarians can treat this condition with the intravenous injection of sodium iodide, but this is only effective in cases that are not too extensive.

In cattle *T. pyogenes* is the most common cause of abscesses, usually as a sequel to a wound or a tick bite. There is no proof that *A. pyogenes* vaccines are effective, so control must be aimed at hygienic practices such as sterilising implements and disinfecting wounds. Tick control will prevent abscessation of udders and scrotums.

A large T.pyogenes abscess in a bovine.

It is most important to identify the causative organism of abscesses as this will determine the control measures. This is done by requesting a veterinarian to submit samples to a veterinary laboratory. The treatment of abscesses with antibiotics is usually ineffective so general abscess problems must be tackled by culling heavily infected animals, destroying infected material by burning or treating with strong disinfectants, using stringent hygiene and disinfection during surgical procedures and eliminating predisposing causes such as thorny grazing. Tick control may be necessary if foot abscess problems are encountered (see chapter on lameness).

Allerton virus

This herpes virus causes a skin condition seen in the summer months in cattle and is often confused with lumpy skin disease which is caused by a pox virus. As with lumpy skin disease, the virus is spread by biting flies such as stable flies (*Stomoxys calcitrans*). However, the skin lesions caused by Allerton virus are coin-shaped, flattish lesions and there are no accompanying systemic symptoms. The skin lesions rapidly disappear and resolve uneventfully without needing treatment. If the virus affects the teats of the udder, this may cause problems during the milking process (see under Dairy). Diagnosis is based on the typical appearance of the lesion, but the virus can be isolated to distinguish the condition from lumpy skin disease by taking a skin biopsy.

Besnoitiosis (Elephant skin disease)

This condition occurs in the northern areas of SA – in Limpopo, the Northwest Province, and the northern areas of Mpumalanga and KwaZulu-Natal. It is caused by a protozoal organism *Besnoitia besnoiti* which can be transmitted by biting flies, but it is now suspected that a wild cat species may serve as the main reservoir for the disease.

Initially, the condition causes severe swelling of the skin accompanied by a fever. Animals are ill, refuse to eat and will avoid exposure to sunlight. Reddening of the skin of white animals may be seen. In bulls the testes may become swollen.

However, this stage may not be noticed by the farmer, who may only recognise that the animal is infected when the skin becomes thickened and hard. At this stage, the skin may develop folds and the hair will be lost. The skin may crack open and ooze serum, and these wounds may be attacked by the cattle blowfly. Bulls become sterile as a result of inflammation of the testes. The diagnosis of besnoitiosis is based

on the typical symptoms and on histopathology of the skin. A course of injectable tetracyclines will help the affected animals to recover, but severely affected animals may need supportive treatment from a veterinarian. A vaccine is available which gives protection against the clinical form of the disease for 4 years. However, very little vaccine is used by farmers and this may lead to its being discontinued.

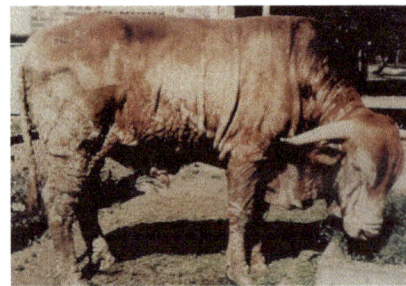

Severe thickening of the skin is seen with Besnoitia infection.

Burn wounds

Animals that get caught in veld fires may suffer mild to severe wounds. Burnt animals should be assessed as soon as possible to decide whether they need to be destroyed on humane grounds. Wooled sheep are generally protected by their fleece and suffer minor skin burns, while cattle, shorn or hairy sheep and goats may suffer extensive injuries. Australian vets recommend grouping animals in three categories as follows:

1. **Poor survival prospects include the following:**
- animals with burns to the legs because the hooves usually fall off;
- animals with breathing difficulties as they will have irreversible lung damage;
- cattle and milk goats with burnt udders, since they will be in severe pain; and have a poor prognosis for recovery.

Allerton virus lesions can sometimes be confused with lumpy skin disease.

Animals in these categories should be euthanased for humane reasons.

2. **Salvageable:** animals with burns to the face, groin, anus, sheath, scrotum and vulva may survive with good nursing and protected from fly strike. Alternately these animals can be sent for emergency slaughter.

3. **Good survival prospects:** sheep with a good fleece cover are often insulated from fire damage and they have a good chance of surviving without intervention.

Bolo disease

Bolo disease is a condition of the fleece of Merino type sheep that is seen mainly in the Eastern Cape area of Stutterheim and Cathcart, although it has also been described elsewhere. The cause is thought to be an unidentified *Corynebacterium* species which invades the skin causing a dermatitis. The condition results in the appearance of dark patches of wool, which when shorn shows chalky white areas. The skin of affected animals is inflamed and scabby, and tears easily at shearing. The condition develops in sheep of two years of age and becomes progressively worse with increasing age. Severely affected animals will lose condition over time.

Bolo disease does not respond to antibiotic treatment but mild cases can benefit from dipping in a solution of 3% flowers of sulphur. Severe cases may not respond and should be culled. Segregation of age groups during shearing may help prevent the spread of the condition and stringent disinfection of shears with formalin is recommended.

Blowfly strike

Blowflies are a group of flies that in nature are adapted to laying their eggs on carrion. Some of these species have adapted to attack live sheep under certain conditions. The problem is seen particularly in fine-woolled merinos when the fleece becomes soiled with faeces or becomes wet. Animals with heavy folds are strongly predisposed to fly strike because the fleece inside the folds retains moisture and results in local areas of "fleece rot". This is the breakdown of fine fleece and the softening of skin. These areas emit a smell that is attractive to blowflies, which settle and lay their eggs on these patches.

The larvae feed on the softened skin, causing large open sores.

Affected sheep are restless and anxious, will bite and kick at their lesions. Heavily infested animals may die if not treated. For treatment and prevention of blowfly strike see the section on Ectoparasites.

Dermatophilus congolensis (Senkobo disease)

The infection of cattle with *Dermatophilus congolensis* is referred to as Senkobo disease and is most commonly seen in cattle in tropical and sub-tropical regions. It is associated with prolonged wetting of the skin for several days during rainy seasons. Cases have been seen in communal areas of Eastern Cape and Limpopo where the latter was misdiagnosed as foot-and-mouth disease. The organism is probably spread at communal dipping tanks. *Dermatophilus* organisms have been isolated from various ticks but whether they play a role in its spread is not clear. The organisms invade the skin and cause dermatitis which results in the reddening, crusting and cracking of the skin. The condition can be localised around the head or feet or can be widespread over the body. The diagnosis should be confirmed by requesting a veterinarian to make impression smears of the lesions or isolation of the organism to distinguish the condition from

Ultratet LA
G2857

Ultratet 200 LA
G3559

A sheep affected with Bolo disease.

ringworm, ectoparasite infestations, or cases of photosensitivity. Treatment of individual animals with injections of long-acting tetracycline is effective. The addition of zinc sulphate to diptanks will control overgrowth of the organism.

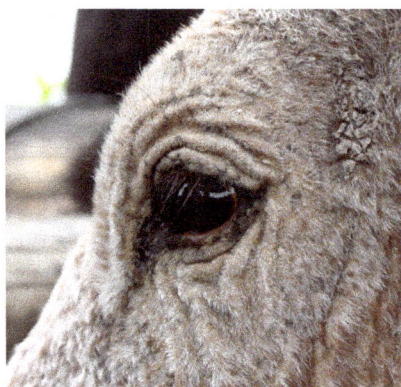

A cow showing the typical crusty lesions caused by Senkobo disease.

Lumpy skin disease

Lumpy skin disease (LSD) is a viral disease of cattle which occurs mainly in the summer months. This is because the stable fly *Stomoxys calcitrans* which transmits the disease occurs in large numbers during late summer. The disease can occur anywhere in the country because, although it may disappear from certain areas temporarily, it can be reintroduced by the transport of diseased animals.

Infected animals develop a fever, show listlessness and they may have discharge from the eyes due to conjunctivitis. They salivate due to the erosions on the muzzle and the mouth. The skin lesions which occur up to 14 days after initial signs, are firm raised round nodules, which can be concentrated in certain areas or spread all over the body. The skin lesions may disappear in mild cases or may become hard or ulcerate. In the latter case they can become infected. Occasionally the virus may affect the cornea of the eye, causing blindness.

Calves are severely affected, developing ulceration of the respiratory and gastrointestinal tract, which often results in death. Cows develop mastitis as a sequel to udder lesions and for this reason outbreaks can be devastating in dairies. The skin lesions cause severe damage to animals intended for hide production. LSD is therefore a very important disease economically.

Diagnosis is based on the symptoms but since these can be confused with other conditions such as Allerton virus infection, virus samples of skin and affected tissue can be taken by a veterinarian for electron microscope examination or culture.

There is no specific treatment but antibiotic therapy is given to prevent secondary bacterial infection. Severely affected animals may need supportive treatment from a veterinarian. The disease is easily controlled by annual vaccination with the lumpy skin disease vaccine. In some herds calves may not obtain colostral protection because their mothers, although immune, do not produce antibodies even when vaccinated. In these herds calves may need to be vaccinated before weaning rather than at weaning as recommended by the manufacturers.

Lumpy wool

This condition results from the infection of the skin or hair with *Dermatophilus congolensis*. It is a serious threat to the wool industry although it also affects non-woolled sheep like Dorpers. The bacterium is carried by infected sheep and transmitted usually by infected dipwash. The organism invades the skin during shearing, or with constant wetting of the fleece due to rain or dipping. Young animals are more susceptible because they have less wool fat which makes the hair more susceptible to wetting. The invasion of the skin causes inflammation which results in the wool forming hard scabby lumps. Removing these lumps exposes bleeding skin lesions.

Lumpy wool can occur either as a generalised or as a localised condition. The localised condition can

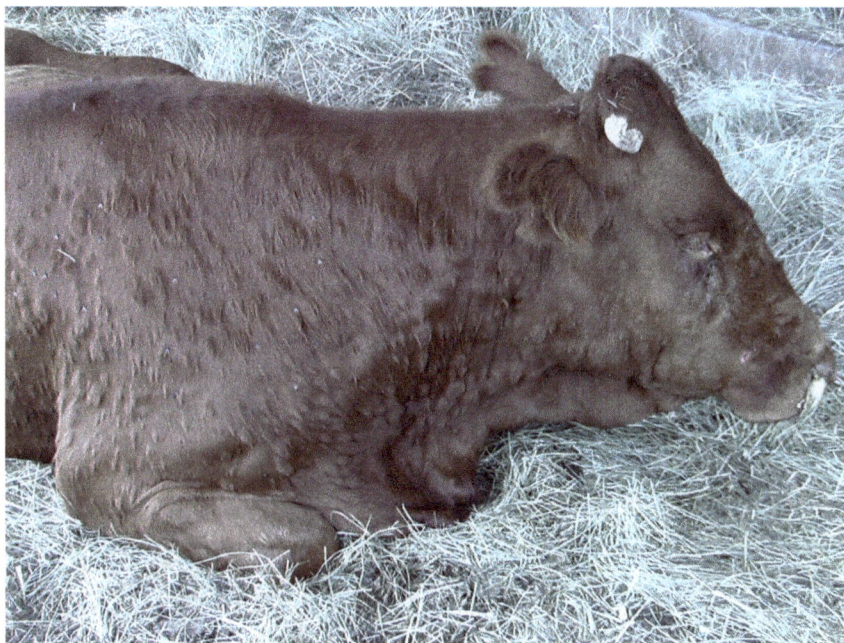

The typical raised, nodular lesions seen with lumpy skin disease.

be seen affecting the topline of the animal, which can include the head and face (the "hardelam" syndrome) or can affect the skin above the claws ("strawberry footrot"). The infection damages the fleece and severely affected animals may die of exposure or loss of weight due to the discomfort. The condition is diagnosed on history and the appearance of the skin lesions but can be confirmed by laboratory isolation of the causative organism or microscopic examination of impression smears made from the scabs. This is important as lumpy wool can be confused with other conditions of the skin and fleece.

Badly affected animals can be treated with a course of penicillin-streptomycin injections or injection with a long acting oxytetracycline. Flocks can be treated with the application of disinfectants containing quaternary ammonium compounds applied as a 1:200 dilution either by hand or in a dip. Treatments should be repeated at 3-week intervals.

To prevent the condition, it is essential to add 5% zinc sulphate to dip wash. The application of zinc sulphate powder along the topline during wet seasons is said to be effective in preventing "hardelammers".

Ultratet LA
G2857

Ultratet 200 LA
G3559

Orf

Orf is a contagious virus infection of sheep and goats which occurs on many farms in SA.

It occurs particularly in young animals since older animals gradually develop immunity with exposure. The virus is very resistant in the environment and can survive in kraals and camps.

Outbreaks occur in lambs grazing on thorny shrubs like "vyebos" or thorn trees, which cause wounding of the mouth. The lesions seen are wartlike outgrowths which develop around the lips, nose and occasionally on the rest of the face and head. Internal lesions arise occasionally. Lambs transmit the infection to ewes and they may develop lesions on the udder, sometimes leading to cases of mastitis. Although the lesions are usually small and localised they can become extensive, may bleed and become secondarily infected.

Lesions resolve within a few weeks but can be treated locally with wound oil or antibiotic spray to prevent secondary bacterial infection. Animals with severe lesions may need veterinary assistance if they cannot feed or walk.

Vaccination of ewes should be done eight weeks before lambing; they must be vaccinated in the axilla (armpit) so that the udder does not get infected. Lambs can be vaccinated from as early as two days old. Vaccination can be repeated 6-8 weeks later. It is accepted that orf vaccines are not as effective as other viral vaccines, so the correct application of the vaccine is most important. Vaccination is done by scarification which entails scratching the skin with a sterile needle and placing a drop of vaccine on the scratches. Disinfectants must not be used at the site of injection because this will kill the vaccine virus. Humans can be infected with orf virus so cases of orf and the vaccine must be handled using gloves.

Futaspray G2715

A severe case of lumpy wool in a sheep.

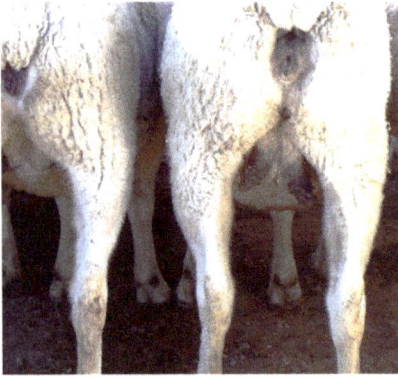
The orf virus can infect the udders of ewes as well as the mouths of lambs.

Parasites

A number of parasites can infest the wool of **sheep** and cause them to show signs of fleece disturbance. The most common problems are sheep scab caused by the mite Psoroptes ovis and biting and sucking mites which affect both **sheep** and **goats**. Australian itch mite and ked flies are less common causes of skin irritation. Descriptions, treatment and prevention of all these conditions are discussed in the Ectoparasite chapter.

Cattle are host to various species of mites and lice which cause itching and rubbing, but these infestations can be confused with other skin conditions causing hairlessness and scab formation. For detailed discussion of mites and lice of cattle, see the Ectoparasite chapter.

Photosensitivity (Light sensitivity)

The most common cause of photosensitivity in livestock is the ingestion of plants or fungi containing toxic components. There are a number of these plants and it is useful to familiarise oneself with local plants which can cause this condition.

Common causes in **sheep** are dubbeltjies (*Tribulus terestris*) which causes "geeldikkop", buffalo grass (*Panicum*), *Lantana camara*, and various Karoo bushes such as *Athanasia* and *Assemia*. The distribution and description of these plants are dealt with in the section on plant poisons.

Plants that cause photosensitivity in **cattle** are *Lantana camara*, *Lasiospermum* ("ganskweek"), *Microcystis* algae and the fungus *Pithomyces chartarum*. For details, see the plant poisoning section. The photosensitivity syndrome arises once the toxic component reaches the bloodstream. Exposure of the skin to sunlight will then cause severe inflammation of the skin, reddening and severe swelling, sometimes causing bursting of the skin. The skin then oozes serum and becomes crusted. The eyes are often red and swollen. With plants which cause primary liver damage such as "dubbeltjies", jaundice will be seen. The diagnosis of photosensitivity is based on the symptoms and a history of eating specific plants. Treatment is the withdrawal of animals from the veld where the plants occur, provision of complete shade and water. Antibiotic therapy can be given to prevent secondary infections. Badly affected animals may need specific veterinary treatments such as fluid and cortisone administration.

Ultratet LA G2857

Ultratet 200 LA G3559

Ringworm

Ringworm, despite its name, is actually a fungal infection of the skin, which is seen in many species including man. In sheep it typically affects those with hair rather than wool. The causative agent is usually a *Trichophyton sp*. The infection is introduced into a flock by an infected animal and spreads with close contact. In cattle the condition is usually seen in calves housed in unhygienic conditions. The lesions

A calf with a severe case of ringworm

are usually circular, scabby or crusty areas of hairlessness. The lesions are usually found on the head but can become extensive and can spread to the rest of the body. The condition is slow and progressive but will cause the animals to lose condition. The diagnosis is usually based on the typical appearance of the lesion, but culture of the organism in a veterinary laboratory will confirm the cause.

Treatment of the affected areas with an iodine wash will kill the fungus, but severely affected animals may need to be plunge-dipped in 2% lime sulphur solutions, once a week for a month.

Warts

Warts in cattle are caused by a papilloma virus and are most commonly seen in calves.

The virus is transmitted directly from one animal to another through breaks in the skin. Cows with warts on the udder may serve as a source of infection for calves. Warts are usually self-limiting, disappearing after a few months, but severe cases of extensive infection are seen particularly in animals in poor health due to malnutrition or parasite infection.

The diagnosis is based on the appearance of the lesion which is typical although it can be confused with *Dermatophilus* infections in the early stages. Autogenous vaccines made from the wart material by veterinary laboratories may

An extensive case of warts in a bovine

be warranted if the problem is widespread. However severe cases may have to be culled.

Wound management

The most serious wounds are those in which large blood vessels have been severed resulting in massive bleeding. In these cases, it is essential to apply pressure to the blood vessel and stop the bleeding. This can be done by applying pressure with a finger until veterinary help is available and the blood vessel can be closed with a forceps. Less serious bleeding can be stopped with pressure bandage made of cotton wool and a bandage. The cotton wool absorbs the blood and applies pressure to the wound when wrapped tightly with a bandage.

Large gaping wounds will need to be sewn up as they will not close properly if left unattended. Smaller wounds can be managed with basic wound management: rinsing the wound with clean water and applying wound oil, ointment or spray is usually sufficient. The use of irritant substances like hydrogen peroxide or disinfectants should be avoided. In areas where screw worm occurs wound oil/spray containing insecticide should be applied to prevent maggot infestation. Injectable antibiotics will only be needed in the cases of large deep wounds or those which have become severely infected due to neglect.

Large superficial abscesses must be left to "ripen" (soften) before they can be opened to drain. This can be done with a sharp sterilised scalpel blade and the cut must be made at the lowest point of the abscess to promote drainage. Once open the abscess it can be cleaned with cotton wool and the inside rinsed with wound oil or wound spray. Once the abscess is open an injection of a long-

acting antibiotic like oxytetracycline can be given to help the wound heal effectively. Note that the lancing of an abscess must be done away from other animals and all pus and cotton wool used during the process must be disinfected.

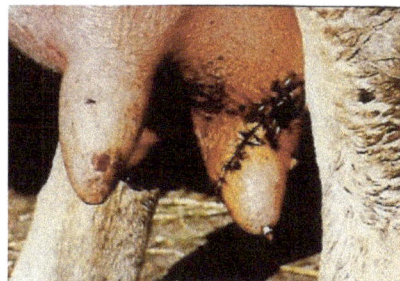

Large wounds like this laceration of the udder require stitching to ensure proper closure.

Futaspray G2715

Expel Wound Spray G3245

Ultratet LA G2857

Ultratet 200 LA G3559

The biology and control of tick-borne diseases is complex and a good knowledge of the lifecycles of the ticks involved as well as the diseases themselves is essential to be able to manage the problem. The vaccines used against these diseases are more difficult to apply than most others and they must be handled and administered correctly, or the desired effect will not be achieved. Farmers who are not familiar with the control of these diseases should consult their local veterinarians before embarking on vaccination campaigns for example when introducing susceptible animals into endemic areas, particularly where adult animals are involved.

Anaplasmosis or tick-borne gallsickness

Anaplasmosis is the most widespread of all the tick-borne diseases because it is transmitted by 5 different ticks, by biting flies and frequently by unsterilised needles. It is caused by a blood-borne parasite called *Anaplasma marginale*. Under feedlot and dairy conditions, the organism is often transmitted by stable flies. Anaplasmosis outbreaks occur in summer and autumn in adult animals as calves under 6 months have a temporary immunity to the disease. However, outbreaks can occur in the winter months if tick numbers are high.

The disease has a long incubation period of 4 to 6 weeks after which affected animals become weak and listless due to a progressive anaemia. They develop constipation because the rumen function becomes impaired. Chronic cases may develop jaundice, show loss of weight and may abort. Death occurs if the animals are not treated. The diagnosis of anaplasmosis is confirmed by finding the organisms in a blood smear.

Anaplasmosis cases can be treated with a long-acting oxytetracycline injection (20 mg per kg intramuscularly) or with imidocarb (at 3.5 mg per kg via the intramuscular route). Neither of the remedies sterilises the infection so they do not interfere with the immunity which develops after recovery.

Supportive veterinary therapy may be required in the form of fluid administration, liver supportive therapy and treatment for rumen stasis.

Ultratet LA
G2857

Ultratet 200 LA
G3559

A post mortem of an anaplasmosis case showing an enlarged spleen, swollen liver, enlarged gall bladder and jaundice.

The control of anaplasmosis
Two options are available:

- **Intensive tick control and no vaccination:** this control option is recommended for dairies because these cows are very susceptible to tick borne diseases and vaccination will interfere with milk production. This requires vigilant tick control as failure of this will be disastrous. Most pyrethroids and formamidine based dips are suitable for use in dairies but the label should be checked for milk withdrawal recommendations.
- **Tactical tick control with vaccination:** this approach can be applied to most other herds with the exception of dairies. It is achieved with low-intensity dipping and vaccination of young animals to ensure immunity. Sporadic outbreaks can still occur in marginal areas or after dry periods. Vaccination is done between 3 and 9 months of age when the animals do not develop severe vaccine reactions. The vaccine is supplied frozen on dry ice and must be thawed carefully as described below in the section on heartwater. Anaplasma vaccine is administered intramuscularly. When vaccinating adult animals, vaccine reactions may develop between the 4th and 6th week after vaccination. During this period animals must be observed for signs of fever (>40°C) and

symptoms of poor appetite, decreased milk production, constipation, anaemia and jaundice. Vaccine reactions can be treated with 10mg per kg oxytetracycline, repeated if necessary, after 24 hours, or with a single administration of a long-acting formulation at 20mg per kg. Anaplasmosis vaccination can be done simultaneously with redwater vaccination. Immunity develops roughly 2 months after vaccination and lasts about 4 years which is basically the productive lifetime of cattle. It must be borne in mind, however, that even when animals have developed a good immunity, under stress such as pregnancy, poor nutrition, etc. the immune system is weakened and cases can occur with heavy challenge. This is true for many diseases including all the those discussed in this section.

Heartwater

The heartwater organism *Erlichia (Cowdria) ruminantium* is transmitted by the bont tick which occurs in warm moist regions of the country, namely the bushveld and the eastern coastal areas (see the section on ticks for a distribution map). The immature bont tick feeds on small mammals and ground birds, and this makes it impossible to eradicate this species. The transmission of heartwater occurs throughout the year but is less prevalent in winter. Losses due to the disease occur in animals introduced into heartwater areas or when animals in heartwater areas are not exposed frequently enough to tick immunisation, usually during drought years.

Cattle begin to show symptoms 9-29 days after being bitten by infected ticks. The incubation period in sheep is 7-35 days. Initially animals show a fever, listlessness, have a high-stepping gait, difficulty in breathing, and later they show prominent nervous symptoms such as chewing and head pressing. They lie down, show frantic "paddling" movements, and death follows soon thereafter. Typical post-mortem signs are the accumulation of fluid around the heart, in the chest cavity, and in the lungs where it is seen as a foamy liquid in the bronchi. To confirm the diagnosis a veterinarian will make a brain smear for laboratory examination. The heartwater organisms can be seen when the smear is coloured with a specific stain.

Treatment of sick animals is most effective when done early in the course of the disease. Once nervous signs have developed the chances of successful treatment deteriorate dramatically. An oxytetracycline injection should be given immediately, preferably intravenously, at a dose rate of 10mg/kg, and this should be repeated at least twice at 24 hr intervals. Slow administration of intravenous preparations is essential to prevent shock reactions. Long-acting formulations can also be used in less severe cases. These are given at 20mg/kg via the intramuscular route and may need to be repeated after 72 hrs.

Supportive treatment can be given by a veterinarian to reverse lung oedema and nervous symptoms. Once the animal's temperature has returned to normal, the stock owner should provide the animal with good quality feed and water.

Ultratet G0296

Ultratet LA G2857

Ultratet 200 LA G3559

A sheep that died of heartwater showing fluid leaking from the nose

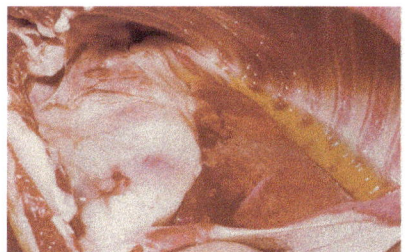

Post mortems on deaths due to heartwater typically show an accumulation of fluid in lungs, heart sac and abdomen.

Control of heartwater in cattle
As with all the tick-borne diseases, there are two alternative options for control:

- **Intensive tick control and disease-free situation:** This is usually practiced in dairies where the farmer cannot accept the risk of diseases which will affect milk production. Intensive tick control is practised and vaccination is not applied.
- **Tactical tick control with vaccination:** This is low intensity

tick control, performed to ensure that there are sufficient ticks on the farm to continue boosting the immunity of the animal and ensure a "stable disease situation". The difficulty lies in deciding how many ticks are sufficient. Using this control strategy, sporadic cases of heartwater may still occur, especially during drought periods when tick numbers are low and there is insufficient immunisation. Another disadvantage is the possibility of tick damage to udders, teats, causing abscesses and tick toxicoses as well as the associated losses of production.

Vaccination is recommended in calves under 3 weeks of age (preferably between 1-7 days)

If done at this time calves become immune and rarely develop the disease. Animals vaccinated later than this period run the risk of developing the disease, and will have to be treated for heartwater. Most calves do not develop severe reactions after vaccination, but they should be observed daily over a period of 30 days and treated if they develop a temperature rise of >1° C in 24 hours or if their temperature reaches >40°C.

Adult cattle will react to the vaccine from day 12 after vaccination. They should be treated with oxytetracycline when a temperature reaction develops as described above. This must be repeated if the temperature does not drop. During immunisation they must be kept tick free. Heartwater vaccination cannot be done in pregnant animals and must not be done at the same time as anaplasmosis vaccination. The immunity conferred by vaccination lasts for as little as 18 months if there is no reinfection from infected ticks during this period.

The heartwater vaccine is actually an infected suspension of blood; it must be stored kept at a very low temperature and for this reason it is despatched to the farmer on dry ice (-70°C). Once the dry ice has evaporated the vaccine can no longer be stored so it must be used as soon as possible after it is received. Storing the vaccine without the dry ice in a freezer or fridge is not acceptable. If the vaccine has not been stored at a sufficiently low temperature, the heartwater organism will begin to die off and vaccination will not provide the desired effect. The vaccine must be thawed before use, either in lukewarm water (rapid method) or by placing it under cold running water (slow method). On no account must it be placed in hot water as this will kill the immunising organisms.

Using the slow method, the vaccine will be effective for 4 hours after thawing. Using the rapid thawing method, the vaccine must be used within 30 minutes. The vaccine is given by slow intravenous injection to prevent a shock reaction.

Heartwater management in small stock

Vaccination against heartwater in small stock as an aid to creating a stable or endemic disease situation has been mostly unsuccessful. Experts in heartwater areas where small stock are kept, report that sustained, intensive tick control will prevent outbreaks. Susceptible animals newly introduced into the area should be dipped by belly bathing with tick remedies weekly for the first 3 weeks. For sustained control, dipping can be done every 2 -4 weeks in summer. The dipping intervals can be extended in winter if tick challenge is low (Dr R. J. Taylor). It should be noted that this intensive tick control renders the flock totally susceptible to heartwater

and dipping must be sustained to prevent outbreaks. A live attenuated vaccine which is safe and efficacious in small stock as well as cattle has been developed by Onderstepoort scientists and will hopefully be available as a replacement for the blood vaccine soon.

Redwater or Babesiosis

Redwater or babesiosis of cattle is transmitted by the two blue tick species (Rhipicephalus (Boophilus) microplus and R. decoloratus). Redwater occurs more widely than heartwater because the ticks occur more extensively. The disease is absent in the extreme west where the conditions are too dry for the tick, and also most of the Western Cape. (See the section r on ticks for distribution maps.) Redwater outbreaks are seen in summer and autumn when the ticks are active. There are two types of redwater – African (Babesia bigemina) and Asiatic (Babesia bovis). There is no cross-immunity between the two diseases, so it is important to know which types occur on a particular farm when vaccination and other control methods are being contemplated.

Cattle develop redwater 2-3 weeks after exposure to infected blue ticks, and they show high fever, jaundice, anaemia and red discolouration of the urine. Asiatic redwater tends to be more acute and animals may also show nervous symptoms such as muscle tremors and convulsions making it easy to confuse with signs of heartwater. If cattle are not treated timeously, they will die. Confirmation of the diagnosis can be done when a veterinarian examines a blood smear and finds the parasites in the red blood cells. In the case of Asiatic redwater the organisms are often more easily found in a brain smear.

Conjunctival anaemia is one of the visible symptoms of redwater due to the rapid breakdown of red blood cells.

Severe congestion of the brain is seen in cases of cerebral babesiosis.

There are two readily available remedies which are effective for the treatment of redwater: imidocarb (which is also effective against anaplasmosis) and diminazine.

Where intensive tick control and a disease-free situation are required (see under control), imidocarb is the drug of choice because it sterilises the infection, prevents carriers and therefore prevents new outbreaks. There is no concern about the drug's effect on immunity under these conditions.

Where the farmer requires a stable redwater disease situation, the choice of drug for treatment will be based on the type of redwater on the farm (see table below).

Animals with advanced cases of redwater may need supportive treatment from a veterinarian: fluid or even blood transfusions may be necessary and corticosteroid administration may be needed to treat the brain involvement in B. bovis cases. If diminizine is used as a specific treatment, oxytetracycline administration may be required to treat concurrent anaplasma infections which often occur. Liver supportive therapy and good quality palatable feed should also be given.

Control of redwater
- **Intensive tick control with no vaccination**: this approach is easier to achieve with blue ticks than with "bont" ticks, but dip resistance can become problematic.
- **Tactical tick control with vaccination**: tick damage and a loss of production may still occur. In practice it is difficult to achieve a stable situation in marginal areas of B. bigemina (western border of the distribution). Similarly, in areas where the blue ticks and multi-host ticks occur (Limpopo Province, Coastal areas of KwaZulu Natal and the Eastern Cape Province), the frequent tick control measures needed for the multihost ticks usually translate into intensive control for the blue tick – making enzootic stability impossible to achieve for redwater. In addition, researchers have found that enzootic stability has never been achieved in the B. bovis areas in SA because of the low prevalence of the organism in ticks. Even where an enzootically stable situation occurs and most animals are immune, redwater outbreaks can occur when there is a massive tick challenge, for example when cattle are placed into new camps with huge tick populations.
- **Calves** should be vaccinated at 6 months of age because at this

Type of redwater	Drug of choice	Revaccination required	Interval between treatment and revaccination (weeks)
B.bigemina (African)	Diminazine	No	N/A
B.bovis (Asiatic)	Imidocarb or diminazine*	Yes	8 or 4*
Mixed/Unknown	Imidocarb	Yes	16

stage, unlike adult animals they usually require no treatment after vaccination.

- **Adult redwater vaccination is risky and requires careful supervision:** After vaccination, cattle must be carefully observed for 21 days for vaccine reactions which must be treated if they become severe. See the table below for selection of the correct remedy. "Blocking" of the *B. bovis* vaccine reaction can be done on day 7 if large numbers of animals are being vaccinated, to avoid having to monitor the temperature- of each animal. However, the immunity achieved with blocking is not as effective as with the standard method. Immunity develops 4 to 6 weeks after vaccination and lasts for life

in the case of *B.bovis*, but only for a short period of less than 1 year for *B.bigemina* if there is insufficient challenge from redwater infected blue ticks.

Two separate frozen redwater blood vaccines are available from Onderstepoort Biological Products (contact details are given in the appendix).

- Frozen Asiatic redwater vaccine for cattle
- Frozen African redwater vaccine for cattle

For this reason, it is of cardinal importance to know which of the diseases occur in an area before embarking on a vaccination strategy. Both these redwater vaccines contain

live, slightly attenuated (weakened) strains of the causative organisms. Redwater vaccination is therefore as with heartwater a form of controlled exposure to the disease making close monitoring and post-vaccination treatment often necessary especially in previously unexposed, adult animals. Being frozen and containing live organisms, the vaccines must be very handled very carefully according to the instructions on the label and package insert. Clear, detailed instructions on handling, thawing (slow or fast methods as described for the heartwater vaccine), dose rate and route of administration (intramuscular) are given on the label, package insert and on the Onderstepoort Biological Products website.

Redwater vaccine	Remedy	Revaccination required
B.bigemina (Africa)	Imidocarb or diminazine	Yes
B. bovis (Asiatic)	Diminazine	No
Both	Imidocarb	Yes

The method of using a third of the normal dose of diminazine to treat vaccine reactions is not recommended

as it has not been proven to be successful. After treatment with certain remedies, revaccination

may be required but only after the recommended time interval (see below).

Redwater vaccine	Remedy	
	Diminazine 3,5mg/kg	Imidocarb 2,5 ml/100kg
B. bigemina (African)	8 weeks*	16 weeks
B.bovis (Asiatic)	4 weeks	8 weeks

*Interval between treatment and revaccination

Summary information on treatment and vaccination for tick-borne diseases

AGE OF VACCINATION

Disease	Species	Age
Heartwater	Cattle	Before 3 weeks
	Sheep	Before 7 days
Redwater (both types)	Cattle	3-6 months
Anaplasmosis	Cattle	3-9 months

VACCINE REACTION INTERVALS

Vaccine	Species	Days after vaccination
Heartwater	Cattle	1-30
	Sheep	1-21
Redwater (both)	Cattle	1-21
Anaplasmosis	Cattle	21-50

BLOCKING VACCINATION REACTIONS (LARGE NUMBERS OF ANIMALS)

Vaccine	Species	Day after vaccination for blocking
Heartwater	Cattle (indigenous breeds)	14
	Cattle (European breeds)	16
	Sheep	11
Redwater (B. bovis only)	Cattle	7
Anaplasmosis	Cattle	Only reacting animals

*Day of vacination is taken as day 0

PERIOD OF INTENSIVE TICK CONTROL REQUIRED AFTER VACCINATION

Vaccine	Period of intensive tick treatment
Heartwater	4 weeks
Redwater (both)	4 weeks
Anplasmosis	8 weeks

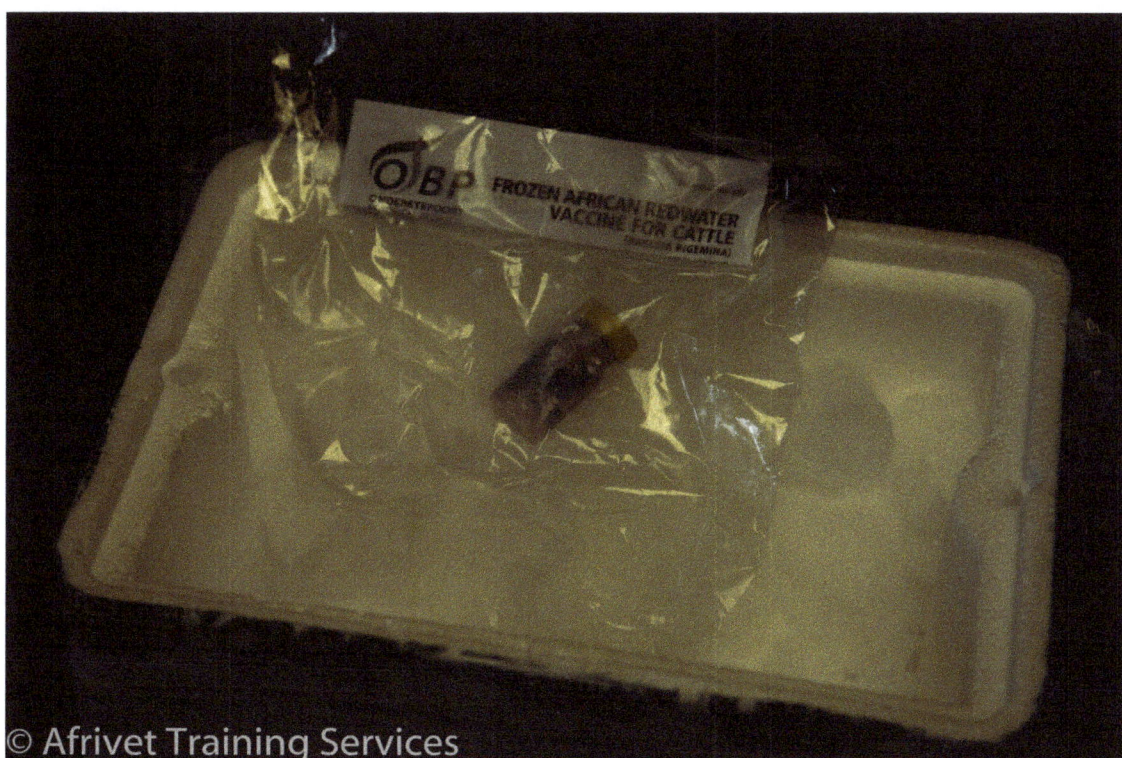

© Afrivet Training Services

The blood vaccines used for heartwater, anaplasma and redwater must be stored on dry ice or in liquid nitrogen.

THEILERIOSES

The theilerioses are a group of tick-borne diseases caused by protozoa (single cell organisms) of the genus Theileria. T. parva is the most important of these in sub-Saharan Africa causing widespread mortalities in tropical areas. Of importance to the South African stock owner are East Coast fever (as a major threat) and Corridor disease which occurs where infected African buffalo and cattle are kept in close proximity.

East Coast fever

Very strict tick control by dipping and cattle movement restrictions eventually led to the eradication of East Coast fever from South Africa in 1955. However, since the tick that transmits this disease is still present in the country, its re-introduction via infected animals is always possible.

East Coast fever is caused by the blood parasite *Theileria parva* which has become adapted to cattle. The brown ear-tick, *Rhipicephalus appendiculatus* transmits the disease from bovine to bovine. The brown ear-tick is widely distributed in the warmer, more humid and bushy areas of central, eastern and southern Africa. These ticks, being 3-host ticks, pick up the infection from an infected bovine in one stage of the tick lifecycle and transmit it to another in the next stage of its lifecycle.

The disease causes a high fever, swollen lymph nodes, lung oedema, severe diarrhoea, abortions and death after 15 days. The diagnosis is confirmed by microscopic examination of the lymph nodes and of blood smears.

Corridor disease

Corridor disease is caused by the original buffalo-derived strains of *Theileria parva*. It is an extremely virulent in cattle. The disease in cattle is called Corridor disease because the first cases were described in the corridor between the Hluhluwe and Umfolozi game reserves in KwaZulu-Natal. It can, however, occur wherever there is close contact between infected buffalo and cattle in the presence of the brown ear-tick. The symptoms are much the same as those of East Coast fever but tend to be more acute with mortalities in excess of 80%. While treatment of Corridor disease is effective, it is not permitted by law in South Africa.

Because of the severity of the disease contact between cattle and buffalo in this area must be avoided by effective fencing.

Cattle with T. parva infections like this case of Corridor disease, show signs of listlessness, depression and lymph node enlargement in the early stages.

TICK TOXICOSES

The saliva of some ticks contains toxins which adversely affect the hosts on which they feed. There are 8 different forms of tick toxicoses including appetite suppression, immune suppression, and paralysis. The various conditions are discussed below:

Depression of appetite and reduced growth rate and production

The saliva of blue ticks (*Rhipicephalus Boophilus spp.*) has been shown to reduce the appetite of the host animals and markedly reduce their growth rate and production. See the introduction to the chapter on Ectoparasites for more detail.

Sweating sickness

Sweating sickness is a disease usually seen in calves, caused by the bont-legged tick (*Hyalomma truncatum*).

The toxin in the saliva of these ticks causes inflammation of the skin and the mucous membranes, including the internal organs such as the respiratory tract and the intestine. Not all *Hyalomma* ticks possess the toxin, but one tick alone can cause severe cases. About 4 days after the tick has fed, affected calves develop a high temperature, lose their appetite and appear listless. A wet dermatitis develops due to the leakage of serum from the skin, which gives the impression of the calf sweating. The affected skin is very sensitive to touch and can be easily injured. The immune system suppression leads to the calves developing secondary infections such as pneumonia.

Specific treatment entails removal of the ticks, which are often found on the tip of the tail. Sick animals should be immediately placed in the shade, given good food, water and an injection with a broad-spectrum antibiotic such as sulphadimethoxine or oxytetracyclines to prevent secondary infections. Prevention requires controlling bont-legged ticks especially during peak summer months. For control of the bont-legged tick, see the section on ticks.

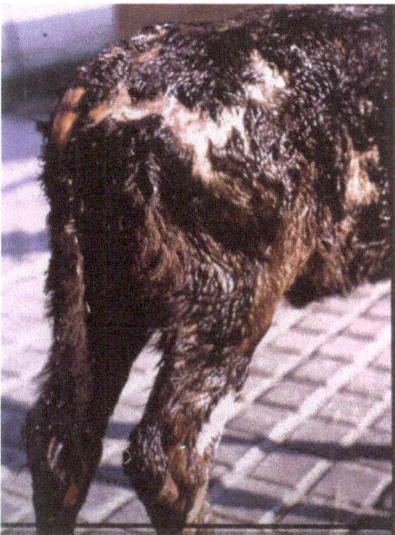

Paralysis in sheep caused by the Karoo paralysis tick Ixodes rubicundus

Sweating sickness in a calf showing severely inflamed and oozing skin.

Tick paralysis

A number of tick species produce a salivary toxin which affects nerve transmission and causes paralysis.

The Karoo paralysis tick (*Ixodes rubicundus*) causes paralysis especially in sheep and goats but also sometimes in calves and antelope. This tick is found in hilly areas of the northern Cape, the Free State and patchily in Mpumalanga, especially on the cooler southern slopes where overgrazing has resulted in the encroachment of unpalatable scrubs (such as "besembos", "taaibos", "renosterbos") and sour grasses ("suurpol"). This vegetation provides an ideal habitat for l. rubicundus which is a three-host tick with a long lifecycle. The intermediate hosts are elephant shrews, the red rock rabbit, caracal and mountain reedbuck which frequent these habitats.

The adults feed on stock and are active from February to November, with peak incidences of paralysis occurring after the first frosts in March, April and May.

Treatment entails timeous removal of the ticks during the early stages of paralysis which will lead to recovery within 1 to 2 days. Control of the Karoo paralysis tick can be achieved by avoiding the affected camps on the southern slopes of the hills during the peak season (March to May). If this is unavoidable the use of dips given by belly bath or pour-ons can be highly effective if applied properly and at the correct time. Amitraz and pyrethroids can be used for control.

Spring lamb paralysis

Spring lamb paralysis is caused by the red-legged tick (*Rhipicephalus evertsi evertsi*). Although the tick is widespread in SA, the toxicosis is seen in the Free State regions. Unlike Karoo paralysis, this paralysis occurs only when large numbers of ticks infest the host. The larger the host, the more ticks are needed to cause paralysis, which is why this form of paralysis is usually seen in small lambs. The peak period of activity of the causative tick is spring, hence the name. Treatment entails the removal of the ticks, while prevention requires effective tick control, especially during spring time.

Angora goat kid paralysis

This syndrome, which is similar to Spring lamb paralysis, is caused by *Rhipicephalus warburtoni* and is confined to the Free State and Northern Cape. The adult ticks cluster in the ears of young Angora kids and cause heavy losses. Prevention must be done as kids may die even if the ticks are removed.

Amitraz is the ideal remedy for use as it causes rapid detachment. It can be applied in the form of a pour-on on the head and ears.

January Disease

Large numbers of *Rhipicephalus appendiculatus* feeding on cattle and engorging rapidly cause acute blood loss anaemia while the toxins in the saliva cause immune suppression and a chronic fatal anaemia. The cattle become listless, lose their appetite and show facial swelling due to a fluid accumulation under the skin of the head. The peak period of activity for this tick is mid -to late summer hence the name. Regular dipping to control tick numbers prevents this disease.

Sand tampan toxicosis

Large numbers of sand tampans *Ornithodoros savygni* supress the immunity, especially in young calves. Cases of severe allergic reactions to tampan bites also occur. Regular dipping with a pyrethroid helps reduce the numbers but as they only take 20 minutes to feed, tampans are difficult to control. Ground-feeding birds (guinea fowl, francolin etc.) should be protected in these areas as they feed on tampans.

AFRIVET ECTOPARASITE REMEDIES

PRODUCT	ECTOPARASITE	SPECIES	ACTIVE
Afrivet Redline Pour on G4245	Ticks and flies	C & G	Flumethrin
Deltapor 5 Pour On G4252	Ticks, lice and flies	C, S & G	Deltamethrin & PB
Deltapor Plus 10 Pour On G4255	Ticks and flies	C (not dairy) and sheep	Deltamethrin & PB
Eraditick Cattle Pour On G4254	Ticks	Cattle (not dairy)	Amitraz
Eraditick Plus Pour On G4251	Ticks, lice, mange mites and flies	C, S & G	Amitraz, deltamethrin &PB
Ecobash plunge and spray G3382	Ticks and flies	C	Cymiazol and cypermethrin
Eraditick Ultra plunge and spray G3976	Ticks and flies	C (not dairy)	Chlorvenvinphos, cymiazol & cypermethrin
Eraditick 125 plunge and spray G3585	See species	C: ticks, lice and mites S&G: ticks, sheep scab, mites	Amitraz
Eraditick 250 plunge and spray G4047	See species	C: ticks, lice and mites S&G: ticks, sheep scab, mites	Amitraz
Deltaforce plunge and spray G4367	Ticks, flies, screw worm	C (not dairy)	Deltamethrin
Expel jetting fluid G4027	Blowfly, sheep scab, red lice	S & G	Ivermectin, novaluron
Eraditick tick grease G3667	Ticks	C, S & G	Deltamethrin, PB.

URINARY PROBLEMS

Bladder stones

Bladder stones occur in rams and bulls as a result of certain dietary factors. The composition of the stones varies depending on the specific circumstances.

Phosphate stones occur most commonly in castrated animals in feedlots, that are fed on high phosphate/low calcium diets. The formation of phosphate stones is promoted further if the diet causes alkaline urine. These stones are chalky, white crumbly and irregular in shape. Because they are fine and crumbly the stones may block the urinary tract usually in the urethra of the penis.

Silica stones occur mainly in sheep on grazing in areas of the Karoo where the plants have a high silica content. These stones are round with a pearly appearance and tend to be confined in the bladder. They are usually found as an incidental finding at post-mortem.

When bladder stones cause the blockage of the urethra, the animals will experience severe pain and will have difficulty urinating. If the urethra is totally blocked it may rupture and urine will collect under the skin around the penis ("waterbelly"), or the bladder may rupture. In both cases the animals will die of ureamia. Animals with clinical urolithiasis will require veterinary help and if the blockage cannot be resolved, emergency slaughter may be necessary. On post-mortem the stones may be found in the kidney, the ureter, the bladder or the urethra. It is helpful to have bladder stones analysed so that the correct control measures can be implemented.

Urethal blockage in steer showing swelling or "waterbelly".

Bladder stones in found in a sheep at post mortem.

To prevent phosphate stones, the calcium: phosphate ratio must be corrected to 2:1. Inclusion of 0,5 % ammonium chloride in the ration will acidify the urine and will reduce the formation of the phosphate stones. In the case of silica stones occurring on pastures, male animals must be moved off the problem pastures and fed an alternative diet.

Copper poisoning

Poisoning known as "geelsiekte" occurs in sheep in certain areas in the Karoo due to a high level of copper in the soil. Copper poisoning can also occur due to the use of chicken or pig manure as a fertiliser on pastures, dosing of copper sulphate or when sheep drink copper sulphate solutions such as dips or foot baths. The epidemiology, symptoms, treatment and prevention are discussed under the chapter on poisonings.

Leptospirosis (see Reproductive diseases)

Oxalate poisoning

There is a wide variety of plants in SA that contain oxalates. If these plants are heavily grazed, poisoning may occur due to primary damage of the kidney. Sheep and goats are more susceptible to this problem than cattle. See the plant poisoning section for details.

Pulpy kidney (see Acute diseases)

Redwater (see Tick-borne diseases)

YOUNG ANIMALS

LAMBS AND KIDS

Surveys of lamb deaths in South Africa have shown that the major causes are starvation due to low birth weight or mismothering (50%), difficult births (25%), and the remaining 25% due to a number of factors such as infectious agents, deficiencies, predation etc. In other words, the majority of losses are due to factors which can be corrected by management, such as nutrition (over- or under-feeding of ewes), supervision of ewes and lambs and selection of ewes for good mothering abilities. The contributing factors to lamb losses, diseases and other conditions are discussed under separate headings below.

Chlamydia or Enzootic abortion of Ewes *(see also Reproductive diseases)*

Flocks infected with *Chlamydia abortus* will initially experience abortion storms but also the birth of weak lambs. These lambs are often too weak to suckle after birth and they die of starvation.

The diagnosis of enzootic abortion is made on the basis of the history of abortions and weak lambs, examination of aborted foetuses, post-mortems by a veterinarians on weak or dead lambs and positive serology.

The main control measure for this condition is vaccination of ewes before the breeding season. During abortion storms, ewes can be treated with long-acting oxytetracycline injections to prevent further abortions.

Ultratet LA
G2857

Ultratet 200 LA
G3559

Coccidiosis

Coccidiosis in lambs and kids is a condition caused by a protozoal organism which colonises the intestine and is excreted in the faeces of healthy animals. There are a number of coccidian species that can affect small stock *(Isospora, Eimeria)* but all have the same general life cycle and cause similar symptoms. The eggs or oocysts of coccidia are excreted in the faeces of infected animals. They need warm moist conditions need to sporulate (mature) which then makes them infective. Susceptible animals ingesting the coccidian oocyst on contaminated pastures will become infected. The organism invades the gut epithelium and completes its development here, in the process causing damage to the intestinal epithelium. On infected farms lambs will pick up infection from older animals which shed the organism but have developed immunity. Unhygienic conditions, crowding and stress can be predisposing factors to coccidial infections. The symptoms seen are loss of appetite, diarrhoea and weight loss. Animals severely affected may die after a few days, or in chronic infections they may last a few weeks. Angora goats may be severely affected and may die without showing marked symptoms.

On post-mortem the small intestine is inflamed and small white raised foci may be seen. The diagnosis can be confirmed by laboratory examination of intestinal smears in

Severe coccidiosis in an Angora kid showing diarrhoea and severe loss of condition.

which the parasites will be seen, or by taking faecal samples from live animals for microscopic examination.

Sick animals can be treated with sulpha remedies (sulpamethazine, sulphadimethoxine) or diclazuril. These are mostly oral preparations but sulphadimethoxine is an injectable which is active in the gut. Treatment may need to be repeated in severe cases. Severely dehydrated animals may need fluid administration.

Prevention in intensive systems is by feeding of coccidiostats such as monensin, salinomycin and lasolacid in rations. These remedies suppress coccidial development but are not suitable for the treatment of sick animals. General hygiene involving manure management and avoiding overcrowding of animals is important is preventing outbreaks of coccidiosis.

Ecosulf LA G3037

Congenital malformations

Congenital or hereditary malformations are primarily due to genetic factors, such as gene mutations. In most cases these occur at a very low frequency. The most common congenital conditions of small stock are underdevelopment of the skin, absence of lower jaw, short lower jaw, cleft palate, deformation or amputation of the limbs.

A high incidence rate of foetal deaths due to malformations indicates the involvement of infectious agents, particularly viruses. During summer months insect-transmitted viruses such as Akabane and Wesselsbron viruses may infect pregnant ewes causing certain malformations. Certain vaccine viruses such as some

Rift Valley fever vaccines, blue tongue vaccine and Wesselsbron vaccine (no longer produced) can cause a small percentage of malformations when given in the first third of pregnancy. A history and post-mortem examination of the foetuses by veterinary pathologists will give an indication of the primary cause.

This lamb was born with extra limbs due to a genetic mutation.

Diarrhoea

There are various causes of diarrhoea in young lambs and kids including E. coli, the lamb dysentery organism *C. perfringens B* and coccidiosis. These conditions are discussed under separate headings.

Dystocia

Dystocia means a difficult birth and this is most commonly caused by overfeeding of ewes in late pregnancy. Ewes with large lambs have a prolonged birth process during which the lamb is deprived of oxygen for considerable periods. These lambs are usually found dead, the head swollen, and the fleece is discoloured from placental fluids. On post-mortem it becomes evident that the lambs were born dead because the lungs are not inflated and the stomach is empty.

A specific cause of "Big lamb disease" or "grootlamsiekte" occurs in certain areas of the Karoo when ewes graze on the plant *Salsola tuberculatiformis* (the cauliflower saltwort). The birth process is delayed

and ewes become massively swollen due to large lambs in the uterus. These lambs have to be removed by caesarian section. Avoid grazing ewes on the plant for the last 50 days of pregnancy. For further information see the chapter on reproductive conditions.

E. coli scours

E. coli infections or colibacillosis occurs in small stock lambing in camps. It occurs in lambs or kids in the first week of life, causing diarrhoea, dehydration and death. There is also a septicaemic form from which lambs die acutely with little or no symptoms. The cause of *E. coli* outbreaks in individuals can be due to lambs not receiving sufficient colostrum because the ewe has swollen or damaged teats, or mastitis,

Outbreaks of colibacillosis are often due to a build-up of bacteria in the camps where the ewes are lambing.

A diagnosis of colibacillosis is made when the symptoms of acute death due to septicaemia or diarrhoea are made in conjunction with the isolation of the bacterium from the organs or the intestine of a pathogenic *E. coli* strain.

Sick lambs must be given fluids as soon as possible either by mouth or intravenously if they are too weak to drink. There are various electrolyte preparations on the market for rehydrating animals. Vaccination of pregnant ewes with an *E. coli* vaccine registered for sheep/cattle can help prevent colibacillosis outbreaks.

Electro Guard NF Oral V28622

Lamb dysentery

This disease occurs sporadically in lambs of 1-7 days of age. It is caused by *Clostridium perfringens* type B bacteria which the lambs pick up via soil and faeces on certain farms. Typically, these lambs refuse to drink, show pain and bloody diarrhoea, dehydration and death. If cases are identified early enough, injectable sulpha preparations which are active in the gut should be given, but usually the diagnosis is too late and lambs die rapidly. On post-mortem these lambs show bleeding and ulceration of the small intestine.

The disease is prevented by vaccination of pregnant ewes with a clostridial vaccine containing *C. perfringens* B or C, since there is cross protection between the two types.

Management problems

The crowding of ewes into camps causes rejection of lambs which then starve to death; disturbance and unnecessary handling of ewes and their lambs will also lead to this problem. Lambing camps need shelter from sun and wind, accessible clean water and sufficient feed. Supervision by a professional shepherd or farm hand is extremely valuable as lambing problems can be handled timeously.

Mismothering

Mismothering is the behavioural tendency of some ewes which leads to the rejection of and failure to feed their lambs which will die of starvation. These lambs usually have to be raised by hand or adopted by other ewes. Mothering in sheep is a genetic characteristic; certain breeds have better mothering abilities and individual ewes should be selected for their mothering abilities. Rejected ewe lambs should therefore not be used for breeding.

Starvation (underweight lambs)

The normal birth weight of lambs varies with the breed, but it should be between 3,5-4,5 kilograms. Underweight lambs are caused by poor nutrition of ewes during the last stages of pregnancy. These lambs are born with poor fat reserves and as a result are weak, unable to suckle and are very susceptible to chilling. They die a few days after birth. They are often found once they have been eaten by scavengers and death is attributed to predation.

The presence of the soft "slippers" on the hoof of the lamb will indicate whether it has walked or not.

On post-mortem these lambs have no fat reserves around the kidneys and have empty stomachs. The problem of underweight lambs can be prevented by ensuring good nutrition of the pregnant ewes especially in the last 6 weeks of pregnancy. Ewes carrying twins or triplets will need more feed than single lamb ewes (see section on Nutrition for further information).

Tetanus

Tetanus is chiefly a condition seen in lambs although sheep of all ages are potentially susceptible. It results from the infection of wounds with *Clostridium tetani* bacteria most commonly after docking and castrating and particularly when using elastrators or "rekkies". Tetanus bacteria grow in these wounds and produce a powerful toxin which affects the nerves, causing a spastic or stiff paralysis. Lambs will develop these 7-10 days after the procedure, the first signs being slight stiffness and collapse of the third eyelid over the eye; eventually the animal lies down and is unable to rise. It typically shows stiff spasms of the limbs and will eventually die when the toxin affects the muscles responsible for breathing.

The diagnosis is made based on the typical symptoms and history of docking/castration since post-mortem examinations are always non-specific.

Treatment with antibiotics or specific tetanus antiserum is almost always ineffectual once the symptoms appear. The best control measure is the vaccination of pregnant ewes with a clostridial vaccine containing a tetanus component. The lamb receives protection through the colostrum and can be safely docked and castrated at three weeks of age.

Tetanus in a lamb on which elastrators were used for docking and castration. Note the typical stiffness of the legs.

Management of breeding flocks

Treatment of chilled or weak lambs: weak but otherwise normal lambs can be treated by injecting 20% glucose (10 ml per kg body weight) by injection through the abdomen wall. Colostrum should be given as soon as possible with a stomach tube. The lambs must be kept warm until strong enough to suckle, when they can be placed back with the mother or a ewe that has lost her lamb.

Vaccination

Pregnant ewes should be vaccinated with multi-clostridial vaccines in the last 6 weeks of pregnancy to ensure protection against diseases of young lambs such as lamb dysentery and tetanus, as well as protection of the ewe against diseases such post-lambing gangrene of the uterus and pulpy kidney. Ewes should be wormed at the same time because they shed large numbers of worm eggs at this time due to a phenomenon called PPRR (pre-parturient relaxation of resistance), which means increased susceptibility to worms during this time. Clostridial vaccines which contain dewormers are very convenient for this purpose and are commercially available.

CALVES

Dairy calf-raising units experience the most disease problems because the calves are removed from their mothers, raised in an artificial environment and usually fed on commercial milk replacements. This presents numerous problems, most commonly diarrhoea of either nutritional or infectious origin, and pneumonia which is usually predisposed by poor housing and nutrition. Management factors and correct housing are therefore essential factors. Beef calves usually experience fewer problems, as long as the cow has no udder defects and can supply the calf with sufficient colostrum and milk. However, these calves may develop navel ill and polyarthritis if they are confined to unhygienic camps. Other possible problems are mucosal disease, worm infestations and diarrhoea due to poor water quality.

Management of newborn calves

As soon as a calf is born one must ensure that its nose is not blocked with membranes and mucous which can prevent it breathing. If there is fluid in the lungs the calf should be picked up and gently swung with its head facing towards the ground, which will dislodge the fluid. The calf must be dried, placed on dry bedding in a place where it is protected from drafts. Rubbing the calf dry also stimulates the calf to breathe.

Colostrum must be given as soon as possible because it contains antibodies which will protect against diseases for 3-6 weeks until the calf has had time to develop its own.

The antibodies in colostrum are effectively absorbed in the gut for the first six hours after birth, and enter the bloodstream. After this, the intestinal absorption stops and the calf starts to secrete digestive enzymes which will digest the antibodies. Colostrum given after this period will then only serve as an excellent source of nutrition. The colostrum must therefore be given within the first 24 hours of life, at 10% of total bodyweight, divided up as 3 to 4 feeds.

Do not simply allow the calf to stay with the cow and hope that feeding will take place. Modern dairy cows' udders are not ideal for feeding calves and the caretaker cannot evaluate whether the calf has had enough colostrum or not. Leaving the calf with the cow will also allow a bond to develop which will later stress both when the calf is removed.

Colostrum can be collected and stored in a freezer for calf feeding. It must never be thawed in hot water as this will damage the antibodies and may burn the calf. The colostrum must be at the same temperature as milk feeds. Do not give any other feed before the feeding colostrum because this will inhibit the antibody uptake.

Feeding the calf

The most common problem of dairy calves is diarrhoea of nutritional origin, either due to poor quality feed or poor feeding techniques. Calves must rather be fed more often than overfed in a single feeding. The ideal is to have the total daily intake divided into two feeds (8-10% of body weight every day). The temperature of the milk/milk replacer must be a constant 37-39°C. The best quality milk replacers are made from whole milk and can be given to calves as early as 4 days after birth, when colostrum feeding is completed. Be aware that milk replacers contain less fat than whole milk, so calves will grow slower than those on whole milk. Milk replacers must be made up strictly according to the directions of the manufacturers, as making milk up under- or over-strength will cause problems.

Housing

Experts agree that calf-raising units should contain separate calf pens or huts for individual calves. This is

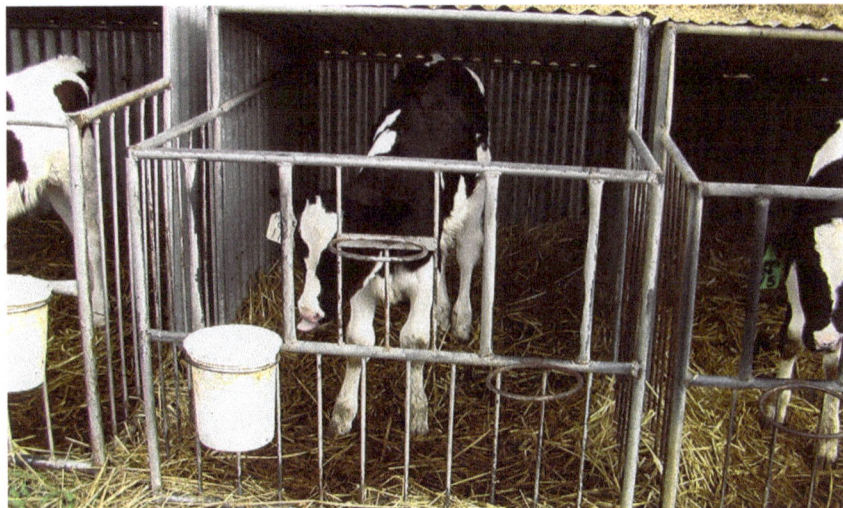

Dairy calves are housed in separate pens or huts for hygiene purposes.

more hygienic than grouping calves together and allows better monitoring of individual animals. Young calves are sensitive to cold and draughts and bedding must always be dry. Poor ventilation will also cause problems, and is one of the predisposing factors for calf pneumonia.

Publications on calf housing can be obtained at agricultural colleges or the Agricultural Engineering Department of the ARC.

Hygiene

Good hygiene is absolutely essential in calf raising units. This includes the regular cleaning of pens and huts to remove manure, and the disinfection and drying of the pens. Clean dry bedding must be provided to keep them clean and warm. Failure to clean calf pens lead to a build- up of infection and may overwhelm colostral immunity.

The meticulous washing, disinfection and drying of buckets and water pails is essential. If bottle-feeding is done the bottles and teats must be cleaned and then sterilised with an appropriate solution e.g. Milton, because washing alone will not remove bacteria from all the crevices.

ACT Cleaning Fluid Act

Calf diarrhoea (scours)

Apart from nutritional problems, infectious agents can also cause diarrhoea in calves. Older calves may experience problems such as mucosal disease and worm infestations. It is important to be able to distinguish the different causes so that the correct control measures can be applied.

An outbreak of calf scours on a dairy farm

Colibacillosis

Colibacillosis is the most important infectious cause of diarrhoea and death in newborn calves (1-7 days). The cause is a group of gut bacteria *Escherichia coli* which will begin to colonise the intestine of the calf almost immediately after birth. These bacteria are present in the manure of adult cattle so calves become exposed at the time of birth. They will receive a massive exposure of bacteria, especially if cows calve in unhygienic conditions.

Certain *E. coli* strains can cause septicaemia (blood poisoning) resulting in acute death, while others cause diarrhoea. The enteric or diarrhoea strains cause a fever, depression and diarrhoea, followed by rapid dehydration and refusal to drink. When the dehydration is advanced the calf will be too weak to drink, will not be able to stand and will die soon if it is not given fluid intravenously.

Primary *E. coli* infections occur only in the first week of life, so vaccination of cows with an *E. coli*

vaccine which contains cattle strains will induce specific antibodies to be shed in the colostrum. Managers must ensure that calves receive sufficient colostrum directly after birth. Cows must initially be vaccinated twice and thereafter with an annual booster 4 weeks before calving to ensure optimal levels of antibodies are shed in the colostrum. For more details on treatment of calf diarrhoea see below.

Paratyphoid (Salmonellosis)

Paratyphoid is a common problem in calf raising systems in SA, particularly where calves are brought in from different sources. This disease is most commonly caused by the bovine adapted strain Salmonella Dublin, which causes problems in older calves of 6-12 weeks of age. However, Salmonella Typhimurium which has a wide host range can cause problems in young calves from 1-3 weeks old.

On farms infected with S. Dublin, adult carriers serve as a source of infection and sporadic outbreaks of diarrhoea or abortions may be seen in the adult herd. Typhimurium infections are usually introduced by other animal species or via the feed and tend not to persist as long as S. Dublin infections.

Paratyphoid in calves causes either acute septicaemia with rapid death or a less acute infection characterised by fever, loss of appetite, depression and diarrhoea, and even some respiratory symptoms such as a nasal discharge and coughing, which can cause confusion with calf pneumonia. Later in the course of the disease the diarrhoea becomes more apparent and may become bloody. Calves may die from the condition or it may become chronic causing stunted animals.

The diagnosis is made based on the symptoms, and post-mortem signs of severe enteritis, but should be confirmed by bacterial isolation which will also allow identification of the causative salmonella organism. The latter is important with regard to selecting control measures.

The treatment of calves with salmonellosis with antibiotics such as sulphas or tetracycline is life-saving, but will not eliminate the bacteria, and these calves will become carriers. The administration of fluids and other supportive veterinary treatment may be necessary.

On farms infected with S. Dublin, young calves must be vaccinated with the live vaccine at the age of 7-14 days to protect them from infection. Disinfection of other stables with phenols, chlorines or infections will therefore have to be performed regularly to reduce the chances of adults infecting young animals. On farms where S. Typhimurium is the cause of problems the killed vaccine must be given to pregnant cows to provide colostral protection. These calves can then be vaccinated at 6 weeks with the live vaccine.

Viral diarrhoea

Rota and corona viruses are widespread in cattle in South Africa. They usually cause diarrhoea in young calves up to a month old. The source of infection for both viruses are older animals that shed the virus without symptoms for the most part. Clinical signs of diarrhoea are seen under conditions of poor hygiene and stress. The symptoms in calves are depression, loss of appetite and then profuse diarrhoea which can lead to severe dehydration and death unless the latter is treated.

To confirm the diagnosis faecal samples will need to be examined or cultured at a veterinary laboratory. This is important to distinguish viral diarrhoeas from other causes such as paratyphoid, *E. coli* and coccidiosis.

Vaccines are available for maternal vaccination but the efficacy of those used for the prevention of corona virus infections are still under debate. For the control of both these conditions in calves good hygiene is absolutely essential. This involves regular cleaning and disinfection of calving and nursery facilities, and camps. Contact between calves must be prevented and particularly mixing calves of different ages. Regular disinfection of equipment and boots and the wearing of clean overalls is essential.

Coccidiosis (see also under sheep)

Calves can develop coccidiosis between the age of 3 weeks to 6 months. Chronic watery to bloody diarrhoea may be seen and the calf will gradually lose condition. Specific treatment with anticoccidials such as sulphmethazine, dimethoxine or diclazuril will be necessary. Fluid administration may be necessary in dehydrated animals.

Cryptosporidium

Cryptosporidia are small coccidia which are normally found in the faeces of cattle of all ages, as well as other species including humans. The organisms cause diarrhoea mainly in young calves from 4 days to 8 weeks, 1-4 weeks of age when they are exposed to infection through contaminated water and feed.

Young calves that become infected show depression, anorexia and then later develop a profuse watery yellow diarrhoea. The disease lasts for 1-2 weeks, causing the loss of weight of the affected calves. The severity of the disease is increased if the calves are also infected with other pathogens such as rota and corona viruses, pathogenic *E. coli* and *Salmonella* spp.

There is no specific treatment for cryptosporidiosis but it can be prevented by ensuring that calves receive sufficient colostrum. Cleaning, disinfection and drying of calf stalls or housing is essential to prevent the spread of infection. Halofuginone can assist in decreasing the oocyst production, however, it is expensive and can have adverse side effects. It is important to support the calf's immune system during periods of stress by supplementing electrolytes, vitamins and minerals.

Diagnosis and treatment of diarrhoea

As soon as calves show signs of refusing food and scouring they must be rehydrated; an early sign of dehydration is the delayed skin fold return (a fold of skin is grasped between the fingers – if dehydrated, the skin fold takes some time to return to its normal position). Later the eyes become sunken and the calf is too weak to rise. Mild dehydration can be treated by giving electrolytes by mouth, but more severe cases must be treated by a veterinarian with intravenous fluid administration. Antibiotic treatment will be needed for cases of paratyphoid or coccidiosis. A variety of commercial electrolyte-containing products are available from farming co-ops. Diagnostic kits are available to help with the diagnosis of the causative agent.

Ecosulf LA G3037

Ultratet G0296

Ultratet LA G2857

Ultratet 200 LA G3559

Electro Guard OraL V28622

Prevention of calf diarrhoea
To prevent calf diarrhoea one must focus on the rapid administration of colostrum in sufficient quantities or specific antibody (BIOINNOVO), the meticulous implementation of the correct feeding procedures (temperature and quantity), the use of quality milk replacers or milk, stringent cleaning of facilities and equipment used for feeding.

The prophylactic feeding of lactobacillus-containing products or those containing bacterial sugars which block the attachment of pathogenic bacteria can be used as aids to prevention of calf diarrhoea.

Causes of pneumonia in calves
After diarrhoea, this is the second most important condition of hand-raised calves. It occurs around 40-50 days of age, when the colostral immunity obtained from the cow is beginning to fall and the calf becomes susceptible to organisms that cause respiratory conditions. There is a wide range of organisms that can cause calf pneumonia – parainfluenza 3, BVD virus, IBR virus, RS virus and *Pasteurella (Mannheimia) haemolytica*. Calves housed in badly-designed facilities with poor ventilation, high humidity and poor hygiene are at risk. Other contributing factors are weaning calves too early onto a solid diet, mixing with older calves, or overfeeding which leads to frequent urination and permanently damp bedding.

Calves developing pneumonia initially show a watery nasal discharge, which later becomes yellow, a dry cough, open mouth breathing, fever and sometimes diarrhoea. Most cases are acute and calves that survive with treatment are often stunted and cannot be used as replacement heifers.

Sick calves must immediately be placed in dry, sunny positions, and must be treated as soon as possible with oxytetracyclines, sulphas or other suitable antibiotics. In advanced cases, fluid administration may be needed.

Combination vaccines which contain a broad spectrum of live respiratory organisms can be given at 35 days and repeated at 60 days of age. It must be stressed that vaccination will not be successful if predisposing factors are not eliminated.

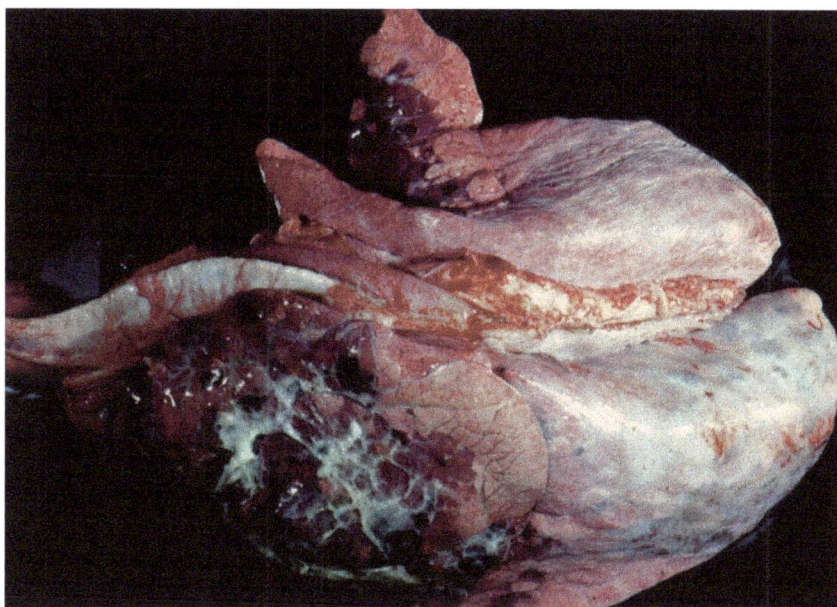

The lung of a calf that died from pneumonia caused by BVD virus and secondary infection with Mannheimia haemolytica.

Ultratet G0296

Ultratet LA G2857

Ultratet 200 LA G3559

Mucosal disease

Mucosal disease is a syndrome which affects calves infected with non-cytopathic BVD virus during the early stages of pregnancy. The non-cytopathic virus does not cause abortion but induces tolerance to the virus. When calves are subsequently infected with pathogenic BVD virus they are unable to mount an immune response and develop a very severe condition characterised by diarrhoea and respiratory symptoms. These calves will invariably die from the disease and there is no economically viable treatment. Control in the herd must be focused on identifying and removing those animals in the herd secreting the virus, the so-called persistently infected (PI) animals. See the chapter on reproductive diseases for more detailed control measures.

Navel ill and joint ill

Navel ill is the infection of the umbilicus with pus-forming bacteria. This takes place soon after birth and is usually a problem when cows calve in unhygienic, contaminated camps. The infection may spread from the umbilicus to the joints to cause a septic polyarthritis. Early treatment with a broad-spectrum antibiotic may clear up the infection, but once the condition becomes chronic, the calf may remain stunted and lame. Control is allowing cows to calve on the veld or in clean calving camps, and where possible disinfecting the navel with an iodine spray or any other wound preparation.

Worm infestations

Worm infestations can cause problems in calves, particularly those raised in camps or grazed on artificial pastures. The type of worm infestation experienced will depend on the geographic region of the country (see Endoparasite section). The symptoms seen will depend on the type of worm infestation but many of the infestations cause diarrhoea, appetite loss and even deaths. The diagnosis of worm infestations is done by doing egg counts or finding heavy worm burdens on post-mortem.

Ectoparasites

ECTOPARASITES

External parasites cause the livestock industry losses amounting to billions of rands in Southern Africa. The losses that are suffered are due either to direct damage caused by ectoparasites, or indirect due to the diseases they transmit. This chapter discusses the appearance, distribution of the most important ectoparasites of cattle, sheep and goats, as well as the control methods for each group. Note that Afrivet remedies for the control of ectoparasites are given in a table at the end of the chapter.

TICKS

The importance of ticks

The dangers of ticks are well-known to most farmers: heavy infestations cause anaemia, ticks with long mouthparts cause abscesses and damage of hides and organs such as the udder, scrotum and ears, and in addition, some ticks transmit disease. But few farmers are aware of the effect of "tick worry" –this is the negative effect on the growth of animals and their production due to the effects of a toxin in the saliva of certain ticks (anorectic effect). Moderate to heavy tick infestations can have a significant effect on the growth and production of animals.

Numerous studies in southern Africa and elsewhere have shown that the production of milk as well as weight gain are reduced in animals infested with various species of

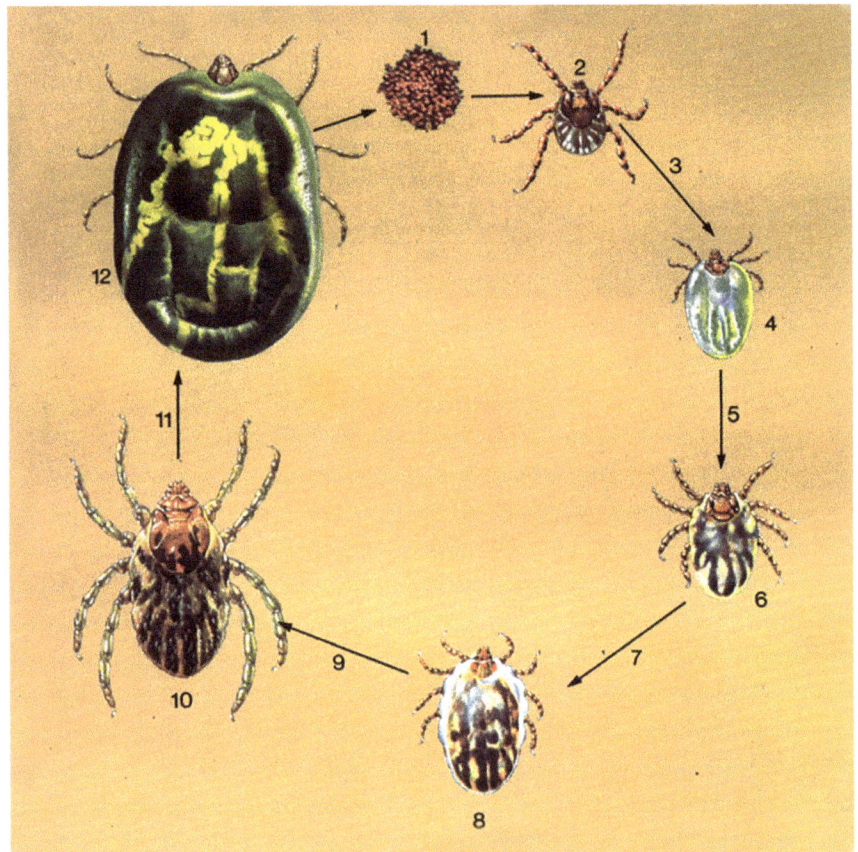

A generalised life cycle of a tick

Various studies on the anorectic effect of ticks on cattle

RESEARCHER	BREED	DURATION OF EXPERIMENT	PRODUCTION LOSS Average per animal Maximum loss*
Norman (1957)	Shorthorn	6 months	13 kg 41 kg*
Francis (1960)	Hereford	30 weeks	9,5 kg 24 kg*
Little (1963)	Hereford/ Friesland	45 weeks	0,75 kg/tick/year
Taylor (1981)	Afrikaner	12 months	48 kg (3 animals died)

ticks. The suppressive effects of ticks are most pronounced in *Bos taurus* (exotic) breeds, although the indigenous and other *Bos indicus* animals can also be affected by production loss. Dairy animals are severely affected by tick worry as studies have shown that uninfested controls produced 3 litres more daily than heavily infested cows and had 10 kg more weight gain.

Structure and biology

Ticks are eight-legged, bloodsucking parasites with a fairly uncomplicated life cycle. When they hatch from eggs laid by the female they are tiny 6-legged larvae. Often referred to as "pepper" or "seed ticks", they climb up grass stalks and sit there waiting for a host to come past. After their first feed on an animal host the larvae moult and become *nymphae* which are slightly larger than larvae but have 8 legs like adult ticks. These in turn feed and moult to become adults. Adults then mate and the females engorge on a host and then drop off to lay their eggs.

Identification of ticks

It is important to recognise that there are different species of ticks, and that distinguishing between them can be difficult. Adult female ticks when they have fed and are engorged (swollen) all look very similar. In addition, the immature and male ticks of many species look very similar. The correct identification of ticks is helpful when monitoring tick control: for example, blue ticks which are one-host ticks are much easier to control with chemicals because they spend more time on the animals than the two- and three-host ticks. Although this is a specialised field which can be quite difficult for the layperson, one can determine which ticks are likely to occur on a certain farm by knowing the geographic distribution of the various tick species, the appearance of some of the more common ticks, the host species they prefer and where they are likely to be found on the animal. Note that some common tick species are discussed here but for more details consult **Afrivet Tick Monographs.**

Life cycles

Ticks can be divided into three groups according to the number of hosts on which they feed during their life cycle:

One-host ticks: All three stages of the life cycle (larvae, nymphs and adults) feed on one single host. In the case of blue ticks this single host is usually cattle.

Two-host ticks: The larvae feed and moult on a host until they become engorged nymphae adults, at which stage they drop off, moult into adults and feed on a second host. The first two stages feed on wildlife species and the adults on large game or domestic stock. An example of a two-host tick is the red-legged tick.

Three-host ticks: Each of the three stages of the life cycle feed on different hosts, including some wild species such as hares, tortoises and ground birds. As a result, these ticks have a long life cycle and are more difficult to control. An example of a three-host tick is the bont tick.

SUMMARY OF IMPORTANT TICKS AND THEIR EFFECT ON ANIMAL HEALTH

Tick group	Species	Importance
One-host	*Rhipicephalus(Boophilus) decolaratus* African blue tick *R.(B). microplus* Pantropical blue tick	Redwater Anaplasmosis Weight loss Production loss
Two-host	*Rhipicephalus evertsi* Red-legged tick *Hyalomma spp* Bont-legged ticks	Spring lamb paralysis Sweating sickness Congo fever Abscesses
Three-host	*Rhipicephalus appendiculatus* Brown ear-tick *Rhipicephalus warburtoni* Brown paralysis tick *Rhipicephalus simus* Glossy brown tick *Amblyomma hebraeum* Bont tick *Ixodes rubicundus*	January disease Theilerioses Paralysis of Angora lambs Foot abscess Anaplasmosis Heartwater Abscesses Karoo paralysis

Lifecycle of 1-host tick: ± 21 days

Larva → Nymph → Adult female / Adult male → Sucking female

Engorged female ← Eggs ← Larva

Blue tick - *Boophilus decoloratus* + *B. microplus*

Lifecycle of 2-host tick: ± 21 days

+ 14 days

Or — Sucking larva → Sucking nymph

Engorged nymph → Adult female / Adult male → Sucking female

+ 7 days

Larva ← Eggs ← Engorged female

Bont-legged tick – *Hyalomma truncatum*
Red-legged tick - *Rhipicephalus evertsi evertsi*

Lifecycle of 3-host tick: ± 21 days

+ 7 days

Or — Sucking larva → Engorged larva → Nymph

+ 7 days

Or — Sucking nymph → Engorged nymph → Adult female / Adult male

+ 7 days

Adult female / Adult male → Sucking female → Engorged female

Larva ← Eggs ← Engorged female

Bont tick - *Amblyomma hebraeum*
Brown ear tick - *Rhipicephalus appendiculatus*

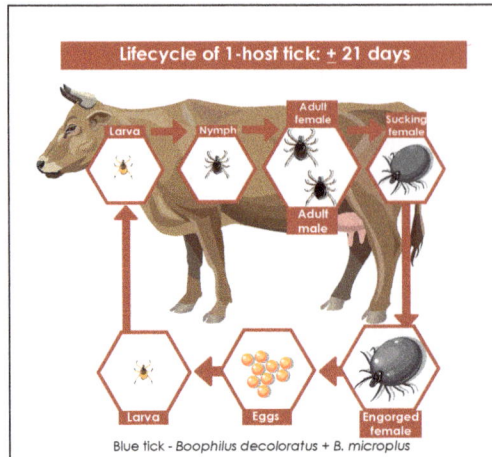

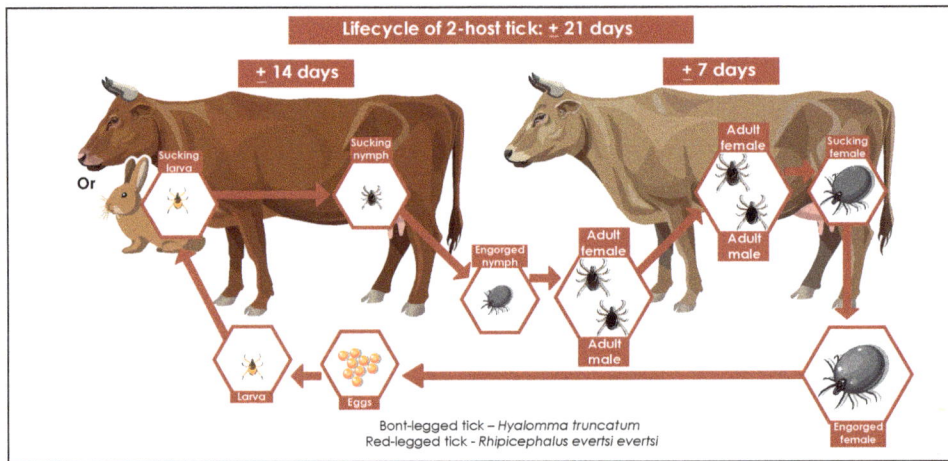

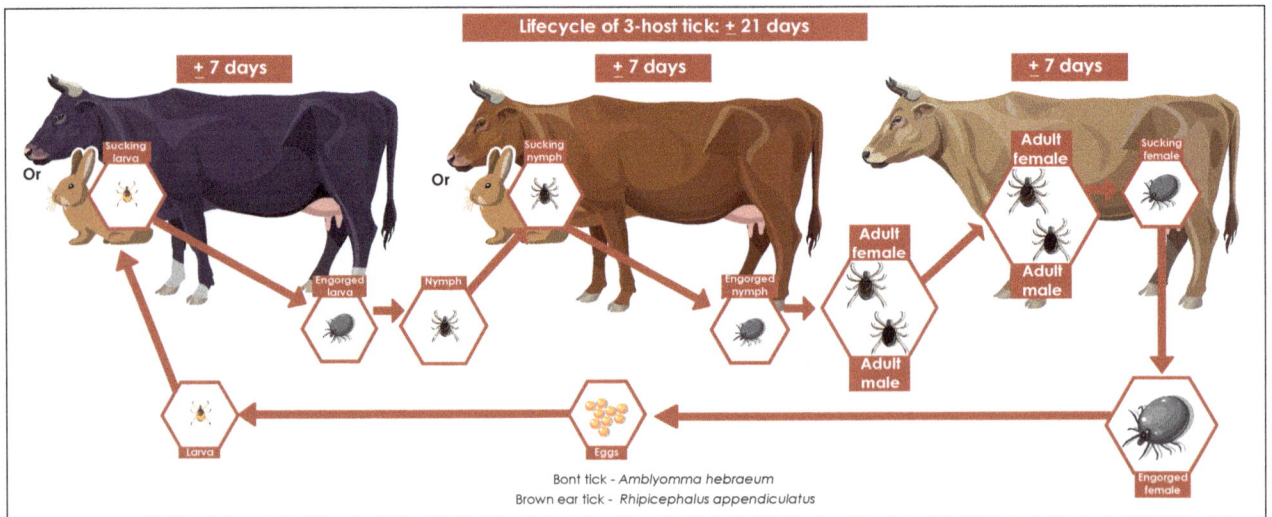

Life cycles of 1-, 2- and 3- host ticks

Ectoparasites

BLUE TICKS

African blue tick *Rhipicepalus (Boophilus) decoloratus*
Pantropical blue tick *Rhipicephalus (Boophilus) microplus*

Important hosts: Cattle are the main hosts of blue ticks, although they can also be found on sheep and goats.

Distribution: R. (B.) decoloratus is the most widespread and is the most common cattle tick in SA. It is found in bushveld, lowveld, and eastern coastal areas, but also focal areas of the Free State and coastal areas of the Western Cape. Its distribution is limited by dry conditions. *R. (B.) microplus* is less common, although its range is widening in SA. The limiting factor for this tick is heavy frost.

Description: These ticks are named for the appearance of the female ticks when they have engorged, but it is important to note that the females of other species will look similar after feeding. The engorged females are an oblong shape and are blue-grey with a greenish tinge.

Life cycle: Blue ticks are one-host ticks with a short life cycle which is completed on a single cattle host within 21 days. The life cycle is roughly 2 months long. Blue ticks therefore have a rapid generation time in comparison with the two- and three-host ticks.

The females lay roughly 2000 eggs.

Season: The eggs of blue ticks can survive the winter and they hatch in the spring. The larvae are therefore found on cattle in the spring. A number of generations then multiply in the summer and, so by autumn blue tick numbers have reached a peak (see graph).

Oct-Dec: Larvae and first generations seen in spring.

Feb-Apr: Ticks have produced 3-4 generations and are present in large numbers in the autumn.

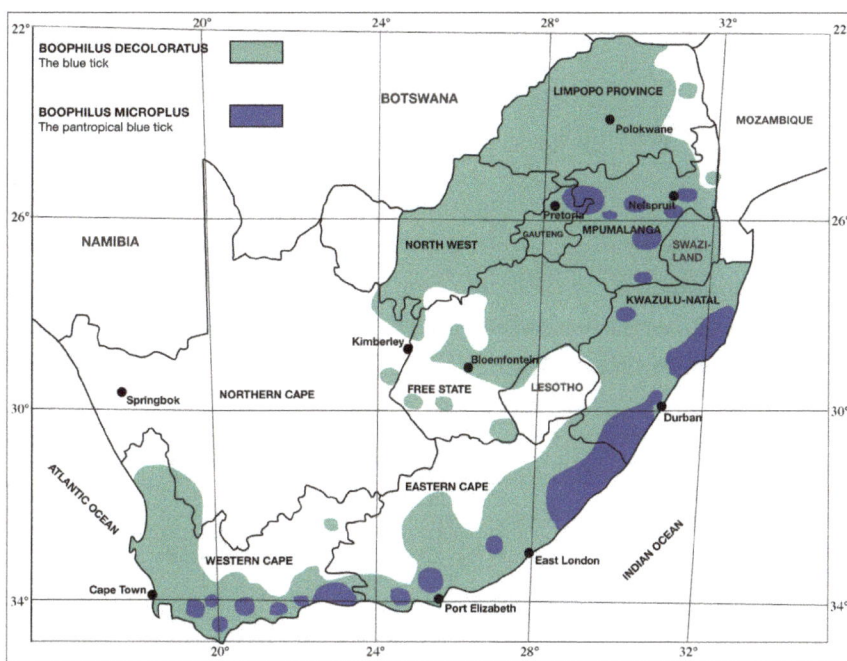

Map showing the distribution of blue tick species.

Seasonal dynamics of blue ticks

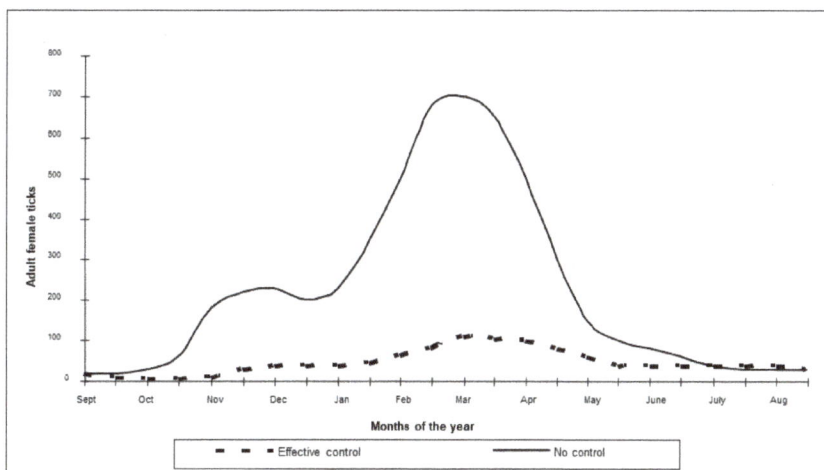

Graph showing the seasonal dynamics of blue ticks and the effect of strategic control.

Site of attachment: Blue ticks prefer the neck, the dewlap, the underline and the flanks.

Importance: Blue ticks transmit babesiosis (redwater) and anaplasmosis, and heavy infestations cause tick "worry" and anaemia.

Control: Three treatments in the spring, 45 days apart, with injectable or pour-on ivermectin will control the first peak and will result in a reduction of tick numbers in autumn. During summer and autumn use any tick dips or pour-ons every 3 weeks to prevent the autumn peak and to limit the transmission of redwater. Blue ticks are exposed to the chemicals more often than the multi-host ticks and for this reason develop resistance more frequently, the spring treatments with ivermectin will help to limit this problem. Note that ivermectin is not suitable for use in dairy cattle.

BONT TICK

Amblyomma hebraeum

Important hosts: Cattle, sheep, goats (immatures on game and ground birds).

Distribution: Bont ticks occur in the eastern parts of the country where the rainfall and the mean temperature is higher. The distribution of this tick extends from the bushveld, down to the eastern coastal areas as far as Port Elizabeth and Mossel Bay. The bont tick needs the shelter of trees and bushes and so is absent from open grassland.

Description: The males have the characteristic "bont" or coloured patterns. The females are a dull mustard colour, with a patterned scutum which becomes more difficult to see once the female has engorged. Both males and female adult ticks have very long mouth parts and orange and brown-banded legs.

Life cycle: The bont tick is a three-host tick with a long lifecycle which can take from 5 months to 3 years to complete. The females lay as many as 18 000 eggs.

Season: The larvae which occur on small mammals, are active in late summer to autumn with a peak in the spring, the nymphae in winter and spring and the adults predominate in summer. However, in wet coastal areas all three stages may be found together at any time of the year.

Site of attachment: On cattle, the adults prefer the hairless areas of the body – the belly, groin, armpit, and the area around the anus and the tail brush. Nymphae favour the feet although they may be found on hairless parts or on the legs. Larvae

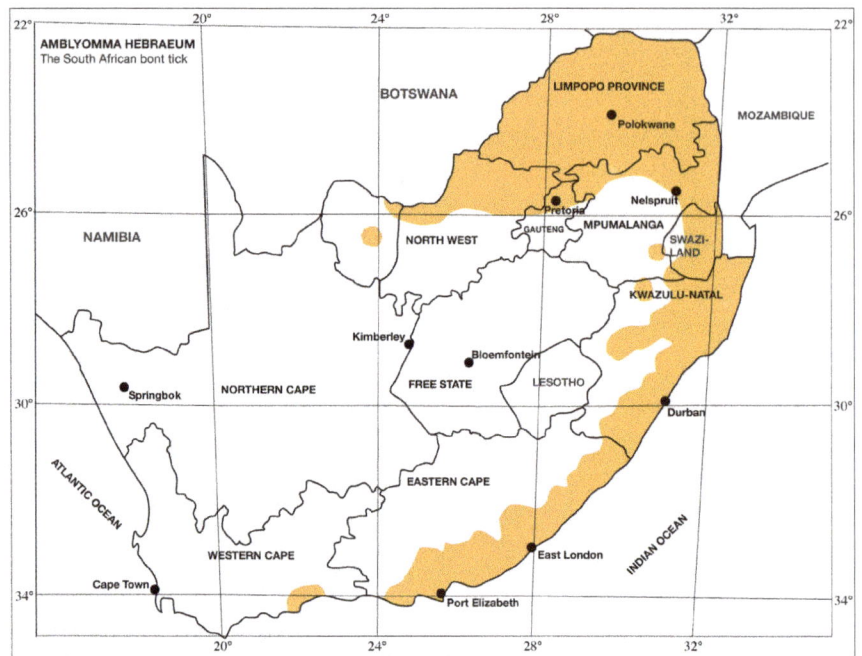

A map showing the distribution of the bont tick.

prefer the head, muzzle, feet, legs and neck. On sheep, adults attach to the groin, armpit, sternum and peri-anal area. Goats tend to have adults on the underline and groin, with nymphae on the feet and legs, and larvae on the feet, legs, and ears.

Importance: Bont ticks are important as transmitters of *Erlichia ruminantium*, the organism that causes heartwater. Their long mouth parts cause damage to hides and also abscesses. They tend to cluster in groups and can therefore cause serious damage to udders, teats and sheath of the penis. The wounds they cause are often secondarily infested with screwworm. Bont ticks transmit the organism that causes tick-bite fever in humans.

Control: Since most multi-host larvae occur on small mammals, intense control of the adults must be done on livestock during the summer months.

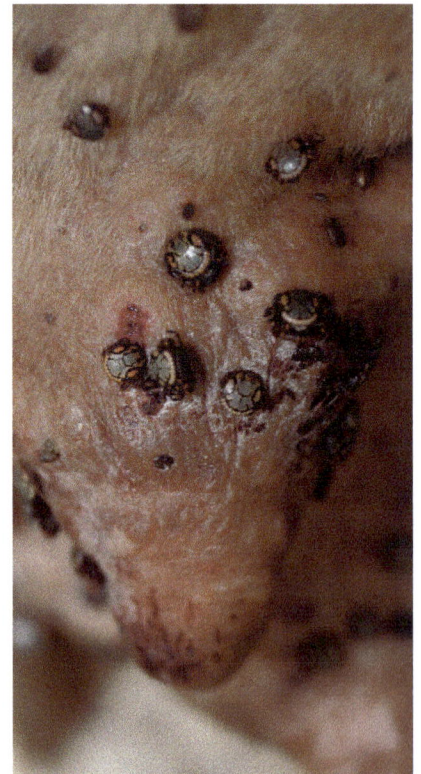

Bont tick infestation showing "bont" males and engorged females.

BROWN TICKS

This group contains the Rhipicephalus ticks, the brown ear-ticks, the red-legged ticks, the brown paralysis tick and the glossy brown tick.

Brown ear-tick
Rhipicephalus appendiculatus

Important hosts: Mainly cattle, although it feeds on a wide variety of animals.

Distribution: Brown ear-ticks occur in the high rainfall areas of the east, central and coastal areas where there is good vegetation coverage. They prefer savannah habitat with trees.

Description: These are medium-sized brown ticks with short mouthparts. The legs of the males increase in size towards the back of the body.

Life cycle: These are 3-host ticks which can feed on wildlife, although all stages are found on cattle.

Season: The adult ticks are numerous in summer from December to March, the larvae in March to July and the nymphs from June to October.

Site of attachment: Cattle may get heavy infestations of all stages; the adults tend to cluster on the ears where they cause the "bleeding ear" syndrome. Immature ticks are found on the head and neck.

Importance: These ticks cause tick toxicosis and damage to ears, which often leads to secondary screwworm strike.

Control: The control is as for bont ticks but because brown ear-ticks engorge so rapidly, a program of 5-5-4 day dipping may be necessary with heavy infestations. For good control of this tick, one must ensure good wetting of the head and ears. Additional treatment with grease or pour-on may be necessary.

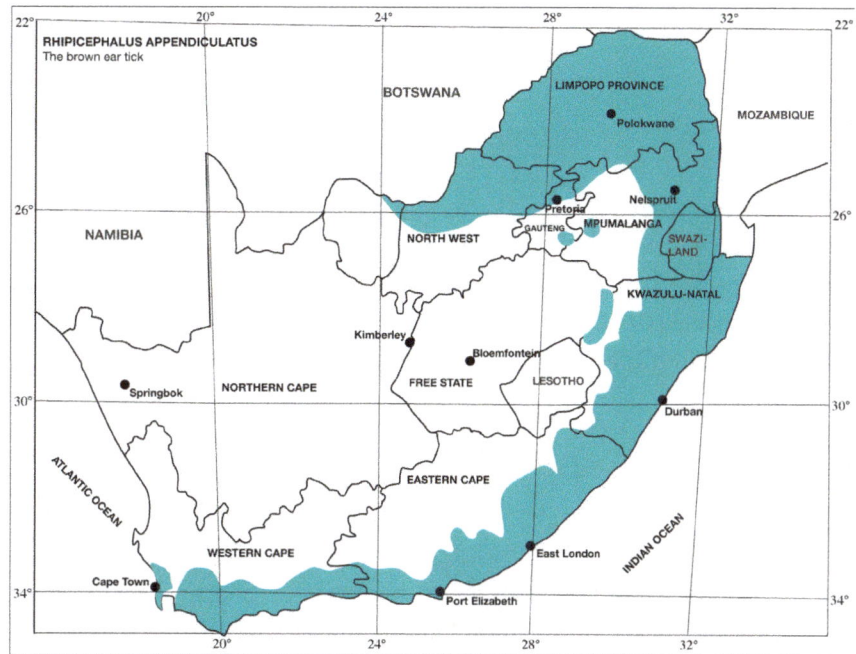

A map showing the distribution of the brown ear-tick Rhipicephalus appendiculatus.

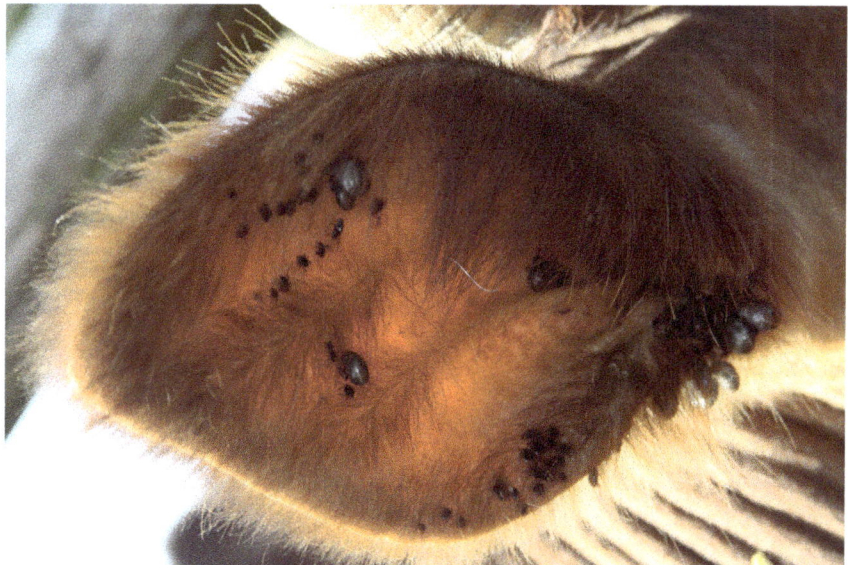

Brown ear ticks showing males and engorged females.

Red-legged tick

Rhipicephalus evertsi

Important hosts: Cattle, sheep and goats

Distribution: The tick is widespread in SA.

Description: This is a glossy brown tick but its red legs are a clear diagnostic feature. It also has beady eyes and a brownish grey body.

Life cycle: These are 2-host ticks.

Season: They are numerous during wet seasons.

Site of attachment: Larvae are found deep in the ear canal, while the adults are seen around the anus.

Importance: The red-legged ticks transmit anaplasmosis, damage ears and in sheep cause spring lamb paralysis.

Control: Since the favourite attachment sites are those which are difficult to wet during dipping, special attention must be given to these areas. Additional spot treatment of the ears and under the tail may be necessary.

The distribution of the red-legged tick Rhipicephalus evertsi.

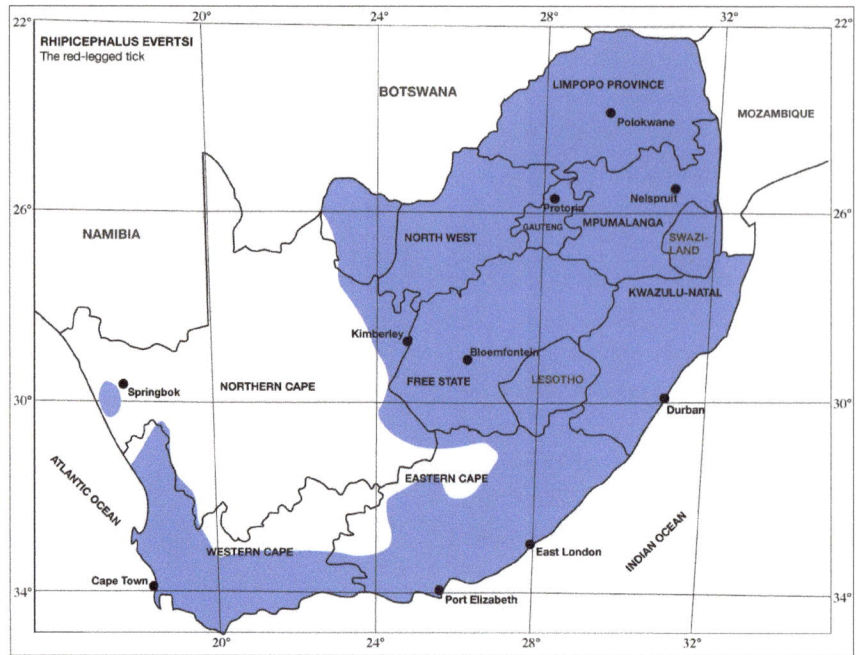

Red-legged tick showing the typical features.

Swelling of the anus due to adult red legged ticks which are most commonly found under the tail.

106

Glossy brown tick
Rhipicephalus simus

Important hosts: Cattle, sheep, goats.

Distribution: This tick occurs in wetter areas, so it is common in the eastern parts of the country.

Description: glossy brown ticks with long mouthparts.

Life cycle: These are 3-host ticks.

Season: Numerous during warm wet conditions of summer.

Site of attachment: The ticks attach in the space between the claws (interdigital spaces).

Importance: Apart from transmitting anaplasmosis in cattle, the bites caused by the ticks serve as a port of entry for bacteria which give rise to the condition called "foot abscess", in small stock; this is a bacterial infection which extends into the joint of the hoof causing chronic septic arthritis which is difficult to treat. The animals suffer severe lameness and lose condition as a result.

Control: Frequent dipping using footbaths or the application of pour-on remedies on the feet will control the problems caused by this tick and others which attach on the feet.

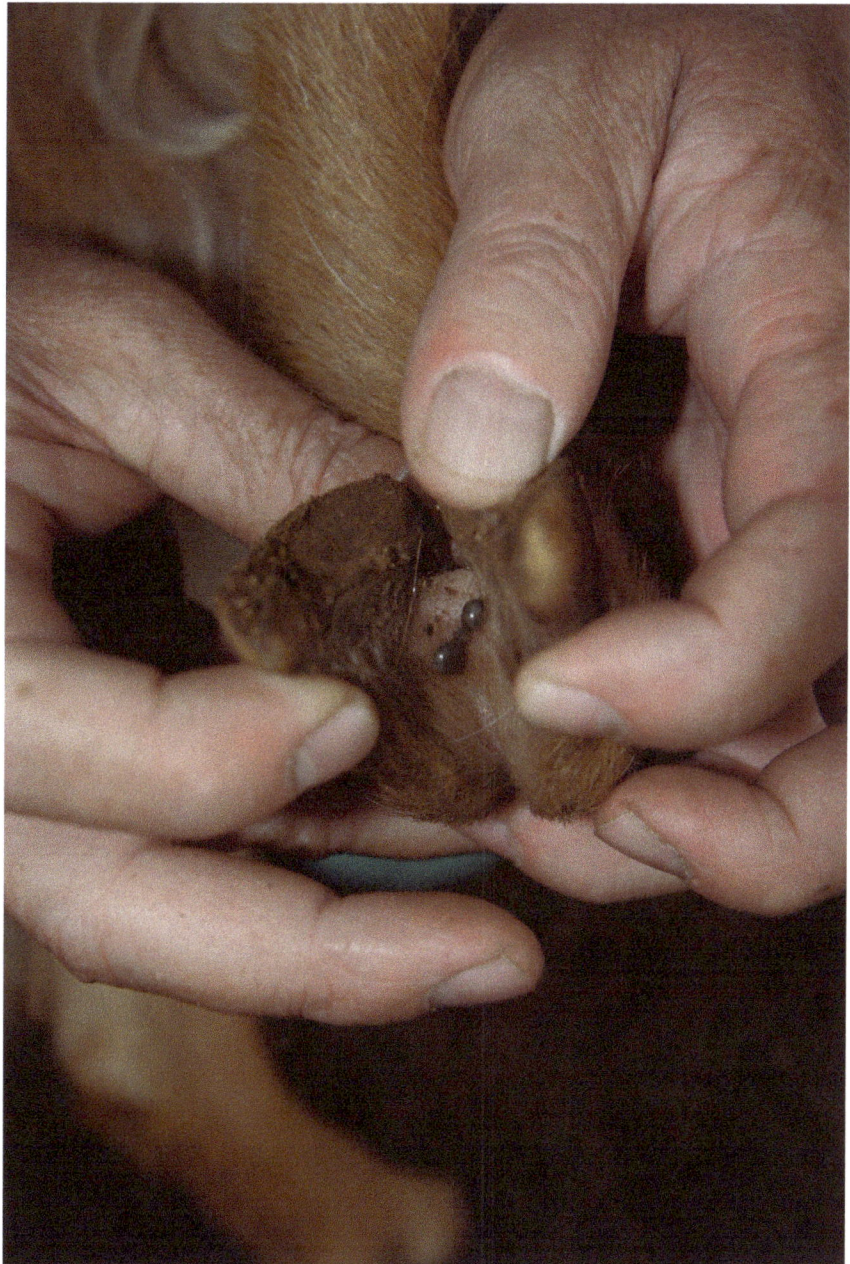

Rhipicephalus simus between the claws of a sheep.

BROWN PARALYSIS TICK

Rhipicephalus warburtoni

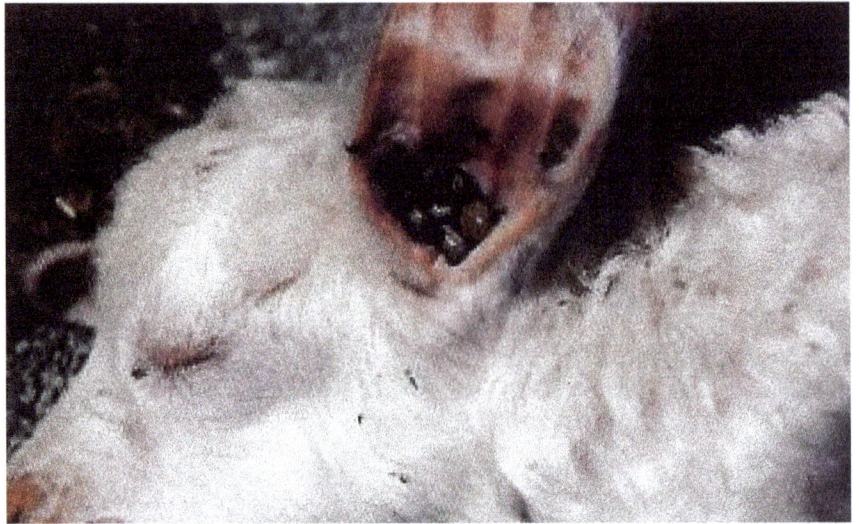

A heavy infestation of an Angora kid with the brown paralysis tick R. warburtoni.

Hosts: The adults infest Angora goats.

Distribution: The ticks are confined to the Free State, the Northern Cape and the Barkly East area.

Life cycle: These are 3-host ticks. The immature stages are found on elephant shrews and all stages can be found on hares. The adults are found on Angora goats.

Site of attachment: The adult ticks creep into ears of young goats while they lie flat in the bush and heavy infestations can occur. They also occur on adult Angoras on the head, neck and brisket.

Importance: These ticks cause heavy losses of Angora kids due to paralysis. The goats may die despite the ticks being removed.

Control: Spot treatment of the head and ears with tick remedies will prevent attachment of these ticks.

BONT-LEGGED TICKS

Hyalomma marginatum rufipes
H. truncatum

Important hosts: Cattle, sheep, goats and wildlife

Distribution: This is a tick of drier areas; it is widespread except in the winter rainfall areas and high-lying areas where snow falls during winter.

Description: These ticks are medium to large, shiny brown with long mouthparts; they have beady eyes and banded red and white legs.

Life cycle: The two-host life cycle takes a year to complete.

Season: The larvae and nymphs are numerous during dry winters and the adults during the wet summers.

Site of attachment: These ticks attach around the anus but also along the underline, between the hooves and on the tip of the tail.

Importance: Bont-legged ticks transmit anaplasmosis to cattle and Congo fever in humans. They cause sweating sickness in calves (see details in chapter on tick-borne diseases). The long mouthparts cause serious wounds and abscesses and can be the primary cause of screwworm strikes.

Control: Because this is a two-host tick, it is more difficult to reduce tick numbers with dipping. Local treatment may be required in addition to dipping.

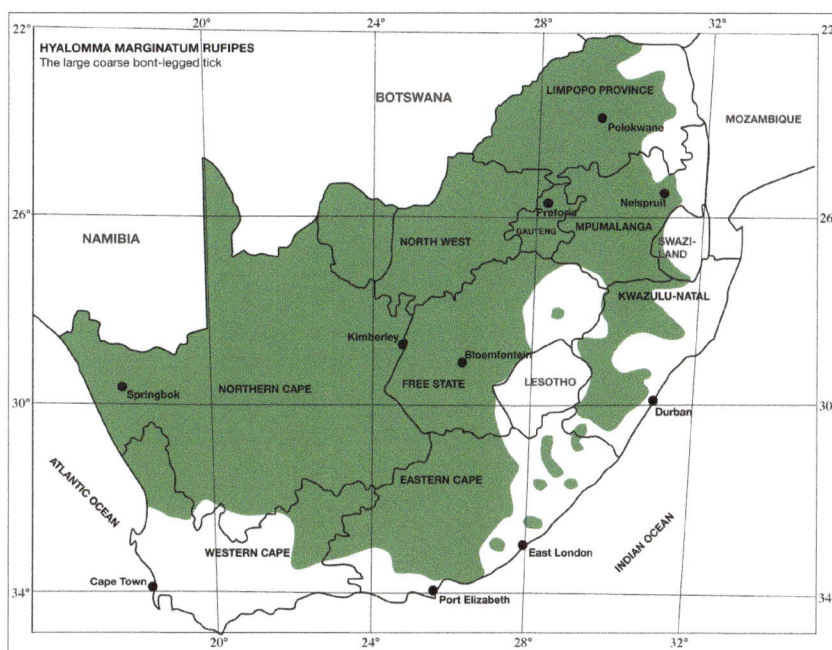

Distribution of the bont-legged ticks

The bont-legged H. rufipes tick has long mouth parts and banded legs.

KAROO PARALYSIS TICK

Ixodes rubicundus

Important hosts: Sheep and goats (antelope, elephant shrews and red hares).

Distribution: This tick occurs sporadically in the Western Cape, widely in central and south-east Free State, sporadically in the Eastern Cape in the Queenstown area, with foci in Mpumalanga. Distribution of the tick is associated with specific vegetation namely "besembos" *(Rhus erosa)* and tussocky grass or "suurpolgras" *(Danthonia disticha)* which occurs on the southern slopes of mountainous areas. The vegetation serves as a shelter for the intermediate hosts of the immature ticks which are red hares and elephant shrews. The distribution of the tick has expanded due to overgrazing of farms which results in expansion of the range of unpalatable vegetation.

Description: These are small reddish-brown, shiny, eyeless ticks, with legs set far forward.

Life cycle: This is a three-host tick with a two-year life cycle.

Season: The adults begin to feed in late summer usually after sudden cold, rain or snow, commencing from February up until May or June.

Site of attachment: The ticks attach along the underline, on the neck, the legs and sometimes the cheeks and the lower jaw.

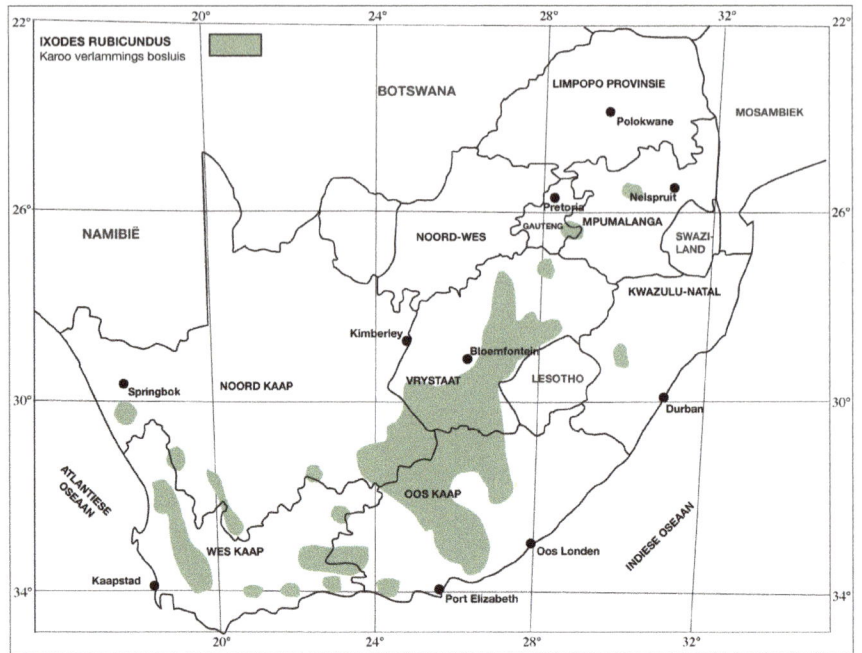

Distribution of the Karoo paralysis tick.

Importance: Once the adult ticks begin feeding, a toxin in their saliva causes paralysis of varying severity, from slight lameness to total paralysis. Large numbers of animals can be affected. The animals will recover within 24-48 hours if the ticks are removed early enough.

Control: If possible, remove animals from hill camps from February until the danger period passes at the end of June. Otherwise, treat sheep weekly to prevent attachment with tick remedies registered for Karoo paralysis tick control. These can be administered in a belly-bath or use pour-on remedies. Note that only water-based pour-on remedies are suitable for woolled sheep and Angora goats. Most remedies have a longer residual action on wool sheep than on hairy sheep or goats.

A Karoo paralysis tick on a sheep.

SOFT TICKS OR TAMPANS

Sand tampan
Ornithodorus savignyi

Hosts: Cattle, sheep and goats (and humans).

Distribution: Sand tampans occur in arid areas of the country such as the Kalahari.

Description: The tampans belong to the group which is referred to as the soft-bodied ticks; these are ticks that have no scutum (the hard shield-like part behind the head). The legs are typically bent forward into little hooks. The unengorged tampans have a flat wrinkled appearance.

Life cycle: Sand tampans lay their eggs in the soil. These hatch into non-motile larvae which never feed but merely moult into nymphae which pass through several nymphal stages before becoming adults. These adults stay buried under the soil in the shade of trees, bushes or rocks and avoid sunlit places. However, they immediately detect the carbon dioxide given off by resting animals or humans and they emerge to attach to these hosts.

Sand tampans can literally survive for years without a meal.

Season: Sand tampans are most active in summer, especially during dry weather.

Site of attachment: Tampans attach to any part of the body but especially the legs; they are commonly found around the hooves.

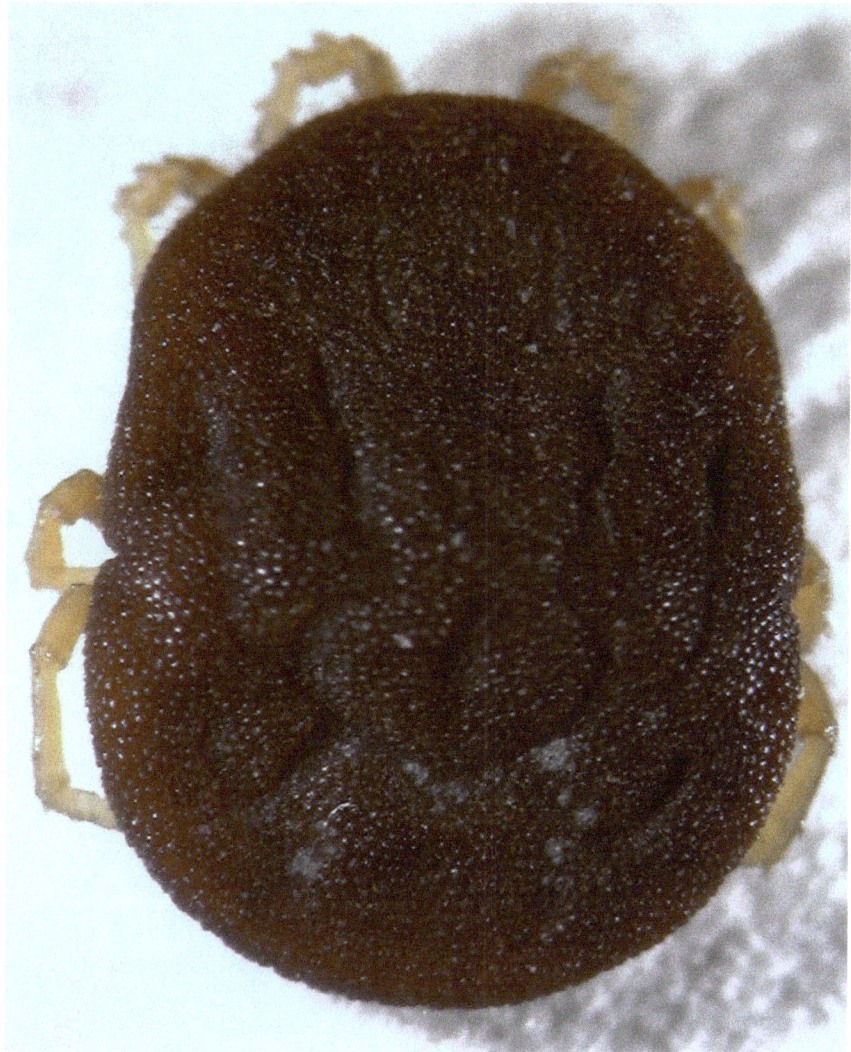

The sand tampan Ornithodoros savignyi

Importance: The bites are painful and the tampans secrete a toxin in the saliva which can kill animals, especially young animals with heavy infestations.

Control: Weekly dipping or dipping every 2 weeks depending on the dip being used. However, chemical control may not be effective because the tampans feed so rapidly. It is impractical to spray infected soil because of the wide areas that need to be treated.

Bantams and ground birds are said to eat large numbers of tampans and are therefore considered important for control.

Spinose ear tick
Otobius megnini

Hosts: The spinose ear tick attacks a wide range of animals including cattle, sheep and goats.

Distribution: It occurs in dry areas of the country. Infestations occur in kraals and stables where they survive for long periods of time.

Description: The nymph stage is covered with hairs and gives rise to the name.

Life cycle: It is a one-host tick and remains on the animal host from the larval to the adult stage. The adults, however, are not parasitic and fall off and conceal themselves in crevices of buildings or other hiding places where they lay their eggs.

Season: Throughout the year, especially during warm periods.

Site of attachment: They feed in the ears of cattle as well as other animals.

Importance: Heavy infestations can cause anaemia, may damage the eardrums permanently and may sometimes cause meningitis. Infested animals are restless and feed poorly.

Control: There is no prevention but affected animals can be treated with tick grease/oil applied into the ears.

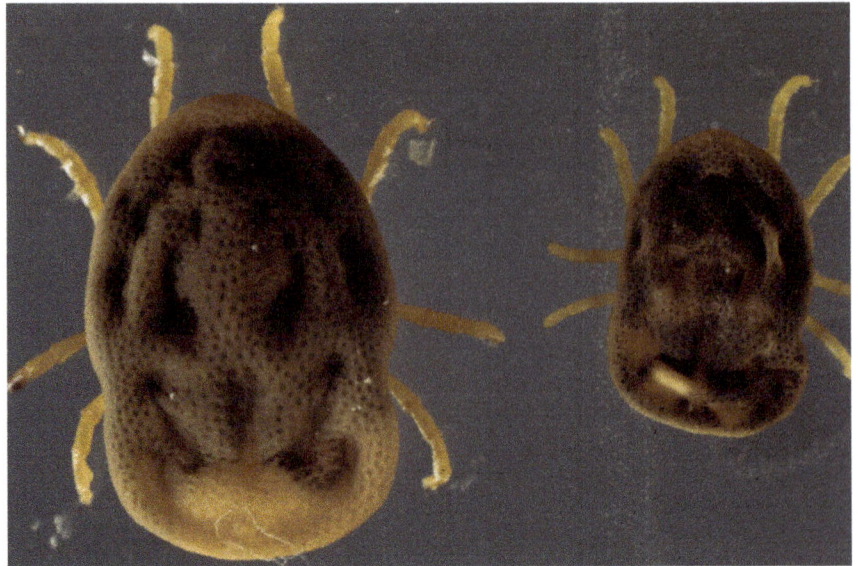

The spinose ear tick Otobius megnini

Tick control in cattle

Approach to tick control

There are two alternative strategies to use for controlling ticks, namely **intensive** or **tactical** control. The choice of the strategy used must be made based on the following factors:

- The type of farming (dairy/extensive/feedlot)
- The species of ticks that occur on the farm
- The tick-borne diseases in the area
- The breed of animal

Intensive control and minimal disease situation

This is the frequent and continuous treatment to minimise exposure of animals to ticks (weekly in summer and every 2 weeks in winter). The animals are therefore not exposed to the tick-borne diseases and vaccination is unnecessary. Intensive control is used in dairies since ticks cause serious damage to udders and tick-transmitted diseases are unacceptable, because of their effect on production. Other advantages of intensive control are the elimination of tick worry and the negative effect on growth and production, no tick damage and a reduction of tick numbers. Good supervision and management are required for intensive tick control.

The disadvantages are that cattle are totally susceptible to tick-borne diseases and if a problem arises with dipping due to poor technique or resistance, large numbers of animals may develop tick-borne diseases. Intensive control is not recommended for those cattle breeds that are "tick tolerant" because their resistance is acquired on exposure to ticks and will be lost under intensive control. Intensive treatment requires substantial capital investment for dipping apparatus initially, and on a continuous basis for dips.

Tactical control and a stable disease situation

Tactical control needs less frequent dipping than intensive control. The aim is to reduce the number of ticks but to maintain sufficient numbers to allow the exposure of animals to infected ticks which will "immunise" animals against the prevailing tick-borne diseases. The advantages are less expenditure on dips and dipping equipment. The disadvantages are that there are still ticks around to cause either damage and tick worry which can affect production, or sporadic deaths due to tick-borne disease. Although tactical control often seems the most attractive option to farmers, it is difficult to achieve in practice because it is difficult to establish the correct dipping intervals, i.e. to know how many ticks are required for sufficient immunisation. This is especially difficult if all three tick-borne diseases are present because they are transmitted by different species of ticks, which require different dipping intervals. For example, dipping to achieve a stable heartwater situation and to reduce damage by three-host ticks, may result in the intensive control of blue ticks and cause insufficient natural immunisation against redwater. To further complicate the issue, droughts may reduce the numbers of ticks below the level needed for natural immunisation. Vaccination of adult animals may be required to re-establish immunity. Stable situations are easier to achieve in areas where ticks are numerous and the farmer is prepared to accept some loss of production.

It is difficult and dangerous to change from an intensive tick-control management system to tactical control with minimal disease, and this must not be attempted without the aid of an experienced veterinarian.

Methods of tick control

Chemical control methods

- *Plunge dip:* If a plunge dip is well designed it is the most effective method of wetting animals. In the long term, plunge dipping is the most cost-effective method if large numbers of animals are involved.
- *Spray races:* Well designed and well managed races will achieve good wetting but spot treatment may still be needed under tails and in ears. There must be sufficient arches and spray nozzles to achieve good wetting.
- *Hand or mechanical spraying:* This is the most expensive and difficult method to do successfully. The minimum volume of application is 5 litres, and it may require as much as 10 litres to achieve good wetting.
- *Pour-ons:* This method is convenient, but the application must be precise. The remedy takes time to spread over the body. This is the most expensive control method. Pyrethroid pour-ons can cause irritation and resistance can develop rapidly.
- *Injection with macrocyclic lactones:* This is a convenient method of control but only works for blue ticks. However, it has the added bonus of controlling intestinal worms.
- *Spot treatment:* The use of tick grease or oils for attachment sites such as the ears and under the tail may be required in certain areas.

For practical management of plunge dips and spray races, see later in the chapter.

Pasture management
Management of pastures can help to reduce the number of ticks on cattle. The resting of camps if done for sufficiently long intervals may be helpful; if the grass can be burnt, this will help reduce tick numbers-especially blue ticks. Burning must be done in spring after the first rains, when the blue tick eggs have hatched. Planted pastures are much less attractive to ticks than natural pasture, but even under zero-grazing conditions, the use of hay can cause the introduction of sufficient ticks to cause disease.

Tick control in sheep and goats

- *Plunge dips:* these are ideal for the post-shearing dipping of small stock to control scab, other mites and lice.
- *Pour-ons* can be used to control Karoo paralysis ticks, and those which infest the ears and between the claws.
- *Belly-bathing:* This is ideal for Karoo paralysis and heartwater ticks.
- *Footbaths* are sufficient for the control of foot abscesses if ticks are the source of the problem. Suitable dips are organophosphates, amitraz and pyrethroids.

Trouble-shooting tick control
Farmers become annoyed when a dip application appears not to be working. It is important to understand the many factors that can play a role in the efficacy of dips. Here is a list of some of these:

Structural or application problems
- The dip tank may be too shallow and does not wet the heads of the animals.

- Wetting in a spray race may be poor due to structural and functional defects.
- With hand or mechanical spraying, problems are almost always due to insufficient dip being used to wet the animal.
- The dip may be too weak due to faulty dilution or replenishment – this often occurs due to the capacity of the dip tank being underestimated. Testing of the dip wash will establish whether the concentration is sufficient.

Time interval
- Pyrethroids can take up to 2 days to kill ticks and some stay attached despite being dead, especially the males.
- Macrocyclic lactones take time to act because the ticks have to feed before there are any effects.
- Pour-ons may take 2-3 days to spread over the animal and their effect on the lower body areas (belly and legs) will be slower than on the head and neck.
- Ticks may climb on animals after the residual effect is past (after 3 days). This occurs especially when farmers put animals in new camps which are alive with thousands of hungry ticks.

Other reasons
- Rain and wet grass washes off dip.
- The animals used for stirring the dip are not returned to the dip when it is at the proper concentration.
- Growth Regulators will not kill adult ticks so treatment with adulticide dips might be necessary initially.
- When there is a massive population of ticks due to warm wet conditions, more frequent dipping is required to reduce the numbers.
- Resistance can be suspected when a dip group has been used for long periods of time. Ticks can be collected and tested for resistance.
- Product may be damaged, sub-standard or expired.

MITES

These are small parasites with 8 legs that are closely related to ticks. The largest of these parasites are 2 mm long, which makes them difficult to see with the naked eye. They are permanent parasites that are only able to live for short periods off their hosts. All are species-specific (adapted to a specific species), with the exception of the *Sarcoptes* mite which is found on a wide species range including on humans, in which it causes scabies. The life cycle of the mite takes roughly 14 days to complete, from the hatching from the egg to the maturation of the 8-legged adult.

Mites are spread by contact between animals and also by inanimate objects. The parasites feed on skin particles and therefore cause skin damage and inflammation (dermatitis). This gives rise to irritation often with severe itching; animals will rub the skin lesions against objects and sheep will pluck vigorously at the wool, causing fleece disturbance. The lesions usually start as small focal areas but if the condition progresses untreated, these can become extensive. Mite infestations can be confirmed by examining hair and skin samples microscopically.

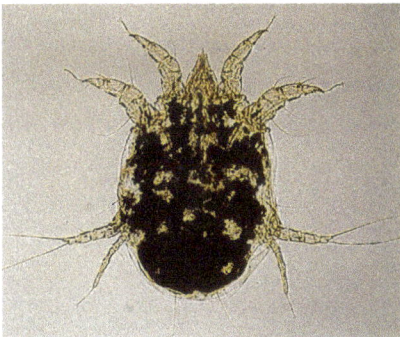

Scabies mite seen under the microscope.

Mite infestations of cattle (Mange)

Mite infestations are seldom encountered when cattle are dipped regularly. However, it is an increasingly common problem in animals that are bought at auctions where they spread due to close contact. Poor nutrition and stress predispose animals to these infestations.

Mite infestations are difficult to distinguish from other conditions such as lice, ringworm and other skin conditions such as plant poisonings which can cause hair loss and itching.

There are a number of species of mite that can affect cattle but because mites are so small, microscopic examination by a veterinarian is needed to identify the species. The treatment is for the most part the same for all species of mites, but it is useful to know the type of mite involved since for example, in the case of *Sarcoptes* the mite can affect other species including man.

Chorioptes: This mite is the most common cause of mange in cattle. It is first seen on the pasterns (feet) and at the base of the tail. In bulls the scrotum can be infested by contact with the feet when lying down. The lesions are usually round hairless patches which may show reddening due to rubbing of the area.

Psoroptes natalensis: Infestations are seen on the neck, the withers, and the tail root.

Sarcoptes scabiei: The mite infests animals in poor condition and targets hairless areas. It is seen on the neck, tail root and back, often with thickening of the skin and fold formation in extensive cases. Cases are seen in late winter and the condition is very itchy. It can spread to other species.

Demodex: This condition is seldom seen in cattle. Since the mite is a permanent parasite in the hair follicles, it is always present but only causes problems when the condition deteriorates. The lesions are hairless with pustule (pimple) formation.

Psororgates bovis: One case has been seen in South Africa. The case occurred in animals that had been treated for a lengthy period with pyrethroid pour-on.

Treatment of mites on cattle
Amitraz as a dip or pour-on remedy is exceptionally effective against mites.

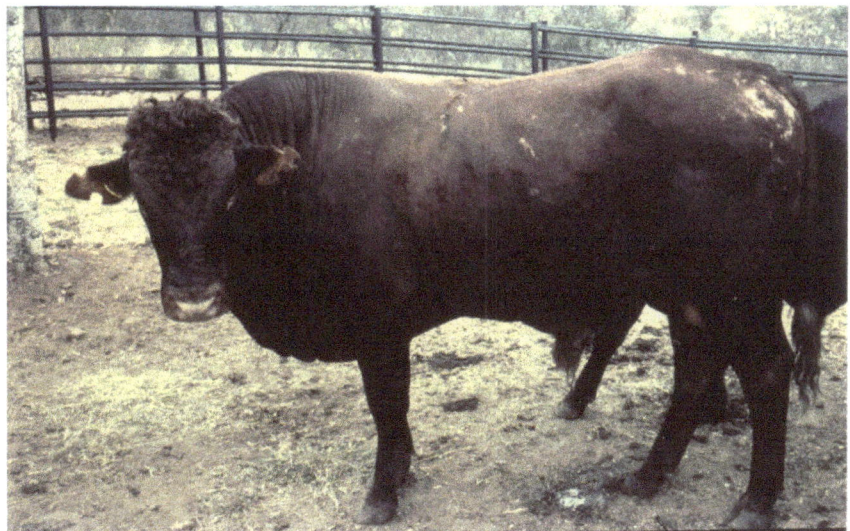

A case of mange in a bovine.

Organophosphates can also be used in dip form. Injectable or pour-on formulations of macrocyclic lactones can also be used. Mite infestations must be treated twice, with an 11-14 day interval. All animals must be treated and camps must be avoided for at least 17 days to prevent re-infestation.

Mites of sheep

Sheep scab

Psoroptes ovis

Sheep scab is caused by the infestation of sheep with the mite *Psoroptes ovis*. It is regarded as the biggest threat to the wool industry in South Africa. The insidious nature of the infestation results from its slow and almost inapparent spread initially which prevents it from being noticed in the early stages. The irreversible damage done to the fleece and the dramatic effect on the overall condition of the animal lead to great economic losses. Because wool is such an important export commodity for the country it is important that outbreaks are declared, and it is therefore a notifiable disease.

The sheep scab mite *Psoroptes communis ovis* is so small that it is almost invisible to the naked eye. The mite is a specific parasite of sheep although it can be carried for short periods of time on the hair of goats, as well as on clothing and implements.

The mite can only be identified by microscopic examination to distinguish it from other mite infestations of sheep such as Australian itch mite. It can infest all sheep of any breed or age. The sheep scab mite has impressive reproductive abilities: the female can lay eggs from the age of 9 days. After mating, she lays eggs on the skin and these hatch within 2-3 days. Within 3 days, the larvae moult to become nymphs and 6

An early case of sheep scab showing bare patches and reddening of the skin.

days later these become adult mites. The life cycle is therefore completed within 11 days.

The adult mite feeds on the sheep by chewing though the skin and feeding on the serum which seeps from these small wounds. The bites cause severe irritation and inflammation and after 4 days, crust form. The lesions enlarge by 2,5 cm per month and the parasites move outwards to the edges.

The most common method of transmission is direct contact with infested sheep, but the mites can be transmitted over a period of 13 days by pieces of wool, overalls, implements, camps and vehicles. Outbreaks occur commonly in winter, but sheep can have inapparent infection during the summer. The mites creep away into places like the "ou oog", the armpit, and the base of the horn. In fat-tailed sheep they hide in the folds of the tail.

Infected sheep show signs of scratching, biting and plucking at the wool. They will lose weight from the constant irritation: rams will not mate and ewes may refuse to feed their lambs due to their discomfort. The diagnosis must be confirmed by a veterinarian identifying the parasite

microscopically. This is important because other conditions may look similar, such as Australian itch mite, red lice and sheep ked infestation.

If a diagnosis of sheep scab is confirmed the outbreak must be reported to the nearest state veterinarian. The farm is then placed immediately under quarantine which means small stock may not be removed from the farm.

Sheep scab has spread in SA due to itinerant sheep shearers who do not practice good hygiene, holding of sheep in auction yards, the use of under-strength dips, and extensive farming which makes regular dipping difficult.

Treatment of outbreaks

All small stock must be treated twice with registered remedies at an interval of 8-10 days.

Dipping

The only acceptable dipping method for sheep scab control is plunge dipping which allows effective wetting of the whole animal. Registered dips for sheep scab include the organophosphate diazinon, and deltamethrin (the only effective pyrethroid for scab). Amitraz-containing dips are very effective but must be made up at a higher concentration than the dilution used for tick control. The animal must be submerged for 60 seconds, and the head must be submerged 3 times to ensure total wetting. The dip must be correctly diluted, and the replenishment calculated carefully. Constant replenishment is the most effective method of maintaining the concentration. Dipping must be repeated 8-10 days later because not all dips will kill of the mite eggs.

Injection

Injection with macrocyclic lactones (ivermectin, moxidectin, etc) is effective against sheep scab at the recommended dose and is a very convenient means of treatment. To be effective, all animals must be treated and the correct dose must be given. All animals must be treated twice with an interval of 8-10 days unless stated otherwise on the label. The accuracy of automatic syringes must be checked beforehand and is of the greatest importance. Not all injectable MLs are suitable for use in goats, so this must be checked on the label.

Prevention of sheep scab

The prevention of sheep scab on the farm is very simple: it requires a single annual dipping or injection of sheep after shearing. Dipping has the advantage of controlling other infestations such as red or blue lice, sheep keds and itch mites.

Newly introduced sheep must be given two treatments with an 8-10 day interval before being introduced to the rest of the flock. Visiting shearers must be provided with clean overalls and must disinfect shearing equipment. Stray sheep must be kept off the property by keeping fences in good condition.

Australian itch mite
Psorogates

This condition is a lot less common than sheep scab but causes similar symptoms of itching, wool plucking and fleece disturbance. Examination of a wool sample under the microscope will identify the mite and allow it to be differentiated from the sheep scab mite. This condition is not notifiable and not controlled by the state. Treatment and prevention are as for sheep scab.

Sarcoptes

Sheep occasionally develop *Sarcoptes* infestations on the face and head. The treatment is as for sheep scab.

Sheep scab and mange in goats

Although the sheep scab mites can survive on goats for short periods, these animals are not permanent carriers. They do however suffer infestations of goat mange caused by *Sarcoptes*, and *Psoroptes* which infest their ears and *Chorioptes* which occur on the legs and fetlocks.

LICE

Lice are small flattened wingless insects with a simple life cycle. They hatch from the eggs or nits within 7-14 days in the form of nymphs which moult three times before they become adults. The life cycle is completed within 2-3 weeks. Lice vary in size from 1-10 mm, so some species can be seen with the naked eye. They are permanent parasites on animals and are species-specific, which makes them easy to eliminate. Lice are more active in winter when the condition of animals deteriorates, and the hair being longer gives better protection. Infestations are most common in young animals, those under stress and those suffering from malnutrition. Infested animals are restless, eat poorly, and scratch and bite at the lesions. The hair is worn off and occasionally the nits or eggs will be seen on the hair around the lesion. There are two main groups of lice, namely biting lice and sucking lice, and distinguishing them can be important for choosing the correct remedy for treatment.

Biting or red lice

These lice have chewing mouthparts because they live on the superficial layers of the skin, causing severe irritation. They are active and may be seen scuttling for cover if the fleece or hair is opened.

Red lice of cattle

Damalinia bovis

Red louse infestation is becoming an emerging problem in cattle. The lice are large enough to be seen with the naked eye, moving around on the animal. Lesions are often found on the shoulders, backline and tail root but can be more widespread over the body. The lice cause severe irritation, hair loss due to scratching and loss of weight.

Red lice of sheep

Damalinia ovis

Damalinia ovis is becoming more common in sheep due to the reliance on macrocyclic lactone injection for sheep scab control. They were formerly well controlled as a single annual dip for sheep scab prevention was sufficient. Red lice can cause severe irritation which results in fleece disturbance due to the animals rubbing, and plucking at the wool. They spend less time eating and lose weight.

Red lice of goats

Damalinia capra and *Damalinia limbata*

Red lice on Angoras (*D. limbata*) are a serious threat to the mohair industry because of the irritation and the loss in condition caused by these lice. The infestation occurs all over the body and causes severe irritation which is manifested by fleece pulling. Control is achieved by a single post-shearing dipping which prevents the problem developing in the winter, when the fleece is long and dipping is difficult.

Red lice visible in fleece.

A sheep with red louse infestation.

Red louse control

A single dipping of sheep and goats after shearing will control the problem and will prevent the necessity for treatment when the hair/wool is long which is difficult. After- shearing treatment is also more effective because the nits are removed with the wool. Treatment with organophosphate and pyrethroid dips are very effective for red lice if done correctly and if repeated within 10-14 days. Pyrethroid and Growth regulator containing pour-ons have good residual action but take time to spread and it may take 2 weeks for the lice to be killed.

For cattle, dips containing pyrethroid or organophosphate are effective, or pour-ons containing pyrethroids or Growth Regulators. Macrocyclic lactones, although registered for red louse control, only suppress and do not eliminate the infestations. Note that Growth Regulators will not kill adult lice but will prevent the development of the nymphs to adults. Results will only be seen 2 weeks after application.

Sucking or blue lice

These lice have piercing mouthparts for sucking blood, which gives them a blue colour. Sucking lice are not very active and are confined to certain areas on the body. Heavy infestations cause severe anaemia in young animals. Their presence is indicated by hairless patches on various parts of the body depending on the species.

Sucking lice of cattle

Linognathus vituli (Long-nosed louse): The lesions appear on the shoulders, neck and chest.

Haematopinus eurysternus (Short-nosed louse): Patches are found around the eyes, the nostrils, horn bases, and the neck.

H. quadripertusis (Tail brush louse): They prefer the switch of the tail but do spread to other parts of the body.

Solenopotes capillatus (Small blue louse): These are found on the shoulders, under the tail and around the anus.

Sucking lice of sheep and goats

Both sheep and goats are prone to sucking lice, and a blue louse species occurs in Angora goats *(L. africanus)* in the eastern Cape, which damages mohair. Heavy infestations cause anaemia, oedema and death or stunting of young animals.

Control of sucking lice

Blue or sucking lice are very effectively controlled with the injection of macrocyclic lactones such as ivermectin. Two treatments should be given at 8-10 days intervals, to ensure that lice hatching after treatment are also killed off. Dipping with organophosphates or pyrethroids, for control of sheep scab after shearing, will also kill off sucking lice. Because lice are not very active, pour-ons do not work very well for these infestations.

FLIES

This group of insects includes those immediately recognisable as flies, namely house-flies, stable flies, face flies, blowflies, nasal flies, as well as those less commonly thought of as belonging to the fly family such as midges (gnats), mosquitoes and louse flies.

Although they all have the same generalised life cycle, they have different habits and breeding sites and therefore the control measures are somewhat different. In some cases, the fly is the problem (as in the case of stable flies), while in other the larval stage is problematic (blowfly strike). As a group, flies are responsible for losses in animal production because they cause direct losses due to irritation, worry or painful bites, and indirect losses due to the transmission of diseases and parasites.

House-flies and their relations

Musca domestica House-fly
Stomoxys calcitrans Stable fly
Fannia cannicularis Lesser house-fly

House- and stable flies are the main species which are found around farmyards. Their populations can reach enormous numbers in summer when the temperature rises and there is plenty of moist organic material (manure and compost) available in which to lay their eggs. These two fly species are important in animal health because they cause annoyance and irritation which interrupt feeding and result in a loss of milk and meat production. Controlled experiments have shown a significant improvement in the production of animals which were treated for flies: dairy cattle showed R 8 000 increase in milk production per lactation, compared with untreated animals in one

Comparison of a house fly (right) -and a stable fly (left): note the biting mouthparts of the stable fly.

lactation and treated feedlot cattle showed a weight increase of R 1 000 per 100 animals.

Experiments in the USA have shown that effective control of flies resulted in an increase in milk production of 1,45 kg/cow/day in dairy cattle in the first 12 weeks of lactation. Yearling cattle treated for stable flies showed a weight gain of 200 g per day when compared with untreated animals.

House- and stable flies are also important because of their potential transmission of diseases such as brucellosis, mastitis, anaplasmosis, eye infections and lumpy skin disease.

The life cycle of the house- and stable fly.

House- and stable flies lay their eggs in organic matter like manure, compost and kitchen waste. In the warm moist organic matter, the eggs hatch and the larvae feed until they are developed enough to crawl out and burrow into the soil where they become pupae. These develop further into adult flies which then emerge when mature. The whole cycle can be completed in 15 days, which means that 12 generations of flies can be produced in one season. The number of adult flies seen are only 15% of the total population on the premises, since the rest are in the form of larvae and pupae, which will develop into adult flies. Every kilogram of compost/

The various stages of the life cycle of a house fly.

manure can contain up to 5 000 fly larvae, which illustrates the enormous reproductive potential of flies and the importance of targeting the immature forms as well as adult flies.

Adult house-flies feed on liquid material of any sort including manure, discharge from eyes, nose or wounds of animals. They can spread micro-organisms mechanically on their feet, mouth parts and by regurgitating their previous meals onto food.

Stable flies look similar to house-flies but have long mouthparts which they use for biting animals and sucking their blood. Their bites cause tremendous irritation, resulting in production animals spending less time feeding as they stamp and swish their tails to rid themselves of the flies. Stable flies transmit lumpy skin disease and anaplasmosis.

To break the life cycle of these flies one must target the different stages and this is always more successful if done early in the season before the fly numbers are high.

Manure and compost hygiene: because manure, kitchen waste, compost heaps (especially those containing mown grass) are the breeding sites of flies, the management of these is the key to fly control. Manure must be collected, turned over and spread out to allow drying. The eggs and larvae will be exposed and will die as a result of dehydration.

If it is not possible to spread manure out to dry, manure piles can be treated with pyrethroid sprays or with Insect Growth Regulators such as cyromazine. Although Insect Growth Regulators do not kill the larvae they prevent their development into pupae and adults.

Control on animals: Pyrethroid-containing dips and pour-ons are effective against flies. They have a repellent effect and prevent the bites of stable flies. The products must initially be applied regularly but as fly numbers reduce the frequency of application can be reduced. Pyrethroids are also effective against ticks.

Control in stables: Powder formulations containing pyrethroids are available for environmental treatment. The powders are made up in water and sprayed onto walls of stables and other buildings where flies habitually rest, usually the walls that face into the afternoon sun. At night flies rest on top of walls, so these places must also be treated. The products are specifically formulated to stay on the surface of walls instead of being absorbed. Paint-on products with a long residual action are also available for walls that are not regularly washed down. They can also be applied to rubbish bins.

Baits: Poisoned baits in the form of coloured granules which are attractive to flies can be placed in certain areas. They must not be used in pig sties and poultry houses because these animals may feed on the poisoned flies. The bait can be used in households and restaurant kitchens, but out of the reach of children and pets.

Traps: Homemade or commercial traps can be used to trap adult flies and reduce their numbers. The traps usually contain strong-smelling bait and are designed so that the flies enter through a funnel shaped tunnel from which they cannot exit.

Dairy parlours can be sprayed with environmental pyrethroid formulations or can be treated with paint-on products.

Face flies

Musca xanthomelas
Musca lusoria

While stable and house-flies tend to congregate around farmyards, the group known as face flies are found in the veld. They stay with cattle herds, breeding in their manure and feeding around the eyes and wounds on the animals. They transmit the worm *Parafilaria bovicola* which causes the phenomenon known as "false bruising".

The *Parafilaria* worms develop in the body of the face flies and burst out of their mouthparts when the flies are feeding. The tiny worms migrate to the eyes of cattle and in this way they land in the bloodstream of the cow. The females settle under the skin, laying eggs and causing small wounds or "bleeding points". This attracts the face flies which pick up the worm eggs and thus complete the worm's life cycle.

"False bruising" reduces the value of the carcase after slaughter because the affected areas have to be trimmed away.

Infestations are easily treated with macrocyclic lactones (ivermectin etc). Prevention using pyrethroid-containing dips and sprays is very effective.

To control these flies, animals can be treated with pyrethroid dips, sprays or pour-ons.

Face flies clustering around the eyes of a bovine

Nasal bot fly of sheep

Oestrus ovis

The nasal bot fly occurs widely in South Africa and parasitises both sheep and goats. The adult fly seeks out an animal and lays tiny larvae around the nostrils. These worm-like larvae migrate up the nasal passages and lodge in the sinuses where they live off the secretions in the nose. They cause severe irritation, causing infected animals to sneeze and shake their heads. There may be a severe discharge from the nose which may cause confusion with other diseases such as *Mannheimia* pneumonia and blue tongue. Heavy infestations will cause severe loss of weight, especially in lambs. When the larvae have matured, they emerge from the sinuses into the nostrils and are sneezed out into the soil where they develop into pupae. After a month or more, the adult fly will emerge from the pupa.

Treatment with macrocyclic lactones such as ivermectin will kill off the larval stages in the sinuses, but it may take some weeks for the nasal discharge to disappear. Treatment should be done in the summer months when the flies are actively laying larvae, but an additional single treatment at the height of winter will kill overwintering larvae. Remedies containing rafoxanide and closantel can also be used for control.

A sheep with nasal worm infestation showing a profuse discharge from the nose.

Sheep ocular fly

Gedoelstia hassleri and G. cristata

The normal hosts of these parasites are the alcelaphine antelope such as wildebeest, hartebeest and blesbok. In sheep, the larvae are deposited into the eye by the female fly and from here they migrate to the circulatory system and to the brain. During their migration they cause severe inflammation of the eyes, which may cause initially inflammation of the conjunctiva, haemorrhages and eventually the bulging of the eyeballs causing blindness ("uitpeuloog"). The condition is often seen in Karakul, Persian and Afrikaner sheep. Treatment with injectable insecticides will kill the parasites but will not reverse serious damage to eyes, the brain and heart.

Blowflies

Blowflies of sheep include Lucilia sericata, *Lucilia cuprina* and *Chrysomya albiceps.*

These large metallic flies initially laid their eggs on carrion where the eggs hatched and the larvae fed, moulted and matured. With the advent of wool sheep farming in South Africa, the flies adapted their breeding habits and now prefer to lay their eggs on live sheep. Although blowflies will lay their eggs on wounds such as tick bites and shearing wounds, they also attack intact skin under certain conditions. They particularly target merino sheep with fine wool, which is prone to fleece rot, a condition that occurs when fleece becomes wet from rain, scouring and urine. With fleece rot, the moisture-softened wool and skin emit a typical smell which is attractive to the blowflies. The flies lay their eggs, and within 72 hours the larvae begin to feed on the skin with their mouthparts. As the larvae feed, they emit a smell which attracts more

blowflies. The larvae feed for 3-5 days and then drop off to pupate in the soil. The adult flies then hatch out some days later.

Often the condition is undetected because it may be concealed by the fleece, but sheep suffering from blowfly strike do show distress by lameness, biting and nibbling at their lesions, or showing constant tail wagging. Sheep may die within a week if their infestations are not treated.

Sheep infested with blowfly larvae must be treated with registered insecticides, either organophosphate or pyrethroid solutions sprayed onto the lesions at the recommended dilutions. Wound oil that contains insecticides like deltamethrin can be used for treatment and prevention of strike on wounds.

Prevention of blowfly strike can be achieved by a combination of management factors and use of chemicals to prevent strike:

Chemical application

- *Post-shearing dipping:* Shortly after shearing animals can be dipped with organophosphates or Growth Regulators and this will give prevention of 6-16 weeks depending on which product is used. Growth Regulators do not kill the larvae (maggots) although they will prevent them becoming adult flies. Post-shearing application (24 hours later) with a Growth Regulator –containing pour-on gives 12 weeks of protection. These products can be repeated but are not suitable once the fleece is long.
- *"Jetting"* or spraying of heavy-fleeced sheep will need to be done during the summer months with organophosphate or growth regulator -containing dips at regular intervals.

Management factors

- Smooth-bodied merinos must be bred in preference to those with deep folds.
- Do trimming of fleece around the crutch (crutching) to prevent soiling with faeces and urine.
- Prevent scours by managing diet correctly and regular dosing of anthelminthics.
- The Mule's operation which removes skin folds from the crutch area was developed in Australia to prevent fly strike on very extensive farms. This drastic operation is not applied much in SA and the need has hopefully been eliminated by the breeding of smooth-bodied merinos.

Lucilia cuprina is a blowfly which attacks sheep.

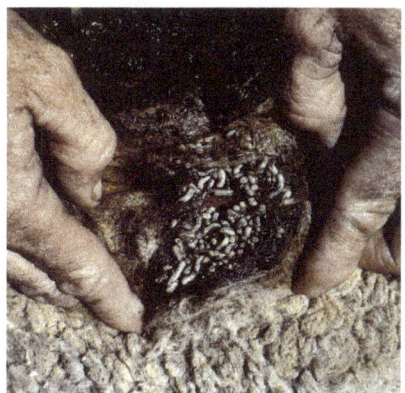

Blowfly strike in a sheep.

Cattle blowfly

Chrysomya bezziana

This fly occurs in the northern and eastern parts of the country namely Limpopo, Mpumalanga, KwaZulu-Natal and the Eastern Cape where they attack cattle, sheep and goats. The flies lay their eggs on wounds of various types, especially surgical wounds, abscesses, bruises and dip scalds, as well as small wounds like tick bites on the ears, under the tail, perineum and the udder. The larvae hatch and begin to feed on the wounds causing further damage as they enlarge.

Treatment of infested wounds with wound oils containing insecticides such as deltamethrin is effective. These wound oils can also be used prophylactically.

In areas where these flies occur, surgery should be carried out during winter months when the flies are inactive.

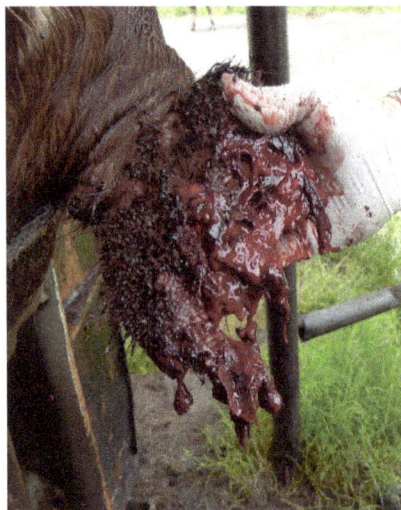

Fly strike in a bovine.

Tsetse flies and Trypanosomiasis (nagana)

Glossina sp

Although they had a wide range over SA in the past, tsetse flies are now confined to the northern part of KwaZulu-Natal. The outbreak of rinderpest in 1890 eradicated millions of cattle and game animals, and the tsetse fly disappeared from most areas. Small foci are still present and were responsible for a major outbreak of nagana or sleeping sickness in cattle around the Mkuzi and Umfolozi Game Reserves in the early 1990s.

The tsetse fly transmits the protozoal blood parasites that belong to the group Trypanosoma. These parasites cause nagana in livestock and humans. The most common type of nagana seen in livestock is the chronic form characterised by emaciation and poor condition. The animals lose weight, show anaemia and laboured breathing. The lymph nodes enlarge and can often be seen at a distance. These animals eventually die suddenly of heart failure. This is a neglected disease which affects the productivity and health of rural cattle in KZN but is largely ignored by veterinary authorities. Control of this disease is essential to promote the upliftment of these poor communities who rely on cattle as a means of subsistence.

Two groups of remedies are used for the treatment of nagana and drugs are also available for the prevention of nagana but their use is currently not permitted by authorities. The regular use of pyrethroid dips or sprays (deltamethrin, cyhalothrin), and pyrethroid pour-on (deltamethrin, flumethrin) which are often used for concurrent tick control, are highly effective in preventing transmission of nagana.

The tsetse fly, Glossina austeni (Diptera: Glossinidae), has replaced various other Glossina species as the main host of nagana in KwaZulu-Natal.

The pupae are encased in the final larval exuviae.

Glossina austeni sucking blood from a human.

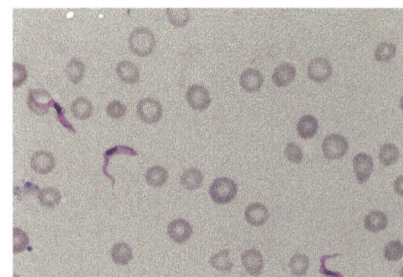

Trypanosome parasites in the blood.

Midges

Midges also known as gnats are a group of small blood-sucking flies.

Culicoides spp

This small midge is plentiful during the summer months in most areas of the country. They breed in manure or other organic matter and are active from sundown until daybreak. The midges frequent moist low-lying areas like vleis, feeding preferably on cattle but also on sheep and horses. In wet warm summer months, they occur in truly enormous numbers – a single night's trapping in horse stables has produced 1 million *Culicoides* midges. Therefore, target animals are at serious risk during summer nights and control measures must be taken against the *Culicoides*-borne virus diseases. They transmit blue tongue in sheep, African horse sickness in horses and three-day stiffsickness in cattle.

Cattle: Chemical control to prevent three-day stiff-sickness is particularly important because of the poor immunity given by the vaccine. The application of pyrethroid products with residual effect such as pour-ons or use of fly repellents, will prevent attacks by midges.

Sheep: Avoid low-lying vlei areas, especially at night, and use the blue tongue vaccine as recommended.

Horses: Vaccinate horses for horse sickness, stable them at night and apply repellents regularly.

Culicoides midge feeding.

Simulium Black flies

These flies breed in fast-flowing rivers, building the larval cocoons under the surface of the water. They breed in vast numbers and can be a particular problem along the banks of the Orange and Great Fish Rivers. Black flies bite and suck the blood of cattle and sheep, and in the process cause severe irritation which gives rise to crusty wart-like lesions developing on the face. Control on animals is difficult because the application of fly repellents is difficult. In severe outbreaks one can apply pyrethroid pour-ons on the head, nose and ears to repel the flies. Usually the authorities are approached to lower the river level for a few days, which kills off the larval stages.

Leptoconops Day-biting midges

These are day-biting midges that breed in the seasonal watercourses in arid areas, especially those that have high levels of salt in the soil. In SA the midges are a problem around Aliwal North, De Aar, and Williston. In Namibia they are a problem around Walvis Bay. These midges attack humans and animals in swarms during the summer months, inflicting painful bites. Control is aimed at draining or treating seasonal watercourses during problem periods.

Mosquitoes
Aedes spp, *Culex* spp

All mosquito species need water in which to breed because their eggs and the immature stages are aquatic. Certain mosquito species which show a preference for livestock, breed in their millions during very heavy summer rain seasons, particularly when pan formation results. This creates the ideal conditions for outbreaks of the virus disease Rift Valley fever (RVF) which is transmitted by these mosquitoes.

RVF is a disease of cattle, sheep and goats which causes abortion storms of 40-100 %, and acute deaths of lambs and kids (30%). Calves may also be affected to a lesser extent. The most practical control measure for RVF is the annual use of the live vaccines Smithburn or Clone 13. During outbreaks unvaccinated animals can be protected by the regular application of pyrethroid dip, spray or pour-ons. For more details on RVF, see the discussion under reproductive diseases.

Sheep ked or louse fly
Melophagus ovinus

The sheep ked is a large bloodsucking parasite which is easily seen when the fleece is opened. The keds are totally dependent on the sheep as they can only survive for a few days away from the host. However, they are now seldom seen because they are very well controlled by sheep dips.

Sheep keds are transmitted by contact between sheep. Heavy infestations cause anaemia, loss of weight, scratching and biting of the fleece. Keds cause fleece damage and staining which lowers the value of the wool.

Dips containing organophosphate or pyrethroids are very effective and have caused the virtual disappearence of the parasite.

GENERAL ASPECTS OF ECTOPARASITE CONTROL

Chemical control

There are currently 5 main groups of remedies registered for the control of ectoparasites in SA. Farmers should become familiar with the members and activities of each chemical group, and the advantages and disadvantages of each.

Pyrethroids

Examples: Deltamethrin, flumethrin and cyhalothrin.

Action: Pyrethroids act on the nervous system of ectoparasites, causing paralysis and death.

Spectrum: Pyrethroids kill ticks; they repel flies and with the exception of flumethrin, have a "knock-down" effect on them. They are effective for biting and sucking lice.

Formulations: Pyrethroids are available as liquid concentrates and are diluted for use in plunge dipping, spray races and handspraying. They are included in many pour-ons and some wound oils.

Advantages: They generally have a broad spectrum and are useful in dairies for tick control because they also have action against flies.

Disadvantages: Pyrethroid pour-ons can cause irritation. Because the pour-ons contain more pyrethroid than dips, resistance is widespread in certain areas. Home-made pour-ons have contributed greatly to this development of resistance.

Safety: Pyrethroids are safe for mammals and birds including oxpeckers, unless they are used in combination with organophosphates.

Environmental effects: Pyrethroids are fairly safe but must not be discarded in rivers or dams as they are toxic to fish.

Amidines/ formamidines

Examples: Amitraz and cymiazole are the only two in this group. Cymiazole has a much lower activity and is only useful in combinations with pyrethroids with which it has a synergy.

Action: This group has a dual effect on the nervous system of ticks, causing detachment and "hotfooting" which is aimless wandering around until the ticks die.

Spectrum: Amidines are effective against all tick species and are very effective against mites. They are not effective against the insect groups (lice and flies).

Formulations: Amidines are available as concentrates for use in plunge dips, handspraying and spray races, and are included in pour-ons.

Advantages: They are safe and there is less resistance to amidines than to pyrethroids.

Disadvantages: Amitraz breaks down in plunge dips and must be stabilised with lime (calcium hydroxide or Ca (OH)2) or must be replenished using a total replenishment system.

Safety: Amidines are very safe for livestock and for humans. Overdosing causes sleepiness which wears off eventually. They must not be used on horses, certain dog species or cats.

Ecological effect: Amidines are safe for the environment, particularly for birds and mammals, as they degrade rapidly, but must not be disposed of into water.

Organophosphates (OPs)

Examples: Chlorphenfinvos and diazinon are the commonly used OPs.

Action: OPs cause overstimulation of the nervous system which leads to its malfunction. Poisoning can be reversed with the administration of atropine.

Spectrum: OPs have a broad spectrum of activity as they are effective against ticks, blowflies, mites, lice and maggots, and they kill all species of ticks. In sheep, OPs are effective against sheep scab, ticks, lice and blowfly maggots. Certain formulations prevent blowfly strike.

Formulations: OPs are available as plunge dips and sprays.

Advantages: They are effective again after a long period of disuse due to the development of resistance and the use of other newer chemicals.

Disadvantages: This is a toxic group and there is also some resistance in ticks and lice.

Safety: The organophosphates are the most toxic of the dips and must be diluted, used and disposed of with extreme care. Do not use in areas where oxpeckers occur.

Environmental: This is the most destructive of all the groups for the environment.

Macrocyclic lactones (MLs)

Examples: This group contains ivermectin, moxidectin, doramectin and cydectin.

Action: MLs affect neural transmission and cause paralysis.

Spectrum: They are registered for blue tick control, the treatment of nasal worm in sheep and goats, as well as treatment of the larval stages of *Parafilaria bovicola*. MLs are also registered for sheep scab control.

Formulations: The MLs are used as injectables, and they work for parasites that suck blood or serum.

Advantages: Useful in areas with blue tick resistant against dips and are active against some roundworms. They are a convenient alternative to dipping sheep against scab.

Disadvantages: Ticks must feed

before the remedy takes effect, so there is still the possibility of disease transmission initially when the remedy is used. Although their use in sheep has almost made dipping redundant, other sheep parasites which are not controlled by MLs such as red lice, sheep keds and itch mite are experiencing a resurgence.

Safety: The MLs have a high safety margin in most livestock, but not all can be used in goats.

Environment: Some MLs may have a negative impact on the biology of dung beetles, and if this is a concern the label must be checked for the extent of the effect.

Growth Regulators (Chitin Synthesis Inhibitors)

Examples: Fluazuron, diflubenzuron, triflumuron, cyromazine and novaluron.

Action: GRs do not kill parasites but inhibit the development of the immature stages of the ectoparasite into adults.

Spectrum: Fluazuron is a Tick Growth Regulator which controls blue ticks. Diflubenzuron, triflumuron and cyromazine control the life cycles of blowflies, house and stable flies and lice and are known as Insect Growth Regulators.

Formulations: Fluazuron is used as a pour-on formulation for tick control in cattle. Insect Growth Regulators are available in dips, sprays or in some cases pour-ons for sheep, for the control of blowfly strike. They can be sprayed on compost heaps and manure for the control of house and stable flies.

Advantages: GRs are non-toxic

to animals. They can be used as alternative control measures on farms with resistance to conventional dips.

Disadvantages: Because they do not directly kill parasites, the remedy will take a while to reduce the parasite population, so no immediate effect will be seen and disease transmission may take place during the initial phase.

Safety: GRs are non-toxic to hosts and operators.

Environment: they break down rapidly in the environment but must not be disposed of in natural water courses.

Combination remedies

Combination products were developed initially to combine the tick controlling abilities of the formamidines with the fly control

COMPARISON OF ECTOPARASITE GROUPS[1]

PARASITE		TICKS		MITES	FLIES		MIDGES	LICE		TOXICITY	
		Blue	Multi-host		Adult	Larvae (Maggots)		Biting (red)	Sucking (blue)	Host	Environment
ACTIVE											
Organophosphates		++	++	+++	++	+++	++	+++	+++	3	4
Pyrethroids	Most	+++	+++	++	++++	++	++++	++++	++++	1	2
	Flumethrin	++++	++++	++	++	+	++	++	++	1	2
Amidines	Amitraz	++++	++++	++++	-	-	-	-	-	1	1
	Cymiazole	++	++	+++	-	-	-	-	-	1	1
Macrocyclic lactones	Ivermectin	+	-	+++	+	+	-	+	+++	1	1
Growth Regulators	Cydectin	+	-	+++	+	+	-	-	++	2	1
	Doramectin	++	-	+++	+	+++	-	++	++++	1	1
	Most	-	-	-	-	++++	-	++++	++++	1	1
	Fluazuron	+++	-	-	-	-	-	-	-	1	1

KEY:
- no effect
+ some
++ moderate
+++ good
++++ excellent

KEY:
1 = low toxicity
2 = moderately toxic
3 = toxic
4 = very toxic

1   These are general comparisons and actvity can vary in different formulations.

of pyrethroids. Although many scientists are of the opinion that the use of combinations may promote resistance, these are popular with farmers.

Tick resistance

The term *tick resistance* refers to the reduced susceptibility of a population of ticks to a chemical group. It is a genetic characteristic which is selected for by the use of a chemical. Resistance is most common in blue ticks because being one-host ticks which spend their whole life cycle on cattle, they are exposed more frequently to dips than two- and three-hosts ticks which have much less exposure. Resistance to the chemicals in tick remedies occurs naturally in tick populations at a very low frequency, but once it has been selected for by use of a specific remedy, these ticks increase in number and can be spread to many other geographic areas by the movement of animals to sales or other farms. Resistance has been seen to most of the remedies being currently used, but the tempo of development varies with the different groups.

Prevention and management of resistance

Resistance typically arises on farms where regular tick control is practised, especially where pour-ons are used for the control of blue ticks. However, resistance is not inevitable on all farms: resistant ticks are usually introduced onto farms with new animals. Avoid introducing resistant ticks by quarantining animals and treating them with at least two different remedy groups (e.g. an organophosphate and then a pyrethroid at a weekly interval).

Resistance should be differentiated from poor control due to application problems (see below).

Ticks can be tested in specialist laboratories to determine resistance.

Confirmation of resistance can be done by sending ticks to a suitable laboratory.

When resistance to a particular group is confirmed, for example, to pyrethroids, the farmer must switch to a completely different group, for example, amitraz or organophosphates. It is no use using a different member of the pyrethroid group (e.g. switching from deltamethrin to cyhalothrin), as this will only compound the problem.

Differentiating resistance from poor efficacy

A quick field test to determine whether one has resistance to a product is to make up 20-40 litres of the product being used and hand spray a small group of animals (at least 5 litres of dip wash per animal). If possible, do the same with a different product group, i.e. if you are using amitraz in the previous group, use a pyrethroid for comparison. Evaluate the tick burdens 2-3 days after hand-spraying. A typical sign of resistance developing is that with the resistant group the animals will have heavy

Blue tick resistance developed to the old arsenical dips causing massive infestations

burdens of blue ticks since resistance is much less common with multi-host ticks.

If the animals that were hand-sprayed with the dip in current use have good control, resistance is not the problem and the following checklist must be used:
- Check dip strength by submitting a dip sample (all SAAHA registered companies will assist their clients with this testing).
- Check the dip dilution for correctness.

- Check the replenishment rate.
- Check the dip capacity – this is often incorrectly estimated and leads to under-strength dipping (see below for method).
- Check that dip is not being washed off by the dew on long grass or by animals wading through rivers or dams.
- Check that animals are being wet properly in the spray race.
- Check that the dosage of pour-ons is correct.
- Check if using amitraz that dip is correctly stabilised (companies will assist with this).

The future of ectoparasite control

The development of chemical resistance is an evolutionary survival mechanism of parasites, and even if totally new chemicals appear on the market, this will also be only a temporary solution to the problem, as resistance will develop to these as well.

However, since fewer new remedies are reaching the market than in the last few decades, farmers and the industry must use chemicals responsibly to prevent resistance getting out of control, rendering current remedies useless and livestock farming uneconomical.

Tick-resistant animals

It has long been known that certain cattle breeds in South Africa are more resistant to ticks than others. The Zebu races and their crosses, and indigenous breeds such as the Nguni, have lower tick burdens than the exotic breeds. On exposure to ticks these breeds mount an immune response which discourages the ticks from attaching, but to maintain tick resistance the animals must be constantly exposed to ticks.

Tick vaccines

The development of vaccines against blue ticks was successful in Australia and South America, but these vaccines were not very efficacious against south African blue tick species. Local researchers are currently performing trials on one- and multiple host ticks.

Methods of control

The selection of a method for controlling ectoparasites must be based on observing various factors, which are summarised in the tables below.

Summary of general ectoparasite control methods in cattle

METHOD	SUITABILITY	ADVANTAGES	DISADVANTAGES	COST
Plunge	Large numbers of animals for tick and fly control	Good wetting	Poor design and management will cause problems	High initial outlay – unit cost low with use
Spray race	Ideal for tick and fly control in dairies	Flexibility if remedies have to be changed	Less effective wetting than plunge	Moderately expensive with initial capital outlay
Mechanical / hand spraying	Used for small numbers of cattle for tick and fly control	Flexible and convenient for low intensity dipping	Less effective wetting	Low capital outlay initially; very expensive per animal
Pour-ons	Tick and fly control; ideal for single treatments for lice/mites	Convenient	Irritation with pyrethroids; accelerates resistance	Expensive per animal
Spot/patch treatment	Only as additional to other methods	N/A	N/A	N/A
Injectables (ML)	Control of blue ticks, sucking lice and mites	Deworming effect for roundworms; no tick resistance yet	Narrow tick spectrum; long meat withdrawal; not suitable for dairy animals	Expensive

Ectoparasite control methods in catttle

Plunge dipping

Plunge dipping of cattle entails the animal jumping into the dip and swimming through the dip wash which contains the chemical. If the dip tank is well-designed, the animals will receive a thorough wetting. Diptanks are an economical if large numbers of animals are being treated for ticks and flies. The advantages are good wetting and only a moderate level of management being required. However sufficient water is an obvious requirement and the dipping process is labour intensive. Although the initial outlay cost is high, the unit cost becomes lower with successive usage. The active ingredient of the chemical in the dipwash is removed or "stripped" from the solution in most cases. This requires replenishment of the dipwash: the method used will depend on the product being applied.

The **conventional replenishment method** is used for organophosphates, pyrethroids and amitraz (bear in mind the latter must be stabilised with the addition of lime).

Tanks using the conventional replenishment method need fresh-filling every 2-5 years or after roughly 20 000 animals have been dipped. The dip is then drained, the tank cleaned and filled with the required amount of water. The dip concentrate to be added according to the capacity. Dip must be replenished to compensate for the stripping (removal of active ingredient by the animals) at a rate specified by the manufacturer. Analysis should be done every 6-12 months to ensure the correct concentration of the dip wash. The best time to sample dips is at the beginning of the tick season (August) or after long periods of disuse.

The **Total replacement (TR)** method is used only for non-stabilised amitraz dips. The dip is fresh-filled each time from scratch because the amitraz breaks down with time. This method is only economical if large numbers (>600) are dipped on a single day, but depends on the tank size. The **Head Count method** was developed and patented by Coopers so that operators can manage dip tanks without having to do complicated mathematical calculations. Since each animal removes roughly the same amount of active ingredient, the replenishment rate is based on the number of animals that have been through the dip.

For more on diptank construction, management and safety see the publication "Practical guide to diptank management and construction" available from Afrivet Training Services.

Typical plunge dip for cattle

Spray races

A spray race is simply a crush over which an arrangement of metal piping is erected. The dip is circulated from a sump through the piping and is forced through small nozzles, thus creating a fine spray. Animals are wetted while passing through the race. The system must be able to maintain 300-500 litres of dip wash in circulation and provide 1,5-2,5 litres per animal. The dip wash must be boosted according to directions on label of product used. Fresh dip must be used at each dipping.

Spray races are ideal for tick and fly control and provide more flexibility if remedies have to be changed due to resistance. However, they provide less effective wetting than plunge dipping and a high level of management is needed. The set-up is moderately expensive to set up initially.

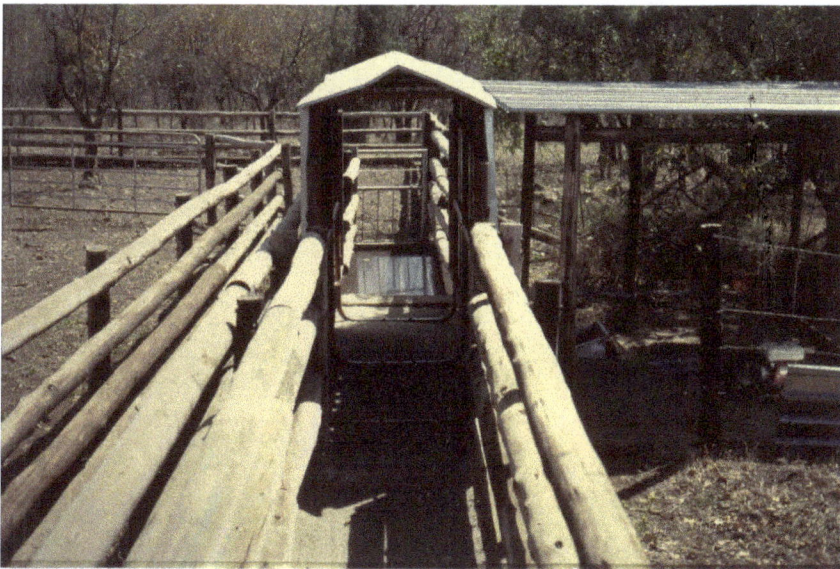

A spray race for cattle

Hand spraying must be done very thoroughly to achieve good wetting of the animal.

Hand spraying

This method is used for very small numbers of animals where limited holding facilities are available. This can be done using a motorised pump with a lance and nozzles, a high-pressure manual pump, a bucket pump or knapsack sprayer.

This is the most difficult method to get right: animals need to be adequately restrained and they must be thoroughly wetted with at least 5-10 litres per animal. For effective application, have animals in single file in a crush pen. Start from underline to top line and tail to head. Pay attention to hooves, tail brush, under the tail, the area between front and hind legs, ears, poll and muzzle. This method is wasteful as it allows a lot of run-off which cannot be reused.

Pour-on application

Pour-on applications are a convenient method for used for tick and fly control and are also suitable for single treatments for example for lice, however it is an expensive means of control compared with above methods. Because of the high concentration of active ingredients irritation is experienced with some pyrethroid applications and resistance tends to develop more quickly than with other methods.

A calibrated applicator must be used because it is essential to apply the correct volume, strictly according to the directions on the label. Pour-on remedies can be used for patch treatment on tick predilection sites (see below). Operators must use suitable gloves to avoid contact with the pour-on liquid.

The application of a pour-on remedy

Patch treatment

Patch treatment is done in addition to dipping or spraying. It is the local treatment of difficult-to-wet sites which are favoured by certain ticks such as the udders, ears, and around the anus. It can be done by applying tick oil or grease, dip, or pour-on formulations.

Injectable

The macrocyclic lactones can be used in injectable form for the control of blue ticks as well as deworming for roundworms. They are especially useful for tick control of dip resistant blue ticks. The injectable form has a long meat withdrawal period and is unsuitable in diary animals. The method is expensive when compared with dipping or spraying.

Patch treatment is used to supplement other methods of ectoparasite control.

Summary of general control methods in sheep and goats

METHOD	SUITABILITY	ADVANTAGES	DISADVANTAGES	COST
Plunge	Only dipping method suitable for scab control; also works for lice and mites	One after-shear dip prevents scab, other mites and lice	Not suitable for sheep with long fleece	Low
Belly-bathing	Karoo paralysis ticks, bont ticks, *Rhipicephalus* ticks.	Applies product to specific area	Not suitable for scab control	Low
Footbaths	*Rhipicephalus* sp on feet	Ditto	N/A	Cheaper than plunge and belly-bath
ML injection	Scab control and blue lice	No dip tanks needed	No action on red lice or ticks	Expensive
Spraying/jetting	Blowfly strike prevention	Focal application	Only prevents blowfly strike	Low
Pour-on /Patch treatment	Paralysis tick, *Rhipicephalus* on feet, red lice, Growth Regulators for blowfly and lice	No dip tank needed. Can target predilection sites of ticks and blowflies	Not suitable for long-wooled sheep	Moderate

Ectoparasite control methods in sheep and goats

Plunge dipping

This method can be used for tick control in small stock but is more commonly used for blowfly and sheep scab control. It is only applicable for short hair of wool or non-wooled stock. One after shear dip prevents scab, other mites and lice. The cost of plunge dipping is relatively compared with pour on applications.

For small numbers of sheep, a 200 litre drum sunk into the ground is adequate, but for larger flocks bigger tanks must be built. For flocks of a thousand or more the capacity should be 4000-8000 litres. The tank must be 0,7-1 m wide and 1-1,5 m deep.

The whole length of the tank must be accessible in case animals get into difficulties. The tank must be carefully calibrated so that the capacity can be correctly determined. Calibration is done with permanent marks or with a measuring stick. Initial fill and replenishment are done using the same principles discussed under cattle dipping. Replenishment must be done to replace the active ingredient removed by stripping. The most effective means of replenishment is

the "constant replenishment method". This method allows a constant stream of replenishment solution to run into the dip and keeps the dip at a constant concentration. If the dip wash is to be used for more than one day, zinc sulphate ($ZnSO_4$) must be added to inhibit the growth of bacteria that cause lumpy wool and post-dipping lameness at a rate of 1 kg/400 litres of dip.

Belly-bathing and foot bathing.

Belly-bathing is an effective and cost-effective method for treating sheep and small stock for ticks which attach to the lower regions of the body. It wets the underline and the breech area of the animal, and sheep walk through the dip wash rather than swim.

Belly-bathing of sheep

A plunge dip for sheep

It is therefore suitable for controlling foot ticks, heartwater control, Karoo paralysis and red legged ticks. It can also be used for blowfly control in sheep. It is not suitable for sheep scab control. Footbathing is suitable only for foot tick control.

Breech-bathing

This method of applying blowfly remedies is sometimes used by farmers. A shallow bath is made by burying half a metal drum in the ground. The dip wash is placed in the bath and the animals are made to sit so that the breech area is well soaked with the dip. It requires the individual handling of each animal and is labour intensive but is suitable for small numbers of animals.

Spraying/jetting

Jetting of sheep using a circular jet spray is not commonly done in SA. Blowfly remedies are applied to the fleece using a pipe connected to a pump and a wide-mouthed nozzle which can deliver a stream rather than a fine spray of remedy, usually to the breech or other target areas. Operators must ensure that the maximum pressure is not exceeded as this can cause skin damage, irritation and poisoning depending on which remedies are used.

Pour-ons/Patch treatment

Pour-on remedies are available for sheep and goats for tick control, red louse infestation and for delivery of Growth Regulators for blowfly control, but the application is labour intensive. The correct formulation must be chosen for wooled/non-wooled breeds. As with cattle, the basic principles for application are the application of the correct volume and in the correct sites. Patch treatment with tick grease of pour-ons can be used to treat tick attachment sites.

Afrivet ectoparasite remedies

PRODUCT	ECTOPARASITE	SPECIES	ACTIVE
Afrivet Redline Pour on G4245	Ticks and flies	C & G	Flumethrin
Deltapor 5 Pour On G4252	Ticks, lice and flies	C, S & G	Deltamethrin & PB
Deltapor Plus 10 Pour On G4255	Ticks and flies	C (not dairy) and sheep	Deltamethrin & PB
Eraditick Cattle Pour On G4254	Ticks	Cattle (not dairy)	Amitraz
Eraditick Plus Pour On G4251	Ticks, lice, mange mites and flies	C, S & G	Amitraz, deltamethrin &PB
Ecobash plunge and spray G3382	Ticks and flies	C	Cymiazol and cypermethrin
Eraditick Ultra plunge and spray G3976	Ticks and flies	C (not dairy)	Chlorvenvinphos, cymiazol & cypermethrin
Eraditick 125 plunge and spray G3585	See species	C: ticks, lice and mites S & G: ticks, sheep scab, mites	Amitraz
Eraditick 250 plunge and spray G4047	See species	C: ticks, lice and mites S & G: ticks, sheep scab, mites	Amitraz
Deltaforce plunge and spray G4367	Ticks, flies, screw worm	C (not dairy)	Deltamethrin
Expel jetting fluid G4027	Blowfly, sheep scab, red lice	S & G	Ivermectin, novaluron
Eraditick tick grease G3667	Ticks	C, S & G	Deltamethrin, PB.

Endoparasites

ENDOPARASITES AND THEIR CONTROL

The internal parasites of cattle, sheep and goats fall into three main groups: roundworms, tapeworms and flukes. Although internal parasite control programs can be integrated, the three categories of parasites are discussed separately in order to give readers a sense of the differences of life cycle and biology. The diagnosis of worm infestation, chemical groups for control, dosing strategies and the problem of resistance are also discussed.

ROUNDWORMS

Most roundworms of importance in farm animals are found in the gastrointestinal tract. There are many species, and because they are mostly rather small, they are difficult to identify without the use of a microscope. "On the farm" identification is done based on the species of farm animal involved, the geographic location of the farm and the part of the GIT where the roundworm is found.

Roundworms vary in size from a few millimetres long to a substantial 30cm *(Toxacara vitulorum* of cattle). They are most often cylindrical in form and have a round cross-section. Most roundworms have a direct life cycle, which means they have only one host during their lifetime. After mating inside their host, female adult roundworms lay eggs which are passed out through the host's faeces onto pastures. A first-stage larva (L1) develops in the egg, which hatches inside a dung pad and feeds on bacteria. The first-stage larva moults and becomes a second-stage larva (L2). When the second-stage larva becomes a third-stage larva (L3), it moves out of the dung pad onto the grass stalks of the pasture. This is the infective stage which now waits for a suitable host to ingest it with the grazing. The development of the larvae is influenced by temperature

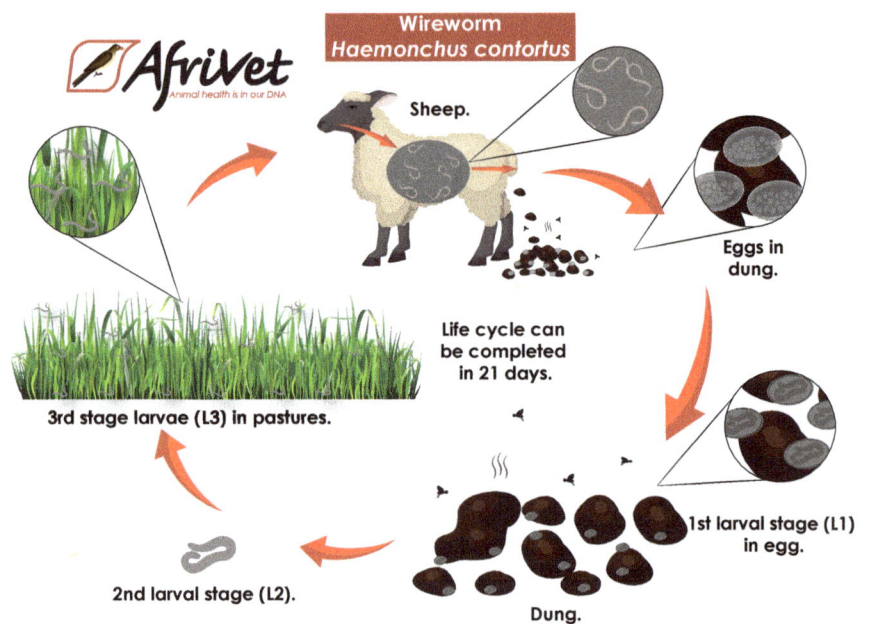

Lifecycle of a roundworm.

and moisture, which when optimal can allow them to complete their life cycle within 1-2 weeks, but generally it takes somewhat longer.

When the infective larvae are eaten by hosts, they migrate to their preferred site in the gut; here they either feed on the surface of the gut, suck blood or they may burrow into the gut tissues. The migration and method of feeding will determine the symptoms which they will cause. The roundworm life cycle is completed when the worms mate and lay eggs.

It is important to realise that there is no multiplication of roundworms within the host. An increase in an existing worm burden can only

result from the intake of additional worm larvae, for example from contaminated pastures.

Distribution and climatic effects

The distribution of roundworms in SA occurs roughly according to the rainfall areas in the country. While some important species like wireworm require heat and moisture to complete their life cycles, others like the brown stomach worm have adapted to cooler conditions, and others have become resistant to surviving dry conditions. The map shows the different rainfall areas and the tables listing the gastrointestinal roundworm species summarise their

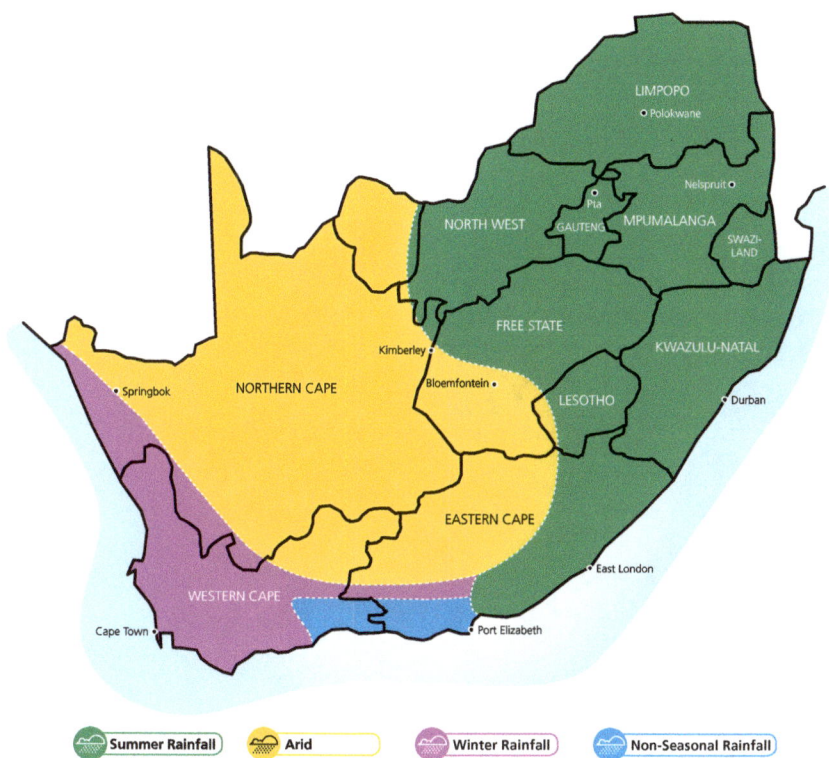

Geographic distribution of roundworms according to rainfall areas.

Summer Rainfall   Arid   Winter Rainfall   Non-Seasonal Rainfall

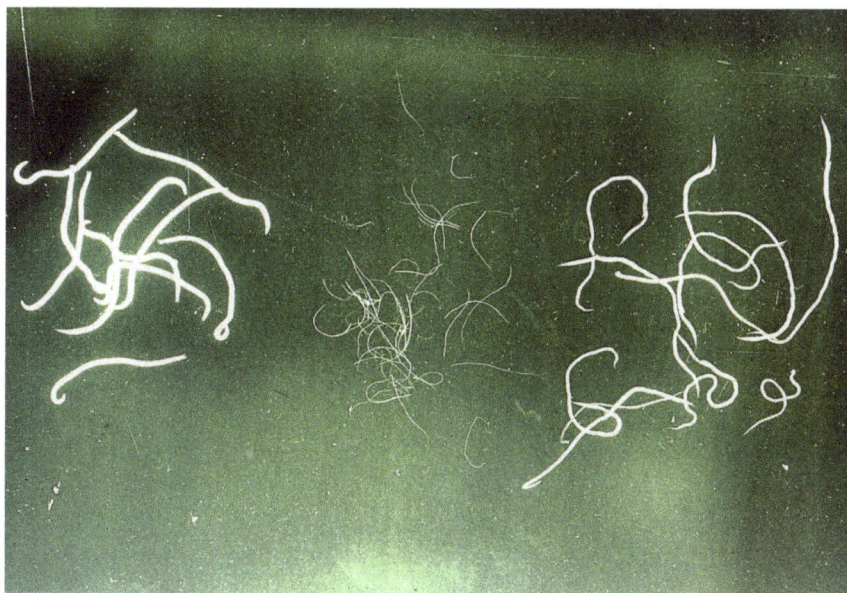

Examples of various roundworms from left to right: nodular worm, bankrupt worm and wireworm.

distribution and symptoms in the animal.

Immunity to roundworms

Young ruminants are born with no immunity to roundworms and are extremely susceptible to infestation. Cattle develop immunity to roundworms fairly rapidly (so-called self-cure) and problems are rarely encountered in adult cattle, although the condition and production of animals under stress (dairy and pregnant animals) can be affected by worm infestations.

The situation in sheep and goats is different: they take a lot longer to develop immunity and both lambs and adults can be severely affected by roundworm infestations. Pregnant sheep and goats shed enormous numbers of roundworm eggs onto grazing due to the so-called **P**eri-**P**arturient **R**elaxation of **R**esistance or PPRR, which is a lowering of resistance during late pregnancy. Although adult sheep may develop a level of immunity to roundworms, this is mostly at very high nutritional levels.

GASTROINTESTINAL ROUNDWORMS

Diagram of the ruminant digestive tract.

Legend: ■ Rumen ■ Abomasum ■ Small intestine ■ Large intestine

ABOMASUM (STOMACH)

Scientific name	Common name	Species	Rainfall area	Symptoms
Haemonchus contortus	Wireworm	Sheep	Summer rainfall	Bottle-jaw, anaemia, wasting, death
Haemonchus placei	Wireworm of cattle	Cattle	Summer rainfall	Anaemia & diarrhoea
Ostertagia (Telodorsagia) circumcincta	Brown stomach worm	Sheep	Winter rainfall	weight loss, diarrhoea, & death
Ostertagia ostertagia	Brown stomach worm	Cattle	Winter rainfall	weight loss, diarrhoea
Trichostrongylus axei	Stomach bankrupt worm	Sheep and goats (cattle)	widespread	diarrhoea, weight loss & death

Haemonchus contortus Wireworm ("Haarwurm")

This is a small worm (10-30 mm long) of which the adult female is easy to identify having the so-called "barber's pole" appearance due to the white spiral of uterus being wrapped around the red, blood-filled intestine. Male worms are small and reddish in colour. All stages are found in the abomasum. The wireworm thrives on warm, moist conditions and is therefore mostly a problem in the summer rainfall areas. Infective larvae on the pastures will hatch and mature rapidly after good summer rains and will infest sheep in November. Conditions are optimal for the hatching and development of the worm in December to May. This is one of the most important roundworms of sheep and goats causing loss of production and death.

The worm has a large spike with which it pierces the abomasum of the host and then sucks blood. The presence of 100-1 000 adults is sufficient to cause a chronic, progressive anaemia, loss of appetite and death. Higher burdens of 1 000-10 000 cause anaemia and weight loss and the typical "bottle-jaw" syndrome which can terminate in death if untreated. Heavy infestations of more than 10 000 wireworms will cause severe blood loss and rapid death. Signs of infection are loss of weight, pale mucous membranes, tarry, black faeces, progressive weakness, loss of appetite and death.

Haemonchus placei the wireworm of cattle has the same biology and pathogenesis as *H. contortus* but rarely causes clinical disease. However, when it does it will cause anaemia, bottle-jaw, black tarry diarrhoea. In more chronic cases animals will show wasting and anaemia.

On commercial farms the frequently needed dosing for control has led to multi-remedy resistance. A vaccine is now available to improve immunity and reduce the number of doses (see also under New concepts) below.

Wirevax G4200

For Afrivet anthelminthic remedies please see table at the end of the chapter.

H.contortus or wireworm in the abomasum

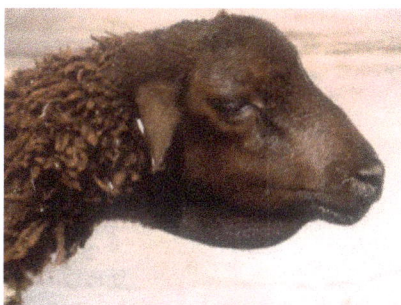

Bottlejaw is a typical sign of wireworm infestation.

Telodorsagia (Ostertagia) circumcinta Brown stomach worm

This is a tiny, brown, thread-like worm (7-12 mm long) found in the abomasum.

Ostertagia is particularly important in winter rainfall areas because they prefer cool autumn and spring conditions. Due to its interference with digestion, it causes an overall protein deficiency and this results in severe wasting; in Angora goats the clinical syndrome is called "waterpens" due to the accumulation of fluid in the abdomen. The worms invade the gastric glands in the abomasum, destroying the acid production function required for digestion. The pH increases and digestion cannot take place efficiently, giving rise to loss of appetite, weight loss, diarrhoea and death.

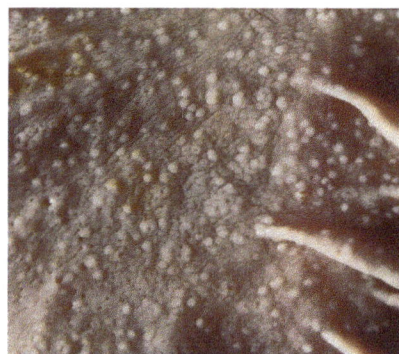

Brown stomach worm of cattle (Ostertagia ostertagi) invades the gastric glands of the abomasum causing their enlargement and prominence.

Ostertagia ostertagi Brown stomach worm

The appearance and pathology is similar to the brown stomach worm of sheep. The damage to the gastric glands causes poor digestion with resultant diarrhoea, and loss of nutrients. Typical symptoms are loss of appetite, wasting, severe chronic diarrhoea, thirst and death.

Trichostrongylus axei Stomach bankrupt worm

These are minute white worms which are almost invisible to the naked eye. Infestations are often missed because of the difficulty of seeing the worms. Its presence inhibits other abomasal worms. Dorpers are more susceptible than other breeds and large numbers of worm are required for significant infestations in sheep and calves. The worms cause inflammation and thickening of the abomasum and an increase in pH. Symptoms are a foul-smelling diarrhoea, wasting, weakness and death.

SMALL INTESTINE

Worm	Scientific name	Species	Area	Symptoms
Hookworm	*Gaigeria pachyscelis*	sheep goats	arid	anaemia
Bankrupt worm	*Trichostrongylus* spp	sheep, goats	winter rainfall and pastures	wasting
Grassveld hookworm	*Bunostomum*	sheep and goats	summer and non-seasonal	anaemia, bottle-jaw
Cattle bankrupt Worm	*Cooperia*	cattle	NW Cape	appetite loss, diarrhoea, death
Long-necked bankrupt worm	*Nematodirus spathiger*	sheep and goats	Karoo & winter rainfall	appetite loss, diarrhoea & weight loss
White bankrupt worm	*Strongyloides papilosus*	sheep and goats	Widespread	diarrhoea, weakness, death
Ascaris worm	*Toxocara vitulorum*	Calves	Widespread	pot belly, diarrhoea

Trichostrongylus sp Intestinal Bankrupt worms

These are tiny reddish brown worms (5-8 mm) which occur in the first few meters of the small intestine, which are difficult to see. This group of worms thrives on cold wet winters and presents a problem on artificial pastures. The eggs and larvae resist drying and can survive long periods until rain falls. These worms are therefore mostly of importance in winter rainfall and non-seasonal rainfall areas. Infestations cause insidious losses, especially in lambs and weaners.

The worms suppress the appetite of the host, resulting in a protein deficiency and resultant muscle wasting. Young growing animals are most severely affected especially when the protein levels in feed are low. Very often the only clinical sign is weakness although weight loss, constipation and diarrhoea can also be seen.

As the name of the worm indicates, the condition causes considerable losses because of the lack of dramatic symptoms. The diagnosis may also be easily missed because the parasite is difficult to see.

Nematodirus spathiger Long-necked bankrupt worm

These are fairly long, red worms (10-23 mm) which show narrowing at the tail end. The eggs and larvae are resistant to drying and extreme temperatures. In the Karoo, infestations occur after rain when contaminated grass around camps greens up and attracts sheep. In winter rainfall areas they are always present on pastures. The worm population peaks in early spring/late winter. There is rapid deterioration in condition after infestation, especially in lambs which pick up massive infestations. The larvae cause severe damage to the intestinal lining, which results in loss of appetite, diarrhoea and weight loss.

Gaigeria pachyscelis Sandveld hookworm

These worms are fairly long (20-30 mm) with a slightly hooked end.

The species is found in arid areas in NW Cape and Namibia. The worm larvae are found around leaking water troughs. They infect sheep through the skin and then migrate to the small intestine. Management practices which prevent water leakage or overflowing will control the problem. Low numbers of worms can cause losses due to the voracious bloodsucking capacity. Five to 6 weeks after infestation, anaemia will develop which results in death. As few as 100 worms can result in fatal anaemia.

Bunostomum sp Grassveld hookworm

They are thick white worms with a hooked end (1-3 cm). These hookworms thrive on hot moist conditions and are seen in summer and non-seasonal rainfall areas. The larvae are ingested either orally or through the skin. They finally lodge in the small intestine where they damage the intestinal epithelium with their large mouthparts. These areas bleed and cause anaemia in the animal. With heavy infestations sheep show bottle-jaw. Dermatitis can be seen at the site of skin penetration.

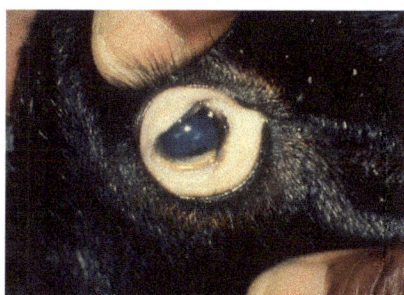

Bloodsucking worms such as wireworm and hookworms, cause severe anaemia which is manifested by pale mucous membrane.

Stronglyloides papillosus White bankrupt worm

These roundworms are widespread through the country but since young animals are most susceptible it is most commonly seen as a problem in lambs and kids housed in kraals, during summer months. Female larvae penetrate the skin, pass to the lungs and finally to the small intestine. Young animals can be infected through the milk of infected mothers. Massive infestations of young animals can cause severe diarrhoea, loss of appetite and death. Adult animals develop resistance and rarely show any clinical signs.

Cooperia spp Cattle bankrupt worm

This is a small (4-9 mm) reddish worm, coiled up tightly. The larvae survive very effectively in the interior of dung pads where they can escape dry seasons. As soon as good summer rainfall arrives, they migrate onto grass in pastures. Massive infestations occur in contaminated calf pens in NW Cape where calves are crowded together. The symptoms are loss of appetite and diarrhoea, and death may occur due to starvation and dehydration.

Toxocara vitulorum (Neoascaris vitulorum) Ascaris worm of cattle

This is a very large white worm. The infective larvae are shed in the milk of infected cows. Suckling calves obtain the worms through their mother's milk and therefore cows must be treated to prevent calf infestation. Infested calves are pot-bellied, show discomfort and diarrhoea.

LARGE INTESTINE				
Worm	Scientific name	Species	Area	Symptoms
Large-mouthed bowel-worm	*Chabertia ovina*	sheep and goats (cattle)	winter and non-seasonal	weight loss, diarrhoea
Nodular worm	*Oesophogostomum*	Sheep, goats, cattle	Widespread	weight loss
Whipworm	*Trichuris sp*	Sheep, cattle		anaemia, diarrhoea, weight loss

Chabertia ovina Large-mouthed bowel-worm

These are large white worms (13-20 mm long) which attach to the mucosa of the colon using their large mouth parts. The eggs can survive low environmental temperatures but drying or exposure to sunlight will kill them. The parasites are therefore restricted to winter and non-seasonal rainfall areas. The worms browse on the intestinal mucosa causing blood loss and leakage of plasma. This contributes to weight loss especially if the animals are on poor feed. Diarrhoea may also be seen due to the damage caused by the worms' browsing.

Oesophagostomum columbianum Nodular worm

These are small whitish grey worms (12-18 mm) with a hooked end. The young larvae require moist and hot conditions and cannot survive drying. The infective larvae invade the wall of the gut where they moult and develop into the next stage. From here the adult worms migrate into the large intestine. The larval invasion of the gut wall results in the formation of nodules which impairs absorption of fluid. These nodules can be seen on post mortem which is a good indicator of the presence of the worm. Nodular worm infestation causes wasting and reduced production.

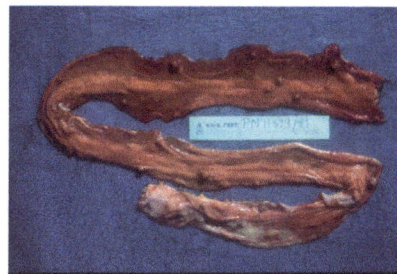

The lesions caused by nodular worm (Oesaphogostomum columbianum) in the large intestine.

Trichuris spp Whipworm

The adult worm is very distinctive with long, thin neck and thick posterior section. This appearance has given it the name "whip-worm". Large numbers are required to produce the discomfort caused by the larvae when they burrow into the gut wall, mature and then migrate into the lumen of the colon. The main discomfort and damage are caused by the migration of the larvae through the intestinal wall but they can cause anaemia due to bleeding. The adults are not thought to cause problems unless they are very numerous, in which case they cause pain, diarrhoea and loss of weight.

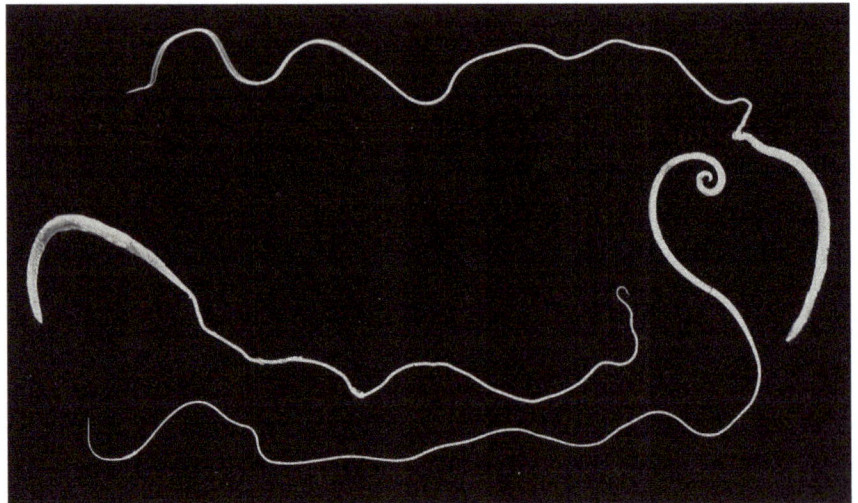

Trichuris, the whipworm

*Note that there are no roundworms of the forestomachs (rumen, omasum and reticulum).

OTHER IMPORTANT ROUNDWORMS

Dictyocaulus filaria Lungworm

This is a long white (3-10 cm) worm with a dark stripe down its length. It has a limited geographic range, being found on isolated farms in cool mountainous or coastal areas. The worms present in the lungs lay eggs, where they hatch and the larvae are coughed up, swallowed and excreted in the faeces. The larvae can survive if conditions are moist and cool enough until the infective stage develops. The infective larvae are taken in with feed, penetrate the gut and migrate to the lungs. Within a few weeks of infestation, the animals show difficult breathing, coughing, nasal discharge and tiredness if chased.

Parafilaria bovicola False bruising

This condition occurs in the warm, wet areas of the country and is caused by the worm *Parafilaria bovicola*. The adult worm is small, white, 2.5-5 cm long and is found under the skin of cattle. The worm is transmitted by face flies (*Musca lusoria* and *M. xanthomelas*) which infect cattle by depositing tiny larvae of the worm in the eyes. From here the larvae migrate to the tissue under the skin. When the female worms lay their eggs, they make a small hole in the skin which causes a "bleeding spot". This attracts faceflies which take up the eggs while feeding on the blood.

The worm larvae develop on the flies and are then in turn deposited in the eyes of other cattle. The subcutaneous tissue where the worms lie becomes discoloured – hence the term false bruising. At slaughter this tissue has to be trimmed, thus devaluing the meat.

These infestations are easily treated with an injection of macrocyclic lactones and further infections can be prevented by treatment with pyrethoid dips which will prevent infection via the flies.

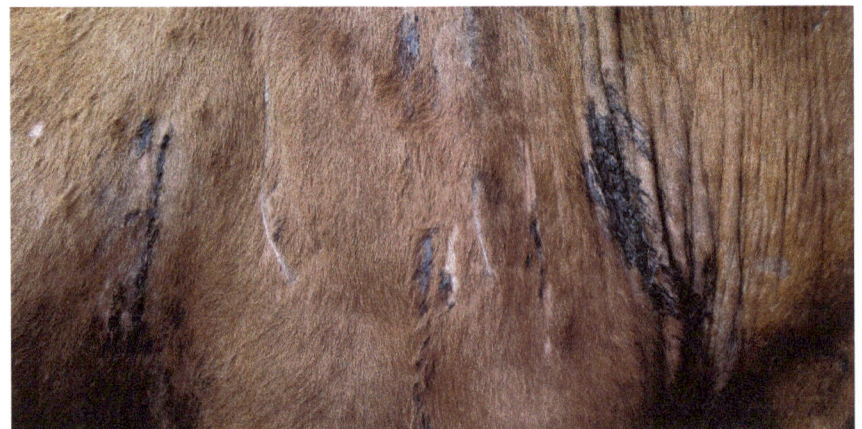

Parafilaria induced "bleeding spots" in a cow.

TAPEWORMS

Tapeworms are economically important in animal health because of their effect on livestock and human health. Adult tapeworms have flattened ribbon-like bodies which can vary in length depending on the species (from 1 mm to 15 m long). The head has suckers and hooks which help it to attach to the host's tissues (usually the intestine). The tapeworm has no digestive system since it absorbs food through its body wall by diffusion. The body is divided into the head (scolex), neck and a series of segments which have both female and male reproductive organs. Growth takes place by the addition of new segments beneath the neck.

Tapeworms have an indirect life cycle, which means they have two hosts, a temporary host in which the larva (cyst) occurs, and the final or definitive host in which the tapeworm itself occurs. The general life cycle remains the same for most tapeworm species, but the intermediate and final hosts differ. The tapeworm sheds segments containing fertilised eggs in the faeces of the host. When these segments containing eggs are ingested by an intermediate host, the embryo hatches and penetrates the intestinal wall. It is carried by the bloodstream to the tissues of the intermediate host for which it has an affinity (muscle, liver, brain). At this stage it is a larva, referred to as a cyst. When the cyst or larval form which

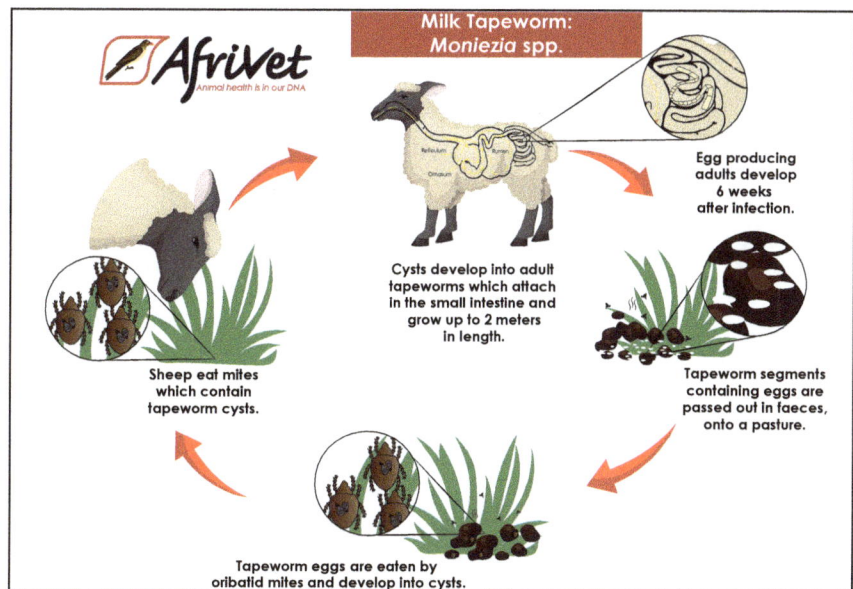

Life cycle of herbivore tapeworm

occurs in the intermediate host is eaten by the final or definitive host, the larval form will develop into the adult tapeworm in its intestine. It is helpful to divide tapeworms of veterinary importance into three broad groups according to their final hosts: herbivore, carnivore and human tapeworms.

Herbivore tapeworms

The adult tapeworm of herbivores is found in the intestine of cattle, sheep or goats. The animals pick up infection when grazing by taking in a tiny soil mite (oribatid) which is common in many areas. The mite contains the larval or cyst stage of the tapeworm which then develops into a tapeworm once in the gut of the herbivore. Here it will grow, increasing its number of segments, and laying eggs which are then shed via the faeces onto pasture.

The soil mites then become infected by eating the tapeworm eggs and thus perpetuate the life cycle.

Significance of herbivore tapeworms

With the exception of the liver tapeworm *Stilesia hepatica* which is believed to be harmless, all the other tapeworms mentioned above can affect their hosts, especially young animals because they compete for nutrition. Calves become infested as soon as they are turned onto pastures and heavy infestations affect their condition especially in the winter when grazing is poor. They often show a rough haircoat and a "pot belly".

Lambs become infested when they begin grazing and heavy infestations retard their growth or may even result in death. Heavily pregnant ewes

Important herbivore tapeworms

FINAL HOST*	TAPEWORM SPECIES	COMMON NAME
Cattle	*Moniezia* sp	Milk tapeworm
Sheep and goats	*Moniezia* sp	Milk tapeworm
	Thysaniezia sp	Ruffled tapeworm
	Avittelina	Thin tapeworm
	Stilesia hepatica	Liver tapeworm

*The intermediate host of all these tapeworms is an oribatid mite

A sheep tapeworm expelled in the faeces.

on poor winter grazing can suffer mortalities when heavily infested.

Carnivore tapeworms

These tapeworms are found in wild or domestic dog species. Dogs become infected when they eat tissues of cattle, sheep or goats in which the larval forms occur, which usually resemble bladder-like cysts. The herbivores become infected by taking in the tapeworm eggs on pastures where dogs have defecated. Depending on the species of the tapeworm the cyst may be found in the brain, the muscle or the liver, lungs, or mesentery.

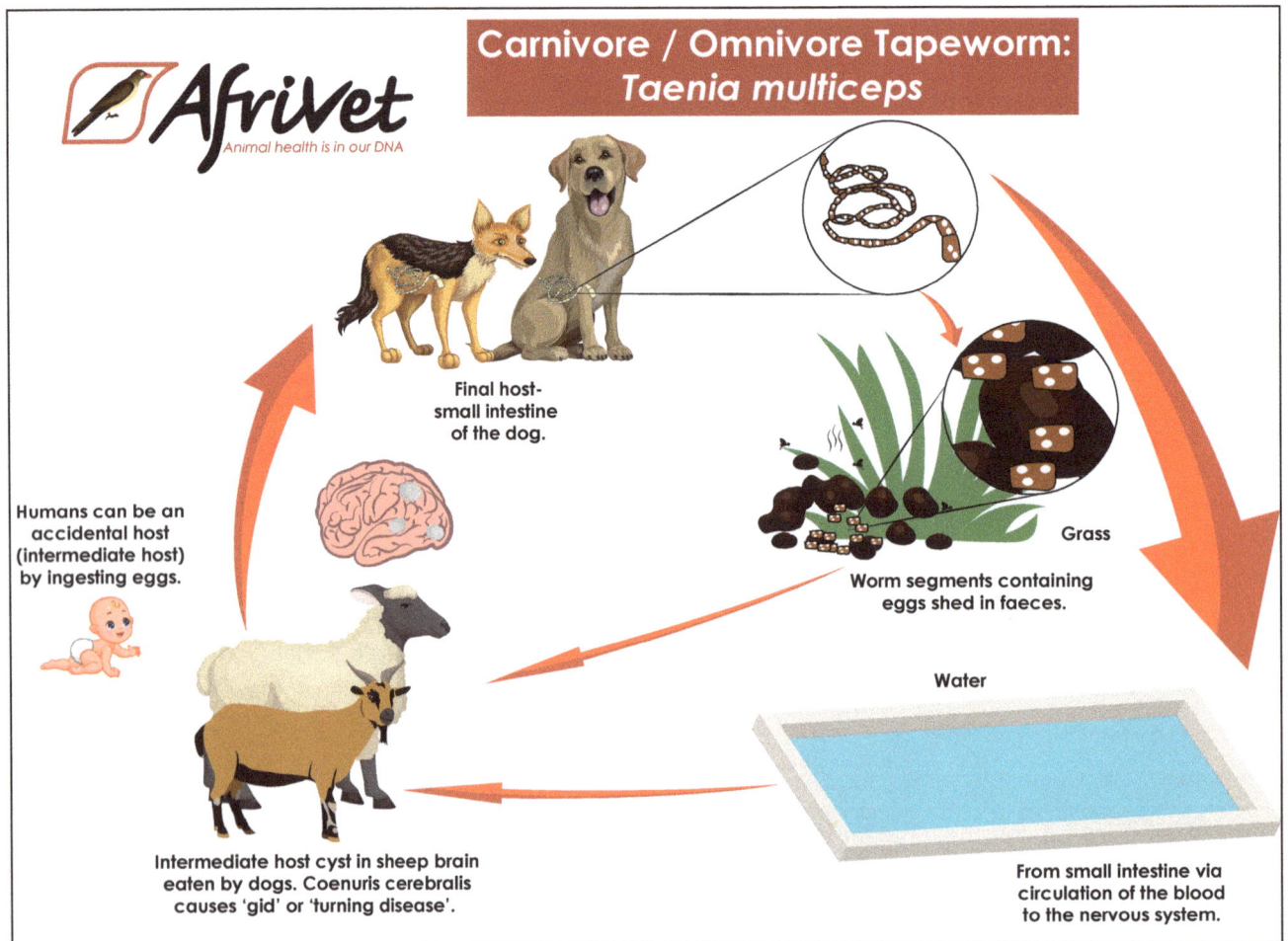

AfriVet
Animal health is in our DNA

Carnivore / Omnivore Tapeworm:
Taenia multiceps

Final host-
small intestine
of the dog.

Humans can be an
accidental host
(intermediate host)
by ingesting eggs.

Worm segments containing
eggs shed in faeces.

Grass

Water

Intermediate host cyst in sheep brain
eaten by dogs. Coenuris cerebralis
causes 'gid' or 'turning disease'.

From small intestine via
circulation of the blood
to the nervous system.

Life cycle of a carnivore tapeworm

Important carnivore tapeworms

Tapeworm species	Final host (tapeworm)	Intermediate host (cyst)
Taenia hydatigena	dogs (domestic and wild)	sheep, cattle, goats
Taenia multiceps	dogs (domestic and wild)	sheep, cattle and humans
Taenia ovis	dogs (domestic and wild)	Sheep
Echinococcus granulosus	domestic dogs	humans, sheep

Significance of carnivore tapeworms

The larvae of the carnivore tapeworms invade the organs of the ruminant intermediate hosts and affect their functions. The larval cysts of *T. multiceps* which occur in the brain of sheep become large fluid-filled sacs and their presence gives rise to "gid" ("malkopsiekte/draaisiekte"). The cysts become so large that they affect the brain function and if large enough, they erode the bone of the skull by pressure necrosis. Humans, although not the usual intermediate hosts, can become accidentally infected.

T. hydatigena cysts are found in the liver and lungs of sheep and other species at slaughter, and lead to the condemnation of these organs in abattoirs. *Echinococcus granulosus* cysts occur in the liver, lungs and brains of a number of species including humans who develop "hydatid disease" of which the most serious form is the infestation of the brain. The cysts will cause nervous symptoms and occasionally death.

Human tapeworms

Taenia saginata is a tapeworm which occurs in the human intestine which can grow to enormous lengths, competing for nutrients, causing weight loss, and reduced appetite. The tapeworm excretes eggs in the faeces which, if ingested by a bovine host, hatch into larvae which then migrate to the muscles where they lodge. Humans become infected by eating contaminated beef in which these larval stages are found. These larval stages, referred to as "measles" are seen as small white nodules which can be detected on meat inspection at abattoirs. Meat heavily infested with measles is condemned at abattoirs, leading to economic losses for the farmer. Lightly infected meat can be frozen to kill off the cysts. The control measure for *T. saginata* on farms is simply to provide toilets to prevent pastures becoming contaminated with infested faeces.

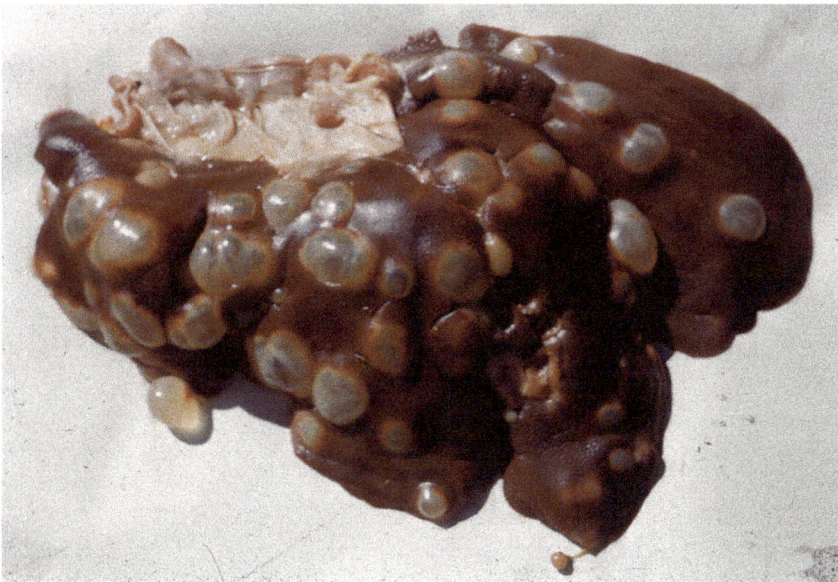

Cysts of T. hydatigena in a sheep liver.

The cyst of the human tapeworm Taenia saginata in the muscle of a bovine.

FLUKES

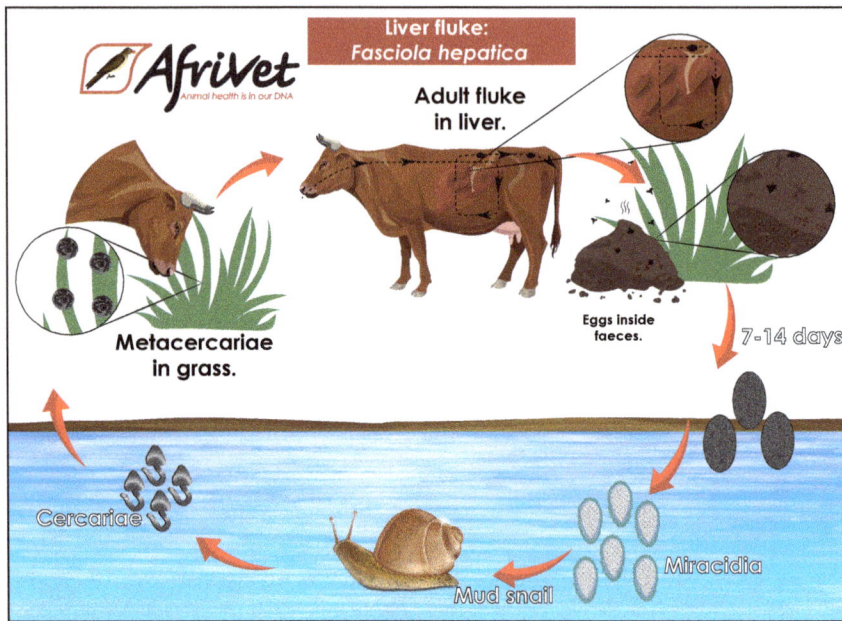

Life cycle of a fluke.

This group includes the liver flukes, conical flukes and the bilharzia parasites. They all have an indirect life cycle, with various water snails as the intermediate hosts, and the final hosts being cattle, sheep or goats.

Some water snail species serve as intermediate hosts for flukes.

An ideal habitat for flukes.

Fasciola hepatica Liver fluke

Fasciola gigantica Giant liver fluke

Adult liver flukes have a flattened leaf-like appearance. *F. hepatica* grows up to 30 mm in length while *F. gigantica* is considerably larger, the mature adults reaching 75 mm. Liver flukes need wet conditions for their existence because their intermediate hosts are small aquatic water snails (*Lymnaea* spp). These snails can live in permanent or semi-permanent water which can be dams, vleis or even continually leaking water troughs.

Animals become infected by the infective forms or cercariae which are shed by the water snails. The cercariae which then form resistant cysts climb onto blades of grass and wait for a passing host. If they are eaten by grazing animals, the cysts penetrate the gut, become young liver flukes and then and migrate to the liver. These flukes then move through the liver tissue seeking out the bile ducts. The young liver flukes then lodge in the bile ducts where they suck blood. Female adult liver flukes lay eggs which are shed via the bile into the faeces. The eggs hatch into a form called miracidium, which then infects the water snail, completing the life cycle. The life cycle takes a long time to complete and this slows

The thickening of the bile ducts caused by liver fluke infestation.

down during winter when the water snails hibernate.

There is scarring of the liver due to damage caused by the fluke migration and the bile ducts become thickened, but heavy infestations can cause fatal haemorrhage in the liver. Sub-acute and chronic liver fluke infection causes loss of condition, weight loss, anaemia, and bottle-jaw. Death occurs 20 weeks after infestation. Sheep are more severely affected than cattle and they do not develop immunity.

Calicophoron (Paramphistomum) microbothrium Conical fluke

The life cycle of conical flukes is similar to that of the liver fluke. Adult conical flukes are roughly 5 -13 mm long, are cone-shaped and pink in colour with a sucker with which they attach to the mucosa of the rumen, where they do not cause any problems. Immature conical flukes which are found in the first part of

Adult liver flukes.

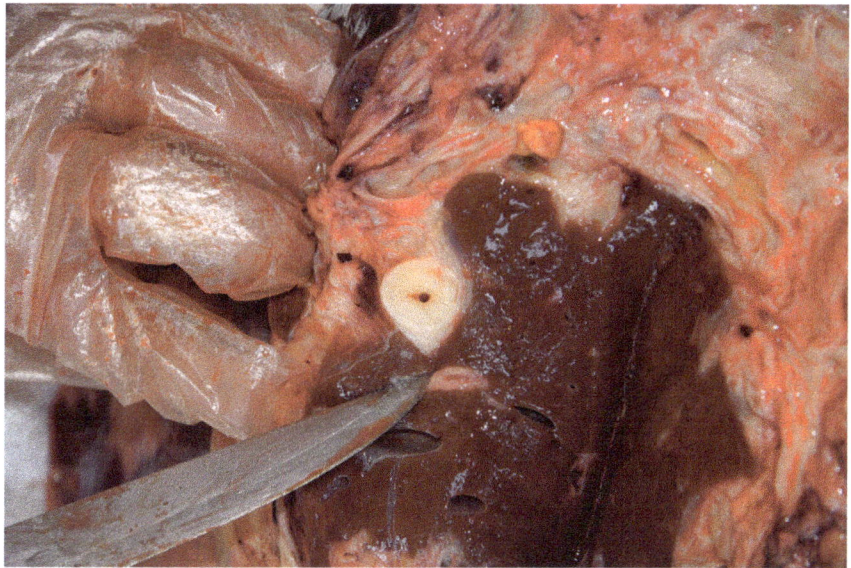

Conical flukes in the rumen where they do not cause problems.

the small intestine look like pink or white rice grains where they do cause problems; they attach to the small intestine by grasping a plug of mucosa and the resultant swelling and strangulation of tissue causes severe discomfort and loss of appetite resulting in progressive weight loss. Foul-smelling diarrhoea may occur due to decomposition of intestinal contents. Occasionally swelling of the head or bottle-jaw is seen and death may occur. Sheep are more severely affected by conical fluke than cattle.

Schistosoma mattheei Bilharzia worms

Bilharzia infestation of livestock is not very common in South Africa, being confined to warm moist sub-tropical areas such as Mpumalanga. Sheep are the most susceptible species, but the fluke can occasionally cause symptoms in cattle. Bilharzia parasites cause a number of syndromes in their host due to the progression of the life cycle.

Ruminants become infected with waterborne cercariae or larvae which are shed by water snails, the intermediate host of the bilharzia worm. These cercariae penetrate the skin, travel to the liver and then enter the mesenteric blood vessels which drain the intestine. The larvae develop into small worms, the male accommodating the thin black female in a groove in his body. Here the worms live off the blood of the host, laying eggs which migrate out into the faeces by penetrating the intestinal wall. The presence of the worm in the blood vessel can cause inflammation of veins and those that die off are carried to the liver where they may cause thrombi. A typical sign of bilharzia in sheep is "grey lungs" which are seen on post mortem. The greatest damage is done by the eggs which on their migration out of the blood vessels, cause severe irritation of the tissues. Sheep are more severely affected than cattle and show loss of weight, sunken eyes, diarrhoea and eventually death. Cattle, although less susceptible, may develop severe diarrhoea.

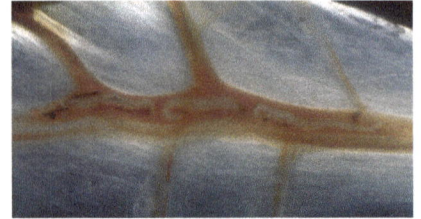

Male and female bilharzia worms in the mesenteric blood vessels.

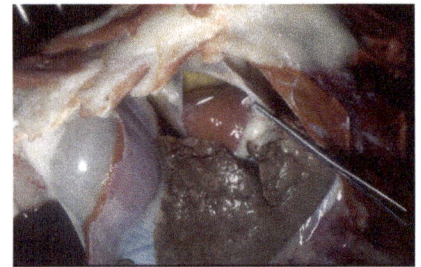

Grey lungs seen with bilharzia infestation in sheep.

DIAGNOSIS AND CONTROL OF WORMS

How do we know that livestock are infected with worms? Although infestations of some types of worms, for example the bloodsuckers like wireworms, hookworms and liver flukes, cause **typical symptoms** like bottle-jaw, much of the time worms cause non-specific signs like wasting, weakness and diarrhoea. In other words, external symptoms are not reliable indicators of worm infestation.

Other methods of establishing whether worms are a problem are by doing a thorough **post mortem examination** of the carcase at slaughter or when animals die. The gastrointestinal tract, liver, head and brain of sheep should be carefully examined by a veterinarian. Establishing the presence of worms and identifying those present will the selection of an effective dosing programme.

Faecal egg counts are an extremely useful tool mainly for monitoring the effect of dosing programmes and can also be used to detect worm resistance (see later).

Local veterinary laboratories and veterinarians are equipped to do faecal egg counts for roundworms and live flukes. The samples taken from a flock or herd for egg counts should represent the group of animals to be evaluated, e.g. 5-10 of a group which are showing signs of suspected infestation or alternately 5-10 animals which were treated 10 -14 days ago. Faecal samples are sent to suitable laboratories preferably in small screw-top plastic containers as soon as possible, since storage will result in decomposition and may affect the tests. At least 2 g must be collected for sheep and goats and 5 g for cattle. The samples must be clearly marked, recording the species of the animal, the identification number of the animal or group (e.g. weaners), and the details of the owner. It is important to specify to the laboratory if fluke egg analysis is required because a different test is required. Tapeworm infestations cannot be diagnosed using faecal egg counts.

The results of roundworm egg counts are expressed as eggs per gram (epg) and are usually interpreted as follows by laboratories:

0:	No worm eggs present
+:	Slight infestation (1-500 eggs per gram)
++:	Moderate infestation (500-5000 eggs per gram)
+++:	Heavy infestation (>5000)

The results of these egg counts however must be interpreted with care, since the number of eggs that occur in a sample is not necessarily proportional to the number of worms present; the animal may also be infested with non-egglaying worms (larvae, non-egg laying adults, sterile adults due to immunity in the animal or a species which lay few eggs). Some species such as wireworms produce massive amounts of eggs while others such as Ostertagia produce low egg outputs.

The egg production of worms is cyclic so it will be low at certain times of the year or even at certain times of the day. Technical problems with eggs counts may also give inaccurate results, so ensure that the counts are being done by a professional. Faecal egg counts must therefore be interpreted taking all these factors into account and are most useful when done on a regular basis as a monitoring tool for building up a history and therefore developing and monitoring a dosing programme.

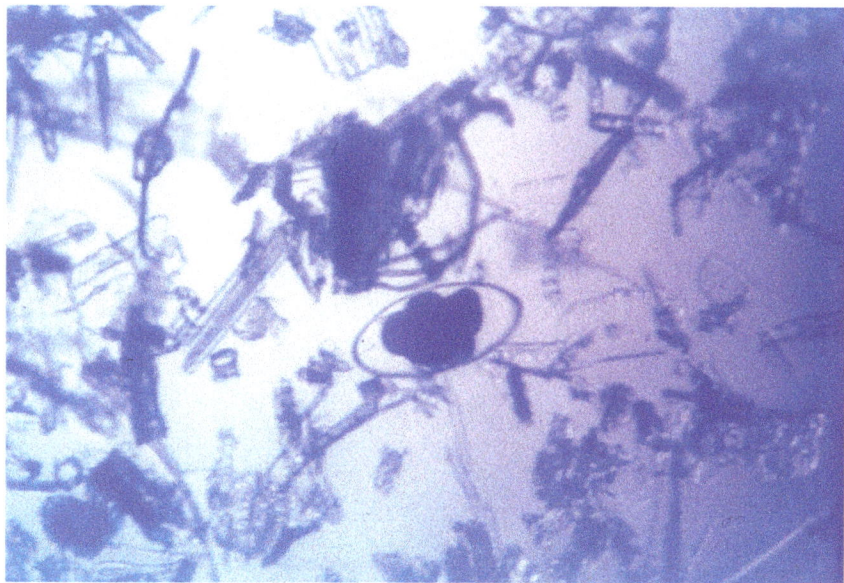

Faecal egg counts are essential to monitor dosing programmes.

CONTROL OF WORMS

Chemical treatment of internal parasites is a powerful tool but must be used judiciously since resistance is becoming a more prevalent problem.

Chemical groups currently registered under Act 36/47 and their spectrum of activity

*1.	CHEMICAL GROUP	REMEDIES	SPECTRUM
	Macrocyclic lactones	Ivermectin abamectin moxidectin	roundworms (also fly larvae)
2.	Benzimidazoles	thibendazole, mebendazole, albendazole triclabedazole fenbendazole	roundworms and eggs
3.	Imidiothiazole	Levamisole	roundworms
4.	Salicylanilides	rafoxanide*, closantel*, resorantel, niclosamide, oxyclosanide	flukes and some tapeworms *roundworms
5.	Phenols	nitoxynil, disophenol	roundworms
6.	Sulphonamides	Clorsulon	flukes
7.	Organophosphates	haloxon, trichlorfon, napthalophos	roundworms
8.	Isoquinaline	praziquantel	tapeworms
9.	Other e.g. Tetrahydropyrimidine	morantel, pyrantel	roundworms

* The number refers to the numbering system on the labels of products (see example of label below).

FOR ANIMAL USE ONLY   SLEGS VIR DIEREGEBRUIK

(2)

OstriDose

Reg No. G2234 Act/Wet 36/1947
A remedy against roundworms in ostriches and horses
'n Middel teen rondewurms in volstruise en perde

STORE IN A COOL DRY PLACE/BEWAAR IN 'n KOEL DROË PLEK

CAUTION/VERSIGITG

Composition/Samestelling
Fenbendazole/Fenbendasool 5% m/v

1ℓ, 2ℓ, 5ℓ, 10ℓ, 20ℓ

† Benzimidazole/Bensimidasool

Date of Manuf./Datum verv.
Lot No.:

Activity of worm remedies

The package insert of the product indicates the extent to which the endoparasite is controlled and the remedies are allocated claims according to their activity against specific worms (see the label example). Label claims are based on evidence presented at time of registration to authorities at Act 36/47.

EXAMPLES OF CLAIMS FOR WORM REMEDIES

ROUNDWORMS AND TREMATODE REMEDIES

Worm species	Effect of the remedy on the worm	
	Immature	Adult
Haemonchus contortus	*	**
Fasciola hepatica	**	*

* Controls (>90% effective)

** Aids in control (60-89% effective)

TAPEWORM REMEDIES

Worm species	Effect of remedy on worm	
Avitelina sp	Class 1	Class 1: 100% effective in 80% of treated animals
Moniezia sp	Class 11	Class 11: 100% effective in more than 60% of treated animals
Thysaniezia spp	Class 111	Class 111: 100% effective in more than 50% of treated animals
Stilesia hepatica	Class X	Class X: Ineffective

Action and spectrum of activity

Anthelmintics are chemicals that are poisonous to parasites but not to the host when given the specified dose. The chemicals are usually absorbed into the bloodstream and enter the general circulation. The parasites are killed when they ingest the chemical through the blood or body fluids of the treated animals. The anthelmintic is eventually broken down by the liver and excreted, finally disappearing from the tissues. The anthelmintics currently used act in one of two ways: either by affecting the neuromuscular system causing paralysis, or by limiting energy by interfering with the respiration pathways. The spectrum of activity may be broad, affecting more than one endoparasite group or may even be confined to just one life-cycle stage of one specific group.

Methods of administration

Most anthelmintics are administered by mouth as "drenches", although some are administered as injections. The dose of anthelmintics given is based on the body weight of the animal to be treated. In order for control to be effective the dose must be accurate as under-dosing will lead to lowered efficacy. Under-dosing takes place when owners do not weigh animals, or the dosing guns used are not correctly calibrated. Overdosing with some remedies can cause toxicity and must be avoided at all costs. Remedies must never be mixed with other anthelmintics or any other products or decanted into other containers.

Registration of remedies

All remedies made available for sale as stock remedies must be registered in accordance with the Act 36/47. This requires proof of efficacy and safety of the remedy for the claims made on the label, in the target species being treated. The label of the remedy must be specific about the dosage, administration, warnings, precautions, side-effects, and the withholding periods before using animals for human consumption.

Generic remedies

When new chemicals are discovered, they are patented by the company which makes the discovery. The patent prohibits any other company or organisation from manufacturing the chemical until the patent expires, usually 20 after years. Once the patent expires, the details of manufacture can be published, and other companies can produce the same chemical – usually at lower cost because the R&D costs do not have to be recovered. Most of the anthelmintics on the market currently have generic equivalents.

Using anthelmintics

Chemical control should be used in a planned dosing program to optimise its efficacy, rather than as a randomly administered treatment.

Tactical treatment is done when worms are causing visible clinical signs: this can be either when the parasites are numerous, or when the animal is very susceptible (late pregnancy), or when there is abnormally high rainfall.

Strategic treatment is aimed at causing the most damage to the life cycle of the parasite, thereby disrupting the population. Animals will not necessarily show any signs of infestation but will prevent the build-up of the parasite populations. An example is the strategic treatment for liver fluke at the end of winter before the first rains. This prevents the shedding of eggs and therefore the infestation of the water snails. This will have an impact which will last the whole year.

The dosing programme must take into account all the parasites which occur in the area of the country (roundworms, tapeworms and flukes), the particular animal group (pregnant ewes, lambs), and the current season (high or low rainfall).

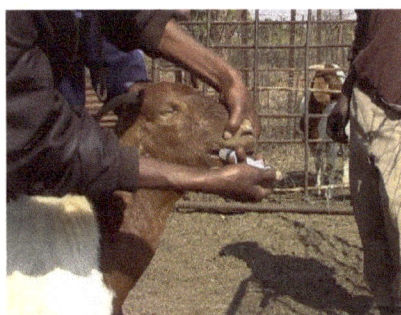

Dosing for internal parasites must be done as part of a carefully planned programme.

Pasture management and hygiene

Since the greatest part of roundworm populations are free-living on the grazing, using pasture management and rotation can control the levels of worm infestation in animals. Resting infested pastures or allowing other species such as cattle to act as vacuum cleaners for sheep parasites can reduce the worm burdens. However, under certain circumstances such as where the parasites are very resistant or where pastures are irrigated, worms may survive very effectively, and rotation and camp resting may not be sufficient for control.

Fluke infestations can be prevented by avoiding vlei areas, especially in summer when the parasites are active and in autumn when the waters begin to recede.

In the case of herbivore tapeworms where the source is a soil mite it is almost impossible to avoid infestation unless the animals can be confined to zero grazing situation.

Camp or kraal hygiene should be practised where possible (especially cattle), removing manure to areas where animals are not grazing. Spreading it out to dry will kill off larval worms. Note that using manure to fertilise pastures can infest them with worms.

An integrated approach should be used, in other words, a combination of judicious chemical usage with pasture management.

Biological control

Dung beetles are helpful in removing manure from pastures, but generally in farming situations there are insufficient beetles to cope with the manure of a few hundred head of cattle. Some chemicals such as the macrocyclic lactones can be harmful to dung beetles.

Other approaches to biological control which are in their infancy are the use of microfungi which, when they establish themselves on pasture, are pathogenic for nematodes. Whether this can be used as a practical control measure is not yet known.

Genetic selection for worm resistant hosts

Within animal populations, some individuals are more resistant to infestations with specific species of worms. This is a genetic characteristic and can be selected by breeding resistant animals. However, there may be limitations on this approach since it may not be possible to select animals that are resistant to more than one parasite. In addition, animals that are selected for worm resistance may not be high producers of wool or meat. A programme to select wireworm resistant sheep in Australia has been set up, but so far it is not clear whether this approach is feasible.

DOSING PROGRAMMES

Dosing programmes should take into account all the endoparasites present on a particular farm, the type of farming and the management. It should ideally be drawn up in consultation with a veterinarian.

Programs for cattle

Since cattle develop immunity to worms with increasing age, dosing programmes are usually aimed at calves and pregnant dairy cows on pasture. Calves should be dosed for roundworm and tapeworms at intervals from 2 months of age until weaning. Pregnant cows should be dosed for roundworms and be allowed to calve on clean camps. The presence of other parasites such as flukes and *Parafilaria* will necessitate additions to the control programme. The incidence of *parafilariasis* will be reduced with the use of pyrethroid dips as it will prevent/reduce transmission of the worm by flies. Effective treatment of *Parafilaria* infestations is achieved with the use of injectable ivermectin preparations. Management factors such as pasture management, kraal hygiene, avoiding marshes and repairing leaking troughs will all aid endoparasite control.

Programmes for small stock

Since roundworms are a problem even in adult sheep, they will have a more intensive control program than cattle. The rainfall area is used as a guideline since this determines the type of roundworms that are prevalent. Tapeworm control must be integrated with the roundworm control, especially in lambs but also in pregnant ewes. Fluke control must be considered if the farm has vleis, dams or irrigation. Some endoparasiticides work for sheep nasal worm and so this can be done at the same time.

Good practices such as **quarantine deworming**, placing dewormed animals on clean pastures, rotation of grazing and kraal hygiene must be used to optimise chemical control and delay the onset of resistance to chemicals.

The guidelines below are used to develop dosing program for endoparasite control in the various geographic areas:

Worm control for small stock in winter rainfall areas

Season	Dosing considerations
Spring (Sept/October)	Liver fluke Nasal worm
	Bankrupt and brown stomach worm infestation Tapeworm and roundworm in lambs Pre-mating dose for autumn lambing
Early summer Nov/Dec	Nasal worm Wireworm Liver fluke contracted in spring Tape- and roundworm in lambs
Summer (Dec/Jan)	Nasal worm Mature large-mouth bowel-worm Pre-mating dose for winter lambing Pre-lambing dose Tape- and roundworms in lambs
Autumn	Brown stomach (mature and immature) Liver fluke Pre-winter dose Tape- and roundworms in lambs
Winter	Bankrupt worm and brown stomach worm Weaning dose for tape- and roundworms in lambs

Worm control programme for small stock in arid areas

Season	Dosing considerations
Spring (Sept/Oct)	Nasal worm and roundworm Tapeworms and roundworms in lambs
Early summer (Nov/Dec)	Nasal worm and wireworm Tapeworms and roundworms in lambs
Mid-summer (Jan/Feb)	Immature nodular and wireworm
Late summer (Feb/March)	Nasal worm and wireworm
Autumn (3 weeks after first frost)	Bankrupt, nodular and brown stomach worm Tapeworms and roundworms in lambs

Worm control programme for small stock in summer rainfall areas

Season	Dosing onsiderations
Spring (Sept/Oct)	Nasal, round and liver fluke
Early summer (Nov/Dec)	Wireworm, nasal worm, liver fluke Tape- and roundworms in lambs
Mid-summer (Dec/Jan)	Nodular worms and wireworms Tapeworms and roundworms in lambs
Late summer (Feb/March)	Flukes Wireworm and nasal worm Tapeworms and roundworms in lambs
Autumn (April/May) or 3 weeks after first frost	Wire- and nasal worm Liver fluke Tape- and roundworms in lambs
Winter	Liver fluke Tapeworms and roundworms in lambs

Dosing according to the production cycle

A more modern approach is to dose according to the production cycle. The schedule is given below.

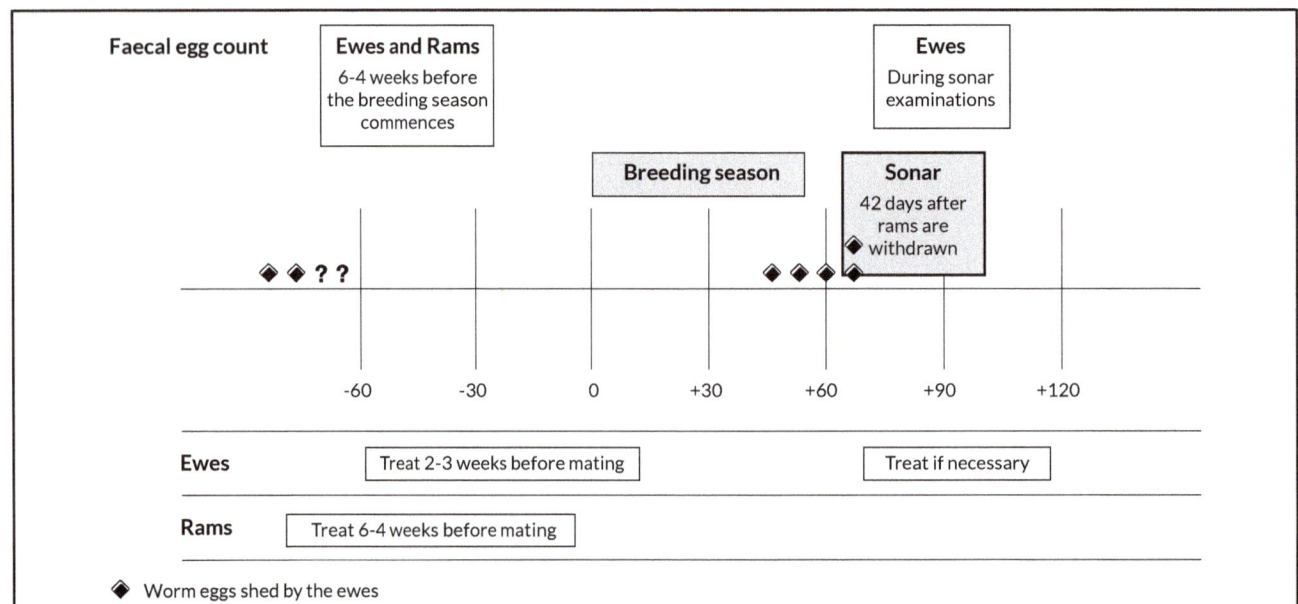

Guidelines for treatment of roundworms before the breeding season

Reason:
Ewes must improve in condition before the breeding season commences. Rams also need improvement in condition for optimal semen production.

Aim:
1. Ewes are usually on good grazing and infestation of camps must be prevented.
2. Nutrients given as supplements must be optimally utilised.
3. The ram must build up condition before breeding season.

Remedy:
Use a broad-spectrum roundworm remedy and include nasal worm treatment if needed at this stage.

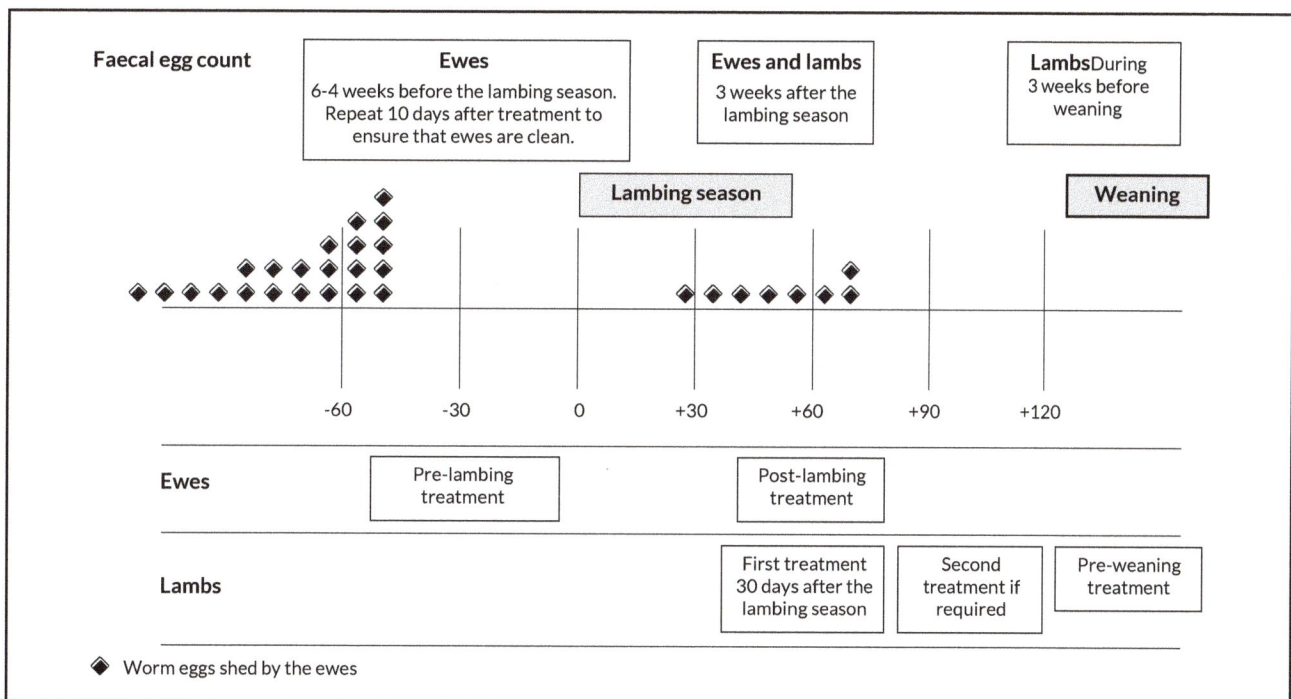

Faecal egg count	**Ewes** 6-4 weeks before the lambing season. Repeat 10 days after treatment to ensure that ewes are clean.	**Ewes and lambs** 3 weeks after the lambing season	**Lambs** During 3 weeks before weaning

Lambing season

Weaning

-60   -30   0   +30   +60   +90   +120

| Ewes | Pre-lambing treatment | | Post-lambing treatment | | |
| Lambs | | | First treatment 30 days after the lambing season | Second treatment if required | Pre-weaning treatment |

◆ Worm eggs shed by the ewes

Guidelines for pre-lambing treatment

Reason:
The ewes natural immunity against roundworms is lowered before lambing and for a period thereafter.
Adult worms will produce a large number of eggs which will contaminate the pasture on which the animals lamb.

Goal:
1. To limit the number of worm eggs shed onto the pastures where the lamb will be born. However this does not solve the problem of the eggs and larvae already present.
2. Improve the supply of nutrients to the heavily pregnant ewe which is required by the rapidly growing unborn foetus.
3. Improve the supply of nutrients so that the ewe has sufficient milk to raise a lamb.

Remedy:
Use a broad-spectrum remedy which works for all roundworms on the farm as well as tapeworms.

Note: For non-seasonal rainfall areas, combine the winter and summer rainfall recommendations.

Selecting a remedy

Using the above tables as guidelines, the farmer and veterinarian decide when to treat animals, and based on this select suitable remedies. The remedy must be selected for activity against the specific parasite concerned, must be suitable for the species, age and status (some remedies cannot be used in lactating animals). Broad spectrum or combination remedies are popular with farmers but the cost must be borne in mind. More careful selections must be made if there is resistance present to one of the remedies. If two different remedies are to be given, e.g. tapeworm and roundworm remedy at one period, allow at least one day interval between them. Pay attention to withdrawal periods if the meat or milk is to be used for human consumption.

Fluke control in sheep and cattle

Integrated control using pasture management and anthelmintic administration will give the best control. Avoid grazing animals on infested pastures if possible and fence these off to prevent access. Snail control using molluscicides is not a long-term solution as they are easily reintroduced. Prevent introduction of flukes onto farms where water snails may be present by treating newly introduced animals before they are turned out to pasture. Select the correct remedy for the problem (liver or conical). If problem areas cannot be avoided, treat for liver fluke every 8 weeks to break the life cycle. Treatment late in winter will break the life cycle as the snail (and parasite) hibernates in winter. Since triclabendazole controls both immature and adult parasites it limits the damage caused by the parasite more effectively than the other liver fluke remedies. Conical fluke infestation can occur during winter and animals should be removed from infested pasture during this time. Treat outbreaks with remedies containing resorantel or oxyclozanide.

Remedies available for fluke control

REMEDY	LIVER FLUKES		CONICAL FLUKES	
	Immatures	Adults	Immatures	Adults
Closantel	-	x	x	-
Rafoxanide	-	x	-	-
Triclabendazole	x	x	-	-
Resorantel	-	-	x	x
Oxyclozanide	-	x	x	x*
Albendazole	-	x	-	-
Niclosamide	-	-	x	-

x: Controls (>90% effective)

* Cattle only

WORM RESISTANCE

"Worm resistance" or more correctly "anthelmintic resistance" refers to the resistance of worms to the chemicals used for their control. The ability of worms to resist chemicals is a genetic one. Under natural conditions genetically resistant worms occur at very low levels in worm populations. These resistant individuals are selected when the chemicals are used, since the susceptible worms are eliminated and the resistant individuals survive to reproduce and increase in their numbers. These resistance genes become prevalent on specific farms and are spread by the sale of animals containing resistant worms all over the country.

Since endoparasites cause losses to farming by causing deaths or decreasing weight gains, chemical control of endoparasites increases the economic production of stock. Once there is resistance to the chemicals available, the farmer will have a smaller arsenal on which to rely. Multi-resistant worms (i.e. worms resistant to more than one remedy group) will be difficult to control.

What practices give rise to resistance?

- Introduction of resistant worms onto a farm (usually stud animals). This is one of the major reasons for the spread of resistance on farms and is preventable.
- Frequent and prolonged treatment with the same chemical group.
- Remedies which have a prolonged (residual) effect may contribute to the development of resistance.
- Under-dosing may cause resistance.

How common is resistance in SA?

In South Africa, resistance has been encountered in some roundworm species of sheep mainly *Haemonchus contortus*, to almost all anthelmintic groups, although some groups show more widespread resistance than others. Benzimidazole resistance is common in roundworms followed by the halogenated nitrophenols (especially closantel); there is resistance but to a lesser extent to

macrocyclic lactones and less in turn to levamisole. Organophosphate resistance is seldom encountered but does occur.

Niclosamide resistance is quite common in areas where there is regular dosing for sheep tapeworms.

Resistance versus ineffective dosing

It is important not to confuse resistance with ineffective dosing. Ineffective dosing can occur due to a number of factors:

- the treatment being ineffective for the type of parasite (check on the label);
- incorrect dose;
- some animals remained untreated;
- animals were able to spit out the drench (poor dosing technique);
- the drenching gun was faulty;
- the drench was not mixed properly according to the label;
- the remedy has expired or had a batch problem.

To determine whether resistance has developed on the farm, the most effective way is using the faecal egg reduction count (FECRT). It should be performed under supervision of a competent person, preferably a veterinarian since the interpretation of the test is critical. To perform the FECRT, sheep are treated with the remedy under investigation as well as another remedy group not used recently on the farm. One group of sheep remains as untreated controls. Faecal samples are collected 10 days

after dosing from all groups. For resistance to be suspected, egg counts before and after treatment must not change significantly. The control sample will establish whether the results are valid.

Prevention of worm resistance

Not all farms experience worm resistance but those most likely to have problems are stud and intensive farming systems where sheep are regularly dosed for wire-worm (*H.contortus*) or brown stomach worm (*Telodorsagia*). Resistance can be managed by applying some basic control measures. **Quarantine dosing,** using two successive treatments with two different groups of chemicals, can prevent the introduction of resistant worms. **Dosing to achieve maximal effect,** for example before lambing and prior to weaning, rather than random treatment will limit the need for frequent dosing. **Monitoring** the effect of dosing by performing faecal egg counts will identify resistance and prevent unnecessary dosing. **Cleaning camps** of manure where possible and **rotating camps** to reduce the survival of worm larvae will limit the exposure of animals to large worm burdens and reduce the need for frequent dosing.

Consult a veterinarian about the ideal times to rest camps. Ensure good nutrition which stimulates the immunity and increases the resistance of animals to parasites.

A registered **vaccine (*Wirevax G4200)* is now available for the control of wireworm (*H. contortus*) in sheep. The use of the vaccine reduces the number of anthelmintic treatments required and therefore the chance of resistance. To achieve good control of wireworm the vaccine must be applied in strict compliance with the manufacturer's directions.

Afrivet endoparasite remedies

PRODUCT	PARASITE	SPECIES	ACTIVE
Eradiworm 25 dose G4249	Roundworms (RW)	C, S & G	Levamisole
Eradiworm +Tape dose G4244	Round- and tapeworm	C, S & G	Levamisole and praziquantel
Eradiworm + Plus dose G4265	Roundworm and liverfluke	C, S & G (not dairy)	Levamisole and rafoxinide
Eradiworm concentrate dose G4250	Roundworms	C, S & G	Levamisole
Ecofluke dose G3383	Liver fluke immature and adult	C, S & G (not dairy)	Triclabendazole
Ecomintic 50 dose G2000	Roundworm C Roundworm and milk tape	- S & G	Fenbendazole
Ecotel 2,5% dose G3162	Tapeworms	Intestinal and hepatic –S Tapeworms -S	Praziquantel
Moxziben dose G4040	RW, liver fluke milk tapeworm, nasal bot	Sheep	Triclabendazole, praziquantel, moxidectin
Closeco 7,5% injectable G3383	See species	Cattle (not dairy): RW and liver fluke Sheep: wireworm, hookworm and liver fluke	Closantel
Ecomectin 1% injectable G2275	Endo- and ectoparasite combination	Cattle: RW, eyeworm and ectos Sheep: RW and ectos (sheep scab)	Ivermectin
Ecomectin sheep drench dose G2630	Roundworm, nasal bot	Sheep & G	Ivermectin

Poisoning

PLANT POISONING

The term poison is given to a substance which causes damage to the animal body. The syndrome of poisoning is dose-dependent, which means that even essential nutrients or normally harmless substances can cause problems if taken in large quantities. Livestock are usually poisoned by plants, water, accidental or malicious poisoning with chemicals or by incorrect application of remedies.

Plant poisoning is a very important cause of stock losses in South Africa; at present there are roughly 600 indigenous plants known to cause poisoning as well as numerous exotic plants. The cost of plant poisoning in livestock is estimated to be R100 million per year as a result of direct losses. The indirect losses due to production loss is thought to be much higher due to loss of productivity of the animals that survive. Plant poisoning occurs under a variety of circumstances, for example when pastures are overgrazed because of drought or overstocking, when animals may be forced to eat toxic plants. Grazing of poisonous plants can also occur when veld has been burnt or when animals unfamiliar with the local plants are introduced. Overgrazing can cause the invasion and dominance of certain toxic plants. In addition, some plants become toxic under certain conditions, either due to damage which causes the formation of prussic acid or due to contamination with fungus which produces mycotoxins.

Plant poisoning must be prevented as far as possible because there are few cases where there is a specific treatment, and supportive treatment to salvage animals is very expensive. Prevention of poisoning must be done by familiarising oneself with poisonous plants and avoiding them, preventing overgrazing and monitoring animals in planted pastures during danger periods.

It is not possible to cover all the plants involved in poisonings so only the most important are discussed here. For more complete information consult Poisoning of Livestock in SA, available online or consult a local veterinarian.

Heart poisons

It is estimated that this group causes almost 40% of all the poisonings of cattle. With the exception of "gousiekte" poisoning in which the heart shows a typical lesion on post-mortem, most heart poisonings are difficult to diagnose and have to be determined on the basis of symptoms seen in live animals and the presence of the plants on the affected farm.

"Gifblaar" (Dichepetalum cymosum)

This plant occurs in the north-east area of the country. It contains a substance which causes acute heart failure. The presence of the plant in the veld is usually indicated by wild seringa (*Burkea africana*) and lekkerbreek (*Ochna pulchra*) trees. The gifblaar plant is characterised by the looping of the veins at the tip of the leaf. It can also be confused with other plants which look similar such as "goorappel".

(*Pygmaeothamnus*), "grysappel" (*Parinari sp*) and one of the gousiekte-plants (*Pachystigma*) (see below).

Gifblaar cases are mostly acute poisonings and animals are usually found dead; occasionally they live longer and may show difficulty in

moving, hypersensitivity, trembling and rapid breathing. These animals may survive if they are rested and kept from drinking water since they often drop dead after this or on being chased. Poisoning can be prevented by camping off areas containing toxic plants. These camps must be avoided

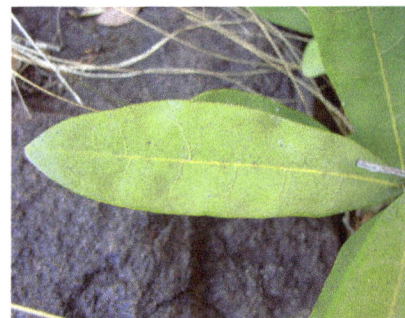

The "gifblaar" plant Dichepetalum cymosum

The plants "goorappel" and "grysappel" can be confused with the "gifblaar" plant.

during dry periods and in spring when the leaves of "Gifblaar" are the only green plants around.

"Gousiekte"

The "gousiekte" plants gousiektebossie, the wild date and "tonnabossie".

There are a number of plants that contain the poison that causes "gousiekte". They occur in the north-east area of the country. The plants concerned are *Pachystigma pygmaeum* (gousiektebossie), *Fadogia homblei* (wild date) and *Pavetta* sp

("tonnabossie"). The toxin causes deaths after a latent period, 4-8 weeks after first eating the plant. The symptoms seen are typical of heart failure, namely weakness, panting, respiratory distress and swelling of the head. Affected animals may drop dead on handling or on exposure to stress. On post-mortem, signs consistent with heart failure are seen. Poisoning by "gousiekte" plants must be prevented by good veld management, preventing overstocking and overgrazing, so that animals are not forced to graze these plants. There is no specific treatment but animals may survive if kept quiet.

Cardiac glycoside plants "Tulp" and "Slangkop"

There are a wide range of plants in SA which contain cardiac glycosides and the group is one of the most important causes of stock poisoning. Most important are the "tulp", "slangkop" and "plakkie" groups. The cardiac glycosides affect three body systems, the heart, the gastro-intestinal system and the nervous system. Generally, the latter is a chronic, cumulative poisoning caused by the plakkie group of plants and will be discussed under the heading "krimpsiekte" under nervous system poisons.

The "tulp" group includes the bulbous plants of the *Homeria* and *Morea* spp. The plants are found in the central and western areas of the country, as well as certain areas of the eastern Cape. Tulp poisoning affects cattle, sheep and goats and most commonly occurs in animals either newly introduced into areas or hungry animals introduced onto barren winter pastures where the only greenery is sprouting tulp blubs.

Animals familiar with the plant do not willingly eat tulp and even stabled animals offered the plants will refuse

them. Control is management of tulp-infested pastures, by camping off or eradication which is difficult because the plants form corms or bulbs.

"Slangkop" plants include *Urginea* sp, *Ornithoglossum* (Karoo slangkop), and *Scilla* sp (blue squill). Animals eating "slangkop" show listlessness, hold their heads down and groan, and show hindlimb weakness and diarrhoea. Diagnosis of these cases is based on clinical symptoms, signs of the plants being grazed, and general signs at post-mortem of heart failure.

Animals suspected of "tulp" or

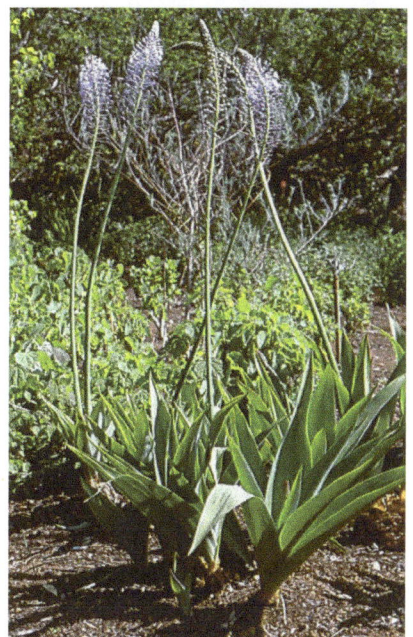

The "tulp" species like Morea plant and Scilla contain cardiac glycosides.

"slangkop" poisoning can be treated effectively with the administration of activated charcoal at 2g/kg body weight. The addition of oils or other substances is not recommended because it deactivates the charcoal. Specific veterinary treatment can be sought for valuable animals.

Other plants containing cardiac glycosides are oleander, poisonous rope (*Stropanthus sp*), milkweed and Bushman's poison bush.

Liver poisons

The liver is the organ most commonly affected by poisonings because it plays a role in detoxifying substances absorbed into the system. The plant poisons that affect the liver may cause an acute condition with sudden death, or a chronic condition with weight loss and jaundice. Some of those that cause liver damage also cause photosensitivity, a condition which causes sensitivity to light and causes inflammation of the skin.

Crotalaria sp Januariebos, Dune bush

C. sparthoides (Kalahari region)
C.globifera (KZN, Mpumalanga and Gauteng)
C. dura (KZN)
C. burkeana (Northern parts of SA)

This broom-like plant causes chronic liver damage in cattle, sheep and goats which is characterised by depression, lack of appetite, constipation and jaundice. Because of the chronic nature of the disease there is no specific treatment except avoidance of pastures on which the plant is found. In cattle *C. burkeana* causes "stywesiekte", a laminitis or inflammation of the hooves. This causes lameness initially and then the hooves grow out and turn up at the ends.

Galenia africana Salt bush "Kraalbos"

Poisoning due to "kraalbos" ingestion occurs in dry western parts such as the Karoo and the plant is eaten mainly during periods of drought. Chronic intake causes liver damage which manifests with fluid accumulation in the abdomen. The condition is known colloquially as "waterpens". On post-mortem the liver is seen to be severely fibrous (cirrhotic) and a diagnosis can usually be made based on the presence of the plant, the typical symptoms of "waterpens" and signs of liver cirrhosis.

Pteronia pallens Scholtz bush
Hertia pallens "Springbokbos"

These are Karoo bushes which can sporadically cause liver toxicity when they are eaten during dry periods or when new sheep or goats are introduced onto farms. Affected animals may show apathy which can be confused with "domsiekte", and jaundice may be seen as a result of the liver damage. Damage to the kidneys and lungs may also be seen.

Seneciosis (Ragwort)

This is one of the main causes of liver poisoning in cattle and to a lesser degree in sheep. The plant *Senecio latifolius* is found in the eastern and north-eastern areas of the country where it can be invasive. It is typically found in open veld, on mountain slopes and in marshy areas. It can also cause problems by contaminating hay. In livestock it causes a chronic damage to the liver which results in progressive wasting. Animals show depression, poor appetite, abdominal pain, constipation and jaundice. By the time the clinical signs are seen, liver damage is extensive

and irreversible. There are various strategies for control: either the avoidance of contaminated pastures, dosing of animals with activated charcoal before grazing, or grazing the pastures in winter when the plant dies back.

The ragwort Senecio latifolius

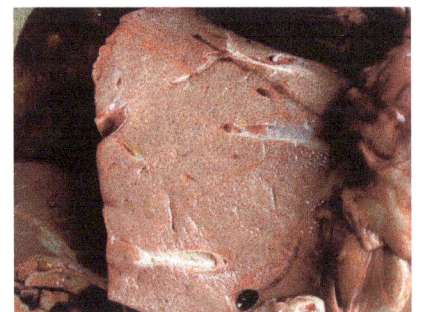

Liver damage caused by Senecio poisoning.

Photosensitivity

There are a wide range of plants in SA which cause this condition: photosensitivity is the sensitivity of the skin to sunlight when certain toxic substances reach the bloodstream. Interaction of sunlight with the toxic substance causes irritation, and inflammation. Affected animals avoid sunlight, scratch, rub and stamp their feet. Unpigmented or unprotected skin areas are affected, showing reddening and swelling, especially of the head. The ears often hang and the lips swell. The skin may crack and ooze serum, which then results in crusting. The eyelids and the lips become stiff and immobile, and skin may actually fall off. In sheep the heads are affected except in black-headed Persian sheep which show swelling of the body rather than the head. Friesland cattle show inflammation of the white areas on the body and Afrikaner cattle show lesions on the muzzle.

When treating these cases, the essentials are firstly removal from the source of poisoning, providing shelter from the sun, fresh water and soft feed. If the skin lesions are mild and non-extensive apply wound oil to prevent infection

A sheep with an early case of photosensitivity showing swelling of the head and jaundice

and soften the hard, crusty areas. Severely affected animals may need injectable antibiotics to prevent secondary infections. If the eyelids are affected use eye ointments to prevent infections and soften the skin. Severely affected animals may need veterinary aid for liver support and cortisone to reduce the inflammation.

A sheep with an advanced case of photosensitivity showing peeling of the skin and irritation of the eyes.

Vuursiekte syndrome

The three plants below cause a similar syndrome in sheep which can be very severe and lead to serious losses: after a few days of grazing sheep begin to seek shade, rub their ears and noses. Their ears, eyelids and lips swell and they may show jaundice due to liver damage. The swelling of the ears and the face may be mild or extreme. After 24 hours, the swelling subsides because the skin begins to ooze serum and this dries to form crusts on the skin. The affected animals lose condition dramatically and the affected skin may peel off leaving smooth pink areas of skin. The plants are seldom eaten voluntarily unless forced by circumstances. Prevention is therefore avoidance of pastures on which these plants are found unless there is sufficient other grazing.

Assemia axillaris "Vuursiektebossie"

This is a woody herb found in arid areas but grows near dams and pans. It becomes an invader especially in overgrazed veld when in becomes inundated by flooding.

Athanasia sp "Klaaslouwbos"

This an unpalatable bush common on ploughed and disturbed lands in the south and south-eastern Cape.

Regarded as a weed, it is unpalatable, and is only eaten when sheep are forced by circumstances to do so.

Lasiospermum bipinnatum "Ganskweek"

These are soft herblike plants with white daisy type flowers. They occur in the eastern Karoo, especially around Graaff-Reinet and areas in the Free State. The plant is unpalatable and mainly eaten when sheep are hungry or overcrowded. It is highly toxic to sheep and causes liver damage and photosensitivity, as well as damage to the lungs. Prevention is avoidance of infested pastures.

Lantana camara Lantana

This is a declared weed of American origin which has spread from gardens to the warm wet eastern and coastal areas all over SA, and invades farms and plantations. It has an enormous potential for spreading since readily eat the berries. Although it has a pungent smell and thorny stems, it is browsed by livestock especially during winter months when natural grazing becomes unpalatable and other browse is unavailable. The plant is one of the most common causes of liver damage and photosensitivity in cattle, since sheep seldom eat it. When ingested by cattle photosensitivity will be noted on white skin patches which show reddening, swelling and peeling of the skin. Other symptoms are rumen stasis, constipation or diarrhoea due to liver damage as a result of continuous intake. The plant should be controlled by cutting it down to prevent the leaves being eaten and the stumps then treated with suitable herbicide.

Lupins

Lupins are cultivated in some areas for fodder, especially in the Western Cape. The plants and their pods become infested with a fungus during wet warm seasons. The fungus produces a poison which causes liver damage, jaundice and mild signs of photosensitivity. Sheep may die a week after grazing on infested lupins. When the weather conditions are favourable use small numbers of animals to check whether the pastures are safe.

When sheep and cattle feed on bitter lupin seeds, they may develop poisoning, specifically an alkalosis. Symptoms may appear a few hours after ingestion and stimulation or exercise causes muscle tremors, staggering and paralysis. Death occurs due to asphyxiation within a few hours. As for urea poisoning, the use of vinegar will reverse the alkalosis.

Microcystis Blue-green algae/ cyanobacteria

This blue-green "algae" is actually an aquatic bacterium which is widespread all-over South Africa but flourishes during the warm summer months. It causes poisoning in Gauteng and the Free State, particularly around the Hartebeespoort and Vaal dams. The bacterium grows on the surface of dams or pans during hot weather when the water is full of nutrients. It is visible as a green, scum-like growth often on the leeward verge of the dam, but may gradually cover the whole surface. As the bacteria begin to die off, they release a toxin into the water which has an extremely unpleasant smell.

Animals drinking water containing *Microcystis* toxin develop either an acute case of massive liver failure which results in death or a more sub-acute condition with photosensitivity, lack of appetite, constipation, weakness and jaundice. The diagnosis is based on a history of Microcystis blooms on drinking water, typical symptoms and liver damage seen on post-mortem.

Microcystis bacteria on the surface of a dam

Lantana camara an invasive alien, is one of the commonest causes of liver damage in cattle in South Africa.

Panicum sp Buffalo grass ("Dikoor")

Buffalo grass pastures can cause the syndrome "dikoor" under certain conditions thought to be similar to those that precipitate "geeldikkop" (see below). This grass is cultivated in the summer rainfall areas of the Gauteng Highveld and Free State and is usually very good grazing. It becomes problematic during dry summer periods when the grass is withered and a fungus is believed to grow on the heads.

Affected sheep show swollen red faces, and very swollen ears (hence the name "dikoor"). The skin then hardens and becomes crusty. The skin around the claws may also be affected and may be confused with cases of blue tongue. On post-mortem the liver is yellow and friable. Sheep on Panicum pastures in late summer must be supervised daily for signs of symptoms.

Panicum maximum grass which can cause "dikoor" under certain conditions.

Tribulus terrestris Devil's thorn ("Dubbeltjies") ("Geeldikkop")

This is a sprawling indigenous weed with yellow flowers which occurs all over the country. It has characteristic thorns which gave rise to the common names. In arid regions such as the Karoo it is a useful grazing plant but under certain conditions, usually when it is wilted, it can cause problems. It is thought that fungi growing on the plant cause it to become toxic and under these conditions huge losses can be suffered in sheep flocks. "Geeldikkop" is the colloquial name used to describe the symptoms of swelling of the head and the jaundice which occurs due to liver damage. The skin swells particularly on the head and the skin around the eyes and the mouth often cracks. "Geeldikkop" must not be confused with other conditions such as clostridial "dikkop" of rams, blue tongue and snakebite which also cause swollen heads in sheep. The diagnosis of "geeldikkop" is made based on the history of animals eating damaged "dubbeltjies", the typical symptoms and the pathology which shows severe liver damage.

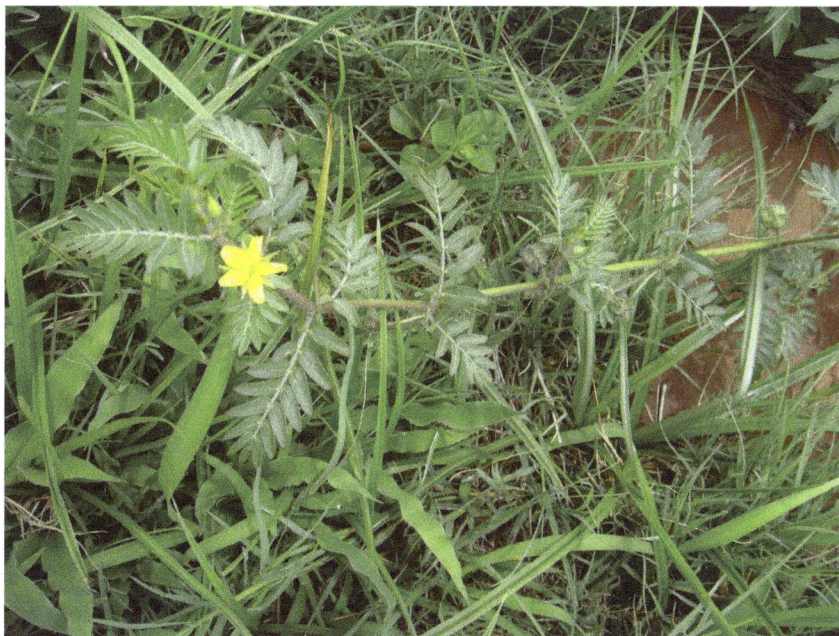

Tribulus terrestris or dubbeltjies causes the syndrome "geeldikkop".

Nervous system

There is a wide range of plants that can affect the nervous system, including the "tremorgenic" conditions caused by fungal infection of certain pastures, "krimpsiekte" and various other plants which are less frequent causes of problems.

Albizia versicolor Poison pod albizia (Eastern KZN and Mpumalanga) Albizia tanganyicensis Paperbark albizia (Waterberg, Limpopo)

The pods of these plants contain a neurotoxin which causes symptoms of hypersensitivity, convulsions and high temperature, which can be confused with heartwater in these regions. The pods are eaten mainly in late winter and spring when they are blown off the trees by wind. The diagnosis is based on the symptoms and finding parts of the pods in the rumen. The condition can be treated with vitamin B6 if given early enough.

Aspergillus clavatus

Sorghum residue or "maroek" which is used as an animal feed rapidly becomes contaminated with fungi after leaving the factory. Contamination with A. clavatus causes a neurological intoxication and a high percentage of mortalities. The animals show hypersensitivity, ataxia, muscle weakness and paralysis. The animals stagger around drunkenly and lie paralysed and trembling until they die. Affected animals are alert but they are unable to eat or drink and show salivation. The diagnosis is based on the history of eating sorghum residue or sprouted maize, the development of nervous symptoms, and on typical lesions that will be seen in the brain on post-mortem. There is no treatment for this condition.

Cynodon Couch grass "Kweek" tremors

Cynodon dactylon is widespread in South Africa and is cultivated as a pasture. Occasionally pastures become infected with fungi in winter months and cause poisoning in cattle and sheep. The syndrome is characterised by muscular tremors, ataxia and paresis, and resembles "maroek" but rarely causes deaths. Although the symptoms can last for a few weeks, most animals recover with no ill effects and continue to eat and drink during their illness.

Cynanchum sp Bobbejaantou/ Klimop

These are creepers that grow in coastal areas from Namaqualand to Port Elizabeth but also in wooded valleys in Limpopo Province. They have bright green, succulent leaves which exude a milky latex when cut. Cases of poisoning have been described in cattle and sheep; animals show staggering, tremors and tetanic convulsions terminating in paralysis before either recovery or death, depending on the amount eaten.

Diplodia maydis (new name Stenocarpella) Diplodiosis

The fungus Diplodia grows on maize cobs (ear and stem rot) and is seen as a white growth. The fungus develops black spore forming heads which distinguishes it from other fungi. This condition is seen mainly in cattle grazing maize lands in winter in the maize areas of the northwestern Free State, Mpumalanga and KZN, especially during cool wet weather. The condition is seen less commonly in sheep.

The symptoms of poisoning are weakness, reluctance to move, a wide-legged gait, high stepping and paralysis. However, recovery often occurs after these dramatic symptoms, mortality rate is low and removal from the affected fields will resolve the problem.

Dipcadi glaucum Wild onion "Malkop-ui"

This bulbous plant is a perennial which grows in focal areas in the Limpopo, Northern Cape Province near Griqualand-West, and adjoining areas in the Free State. The plant causes losses in sheep that eat the bulbs. They show loss of appetite, diarrhoea, and typical head-pressing – which gives the plant its name.

Helichrysum argyrosphaerum Wild everlasting, "Poprosie"

This creeping annual with papery flowers has a wide distribution in South Africa but is concentrated in the central and eastern parts of the country. However, outbreaks of poisoning in livestock have so far only occurred in Namibia. Poisoning is most commonly seen in sheep which develop blindness due to damage to the optical lobe of the brain. Apart from blindness, the animals may have nervous signs such as circling, "star-gazing" and various degrees of paralysis. Cattle are occasionally affected but do not develop blindness; they become weak and paralytic. Blindness in sheep due to brain damage also occurs with rafoxanide or closantel poisoning.

"Krimpsiekte"

This is the chronic poisoning by certain cardiac glycoside containing plants, specifically the "plakkie" group which includes Cotyledon sp, Kalanchoe and Tylecodon.

These plants occur mainly in the dry western areas of the country, the

Little Karoo and the southern fringes of the Great Karoo. The incidence of krimpsiekte is highest in goats, but sheep and cattle are also affected. Poisoning often affects newly introduced animals not familiar with the plants that cause krimpsiekte. It can occur throughout the year but is most common in spring during drought years when animals are inclined to eat plants they normally would avoid.

Symptoms of "krimpsiekte" are varying degrees of paralysis: in early stages animals lag behind the flock, tire easily when driven and lie down trembling with feet held together, the back arched and head low. The neck may be twisted and held low. There is also a bloat form called "opblaaskrimpsiekte". There is no treatment for "krimpsiekte" and **the meat of animals that have died from "krimpsiekte" is not suitable for eating as secondary intoxication can result.**

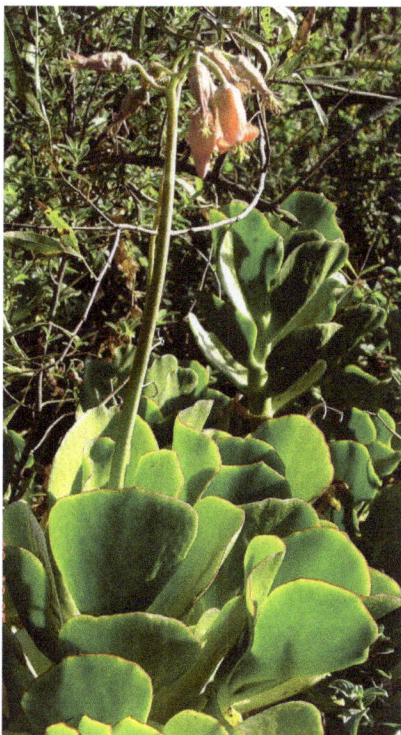

Krimpsiekte plant or plakkie (Cotyledon).

"Paspalum staggers"

A fungal infection of *Paspalum dilatatum* (Dallis grass) grass causes non-fatal nervous symptoms in cattle, and less often in sheep. This grass grows on clay and loam soils, mainly in the eastern and coastal areas of the country, either in cultivated lands, roadsides or marshes and vleis. After a few days of grazing on infected pastures animals show hypersensitivity, tremors and poor coordination. The grass should be grazed heavily in spring and summer to prevent the development of seed heads. Toxic pastures can also be rendered safe by mowing.

Phalaris Canary grass

Phalaris poisoning or "staggers" occurs on cultivated pastures of these exotic grasses when grazed predominantly. *Phalaris* poisoning can cause sudden death, an acute form with temporary nervous symptoms or a chronic fatal nervous condition in sheep which occurs 2-3 weeks after grazing the pastures. The number of animals affected varies from 5-50%. Cattle are less severely affected, showing stiffness and dragging of the feet.

Remove animals from the pasture as soon as they show signs of poisoning. Animals can be dosed with cobalt bullets to prevent the condition.

Melia azedarach Syringa

This is a commonly cultivated exotic tree with scented purple flowers and yellowish fleshy berries at the end of summer. It causes occasional poisoning in cattle and sheep. Poisoned animals show restlessness and muscle tremors before dying soon after ingestion. There are no typical lesions on post-mortem but finding the seeds in the digestive tract can confirm the diagnosis. There is no specific treatment.

Melica decumbens Staggers grass

This tufted grass occurs in the eastern part of the Karoo and Free State. It causes problems in cattle and occasionally sheep, particularly late in winter and spring just after the rain. Poisoning causes unsteadiness and high stepping gait. Animals still have good appetites and usually recover if removed from the pastures and given good care.

Ryegrass poisoning "Annual Ryegrass Toxicity"

Ryegrass, or annual ryegrass (*Lolium sp*) as it is commonly known, is widespread in SA – either as a cultivated pasture or on stubble or fallow lands. When ryegrass becomes infected with tiny nematodes, they sometimes carry bacteria into the plant. These bacteria are responsible for poisoning of stock grazing on the pastures. Animals develop nervous signs, show abortions and a high percentage of mortality. Veterinary treatment is required for animals showing severe nervous symptoms. The diagnosis of outbreaks can be made on microscopic examination of the ears of ryegrass at a veterinary laboratory with experience. Control of the condition is grazing these lands before they develop seeds, burning these fields or using selective herbicides to control the ryegrass.

Solanum kwebense Red berry "Maldronksiekte"

This plant produces fruits which contain a toxic substance, which causes the condition called "maldronksiekte" in cattle. This small shrub occurs in the extreme north of the Limpopo Province, particularly under Acacia erubescens ("geelhaak") trees. It resembles the other Solanum sp with grey green leaves and blue star-shaped flowers, but has red berries. The toxin causes a specific type of damage to the nerve fibres in the brain, causing seizures in cattle. The symptoms are seen when the animal is disturbed or frightened, causing epileptic attacks from which they recover rapidly. Early emergency slaughter of affected animals will prevent loss of condition.

Affected animals may drown in dips or may suffer serious injuries during attacks. The brain lesions seen at post-mortem are characteristic and can be used for diagnosis. Good veld management to prevent overgrazing and overstocking will prevent these plants flourishing.

Sarcostemma viminale Caustic bush "Melktou"

This is a leafless succulent climber which grows in trees all over SA including the arid western areas. Cattle and sheep eat these when grazing is scarce. Angora goats are apparently partial to "melktou". Poisoning causes animals to show hypersensitivity, tremors and uncoordinated gait. They become recumbent and show tetanic spasms. More chronic cases may show paralysis and this may last for weeks.

Digestive system

Chrysocoma "Bitterbos" "Kaalsiekte"

This indigenous Karoo bush proliferates with overgrazing, especially during wet years when it becomes palatable. The plant causes two conditions of small stock. Adult sheep and goats develop diarrhoea, weakness and death. Lactating ewes or does shed the toxin in the milk and this causes skin irritation in the suckling lambs or kids. These animals constantly lick their skin causing hair loss and sometimes even impaction due to hair balls. Lambs with hair loss may die of exposure and lung infections. Lambs between 2-4 months may develop "valsiekte" which causes them to fall and drag themselves around.

Cucumis sp Wild cucumber

Wild cucumbers occur widely throughout SA (with the exception of the coastal areas), mostly on old lands and disturbed ground. The cucumbers are quite bitter and are usually only eaten by very hungry animals. They are very poisonous and many animals die without any symptoms, while milder cases show diarrhoea and weakness.

Geigeria sp "Vermeersiekte"

This is an important cause of losses in sheep in the Griqualand-West area in SA. The plant is palatable and valuable grazing when eaten together with other plants, and only becomes a problem when it forms the bulk of the diet. This situation arises when veld is degraded and the plant dominates over grass in grazing. Merino and Karakul sheep appear to be more susceptible than other breeds. Cattle and goats develop paralysis when ingesting this plant. In sheep, the toxin damages the muscles of the oesophagus causing, it to widen and preventing swallowing. Affected animals regurgitate rumen content and their lips and nose are usually smeared with rumen content. The cud may collect in the cheeks. In addition to regurgitation, animals may cough, have diarrhoea, bloat and show stiffness and paralysis. On post-mortem the dilated oesophagus can be clearly seen. Animals mildly affected will recover if removed from the problem pastures. There is no economically viable treatment for badly affected animals. Prevention is resting the pastures in which Geigeria sp dominate and allowing the grass and other herbs to re-establish themselves.

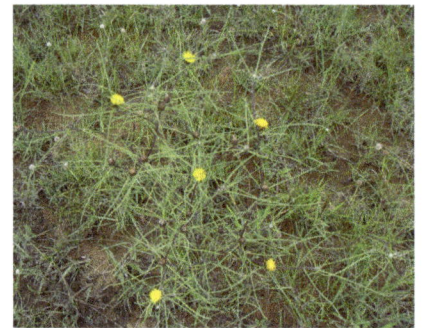

Geigeria the "vermeersiektebossie"

Ornithogalum sp Chinkerinchee

This bulbous plant occurs in focal areas in the Western Cape where it is a common cause of problems. However, it is found widely throughout South Africa. This is a highly toxic plant for humans as well as livestock. Animals ingest the plants when it is accidentally included in cattle feeds, or when they are extremely hungry. The plant causes very severe diarrhoea which may last for weeks and can eventually cause death. Cattle may develop temporary or permanent blindness. Animals can be treated by dosing with activated charcoal, fluid administration and supportive therapy.

Pennisetum clandestinum "Kikuyu poisoning"

Kikuyu pastures that are attacked by army worm infestations (Spodoptera exempta) become highly toxic, probably due to secondary infection by fungus. The pasture becomes toxic roughly 10 days after the initial worm damage. Cattle are the species usually affected. Early signs of intoxication are drooling and "sham drinking" – animals dipping their mouths in the water but not actually drinking. The animals become severely dehydrated because of the paralysis of the tongue. They also show bloat and later limb weakness which causes a wobbly gait and collapse. The mortality rate of affected animals can be as high as 80%. The diagnosis is based on the history of grazing on kikuyu pastures and the typical symptoms. On post-mortem, the forestomachs typically show necrosis of the mucosa.

Cattle must be removed from the pasture for roughly 40 days and animals of low value must be used to test whether the pasture is safe.

Ricinus sp Castor oil

This is a large shrub which was grown in gardens as an ornamental plant and is now a declared invader. It produces decoratively patterned seeds which are very toxic, but the leaves are also reported to be poisonous for livestock. Although castor oil is not very toxic because of the heating it undergoes during processing, the seed cake which remains after pressing to extract oil, is sometimes accidentally included in livestock rations. The symptoms of poisoning are collapse and severe diarrhoea, which terminates in death. There is no specific or economical form of treatment and only the symptoms can be addressed.

Kidneys and bladder
Oxalate-containing plants

There are a number of plants in SA that contain oxalic acid: *Oxalis sp* (suring), *Rumex* (sorrel),

Mesembryanthemum (vygies), *Amaranthus* (marog), *Opuntia* (prickly pears), *Portulacaria* (spekboom) and *Agave* (garingboom), as well as certain vegetables namely rhubarb, beetroot, and spinach. Sheep are most commonly affected when they are forced to eat these plants but whether poisoning develops or not, depends on the level of oxalic acid in the plants and how much is eaten by the animals. Oxalic acid forms insoluble oxalate crystals which accumulate in and damage the kidneys. In acute forms there is milk fever-like syndrome, reduced motility of the gut, depression, weakness, and coma. Chronic poisoning will cause depression, lethargy, stiffness, recumbency and death. The diagnosis of oxalate poisoning is usually confirmed by doing histology on animals that have died or been sacrificed. Oxalate poisoning can be prevented by rotating pastures or if this is unavoidable, the animals can be fed a 25% dicalcium phosphate in a salt lick as a preventative measure.

Tannic acid poisoning

Exotic *Acacia* sp (wattles) contain tannic acid which initially causes constipation and then diarrhoea. Massive quantities of tannic acid can cause liver and kidney damage. In addition to these effects, tannic acid inhibits protein metabolism in ruminants. This is a problem especially in antelope when they are forced to browse heavily on small properties, during droughts or winter seasons. These animals may die from starvation despite the apparent presence of sufficient browse.

Reproductive system
Salsola tuberculatiformis

This is a Karoo bush which when

eaten by sheep in the last stages of pregnancy will delay lambing. This results in the foetus growing very large and sometimes being unable to be born naturally. This condition is discussed in more detail under "Reproductive diseases".

Trifolium sp Clover
Medicago Lucerne

Clover pastures contain substances with oestrogenic effects and may cause reproductive disturbances such as vaginal prolapse in sheep (see reproductive sections). They are not often used in SA because of these potential problems. More commonly, lucerne pastures may be implicated in low-grade fertility problems due to the production of oestrogens. Consult a veterinarian to establish the diagnosis if this is suspected.

Prussic acid poisoning "Geilsiekte"

Plants that contain substances called cyanogenic glycosides become toxic when trampled, frosted or damaged in some way because this process releases enzymes which then release hydrogen cyanide (prussic acid). Examples of plants that can potentially cause this poisoning are sorghum, *Cynodon* (couch grass or "kweek"), Namaqua daisies (*Dimorphotheca sp*) and some of the acacia species (*caffra, erioloba, sieberiana*). Symptoms of prussic acid poisoning are difficult breathing and convulsions, but most of the animals affected die acutely with minimal signs. On post-mortem examination, these cases can be confused with pulpy kidney, as the kidneys decompose quickly. Prevention of prussic acid can be achieved by feeding sulphur in the form of flowers of sulphur in a lick at 5-7%, or hypo (sodium thiosulphate) in drinking water at a rate of 1kg/2000 l in summer, or 1kg /1000l in winter.

Couch grass or "kweek" can cause "geilsiekte" or prussic acid poisoning.

Nitrate poisoning

Some plants accumulate nitrates especially *Amaranthus* (pigweed), *Brassica sp*, oats, ryegrass, sorghum and wheat. In addition, pastures fertilised with nitrate-containing fertilisers can raise the nitrate levels and are becoming increasingly important as a source of low-grade poisoning. Chronic nitrate poisoning symptoms are the suppression of appetite, abortions and bloat. Nitrate fertilisation can also lead to vitamin A deficiency. Deaths due to nitrate poisoning occur often when hungry animals are chased into nitrate fertilised pastures. Avoiding pastures for 21 days after they have received nitrate fertilisation is an important preventative measure.

Acute nitrate poisoning causes difficult breathing, weakness, brown discolouration of the mucous membranes and diarrhoea. On post mortem the blood is a characteristic brown colour. Veterinary help must be sought when nitrate poisoning is suspected to establish a correct diagnosis and give specific treatment to affected animals. Methylene blue can be administered by a veterinarian for treatment of clinical cases of nitrate poisoning.

Amaranthus spp or "marog" contain high levels of nitrate.

CHEMICAL POISONING

Agricultural chemicals

Chemicals such as herbicides and insecticides are still an important cause of stock poisoning in livestock either accidentally or as a result of malicious actions. According to the toxicology section of Onderstepoort, aldicarb, carbofuran, terbuphos, tetrachlorphinvos and endosulphan are the most common chemical causes of livestock poisoning. The safe application, handling, and storage of these chemicals is therefore of cardinal importance. Overdosing animals with dewormers and making up dips incorrectly still cause poisonings of stock and underlines the importance of reading labels carefully. Organophosphate poisoning can be treated with veterinary help if given timeously, but for most there are no specific antidotes.

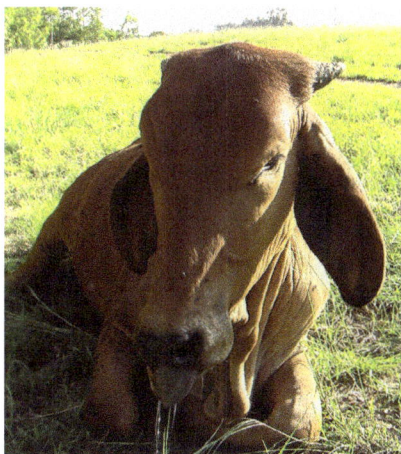

Organophosphate poisoning in a bovine showing salivation and paralysis of the tongue.

Copper poisoning

Sheep are more susceptible than cattle to copper poisoning; they are most commonly poisoned by the feeding of poultry manure, the administration of copper sulphate to correct deficiencies in certain areas, and high levels of copper in the soil in some areas of the Karoo ("enzootic icterus").

Cattle are sometimes poisoned by drinking water from footbaths containing copper sulphate. Acute copper poisoning causes abdominal pain and green mucoid diarrhoea. Affected animals usually die within 12 hours of ingesting the copper source. Chronic poisoning (enzootic icterus) often manifests with an acute haemolytic disease when animals are stressed. These animals show anaemia, haemoglobinuria and jaundice. On post-mortem the carcase is typically yellow and there is a black discolouration of the kidneys. There is no specific treatment but in areas with high copper levels in the soil, dosing the animals with molybdenum pellets may be used to prevent chronic poisoning.

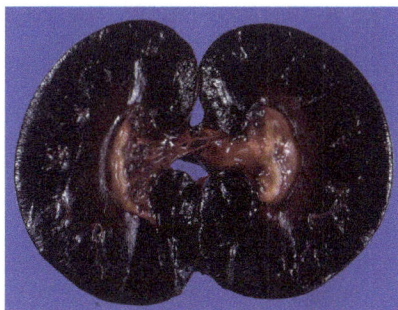

The typical black kidneys seen with copper poisoning.

Lead poisoning

Lead poisoning still occurs sporadically in livestock as a result of ingestion of batteries, lead soldering and insecticides containing lead. It is a nerve toxin which affects young animals more severely than adults. Symptoms seen are rolling of the eyes, convulsions and a high-stepping gait, but blindness and tooth grinding may also be seen. The diagnosis of lead poisoning can be done by taking liver and kidney samples for analysis. Chronic cases are seldom salvaged by treatment due to the irreversible nerve damage.

Urea poisoning

The use of urea as a non-protein source of nitrogen for ruminants is useful but if not properly managed can cause poisoning. This occurs when urea is not properly mixed in rations, or lick blocks disintegrate and fall into water sources. Urea blocks in drums may dissolve in rainwater and be drunk, causing poisoning. Urea licks should have salt added to limit the intake. Cattle do develop tolerance to urea but should be allowed to adapt slowly.

Urea poisoning results in a generalised alkalosis (increased pH) of the system which causes nervous symptoms such as lack of balance, and signs of difficult breathing due to an accumulation of fluid in the lungs. Confirmation of the diagnosis is based on a history of feeding of urea, typical symptoms and a high rumen pH.

Deaths can occur rapidly if the animals are not treated promptly by administering vinegar to neutralise the alkalosis. In cattle, give 2 litres which can be repeated again after a few hours. If animals are so severely affected that they cannot breathe, the vinegar must be delivered into the rumen. Per acute deaths with rapid post mortem bloating and subcutaneous "swelling" is also seen. On post mortem the carcases of affected animals give the impression of advanced decomposition although they may have died recently.

WATER

The quality of drinking water given to livestock is often overlooked. Dairy cattle are particularly affected by poor quality water because of their high daily intake. Poor quality water occasionally causes severe clinical disease and production losses in dairy herds.

Brackish water

One of the main water problems in certain areas of the country is brackishness: this is caused by the presence of high levels of various salts in underground water, as a result of local geological conditions. The salts involved can be sodium chloride, magnesium chloride, sodium sulphate or magnesium sulphate. Animals forced to drink brackish water show decreased water- and also food intake; they can also suffer from diarrhoea due to high concentration of magnesium salts. The brackishness of water is aggravated when it is pumped into troughs and evaporates during the day, increasing the concentration of salts. Regular cleaning of troughs will result in less unpalatable water. Since not all boreholes in these areas are brackish, one should look for the most palatable water for livestock drinking water or make use of rainwater. Salt (Na Cl) poisoning is occasionally seen in ruminants exposed to contaminated water.

Nitrates

Certain areas in the country have high levels of nitrates in underground water, particularly areas like the Springbok flats near Pretoria, certain areas in Limpopo and the north-western Cape. Nitrate contamination of water sources such as streams, dams and underground water can result from run-off from fertilised lands or sewerage contamination. Chronic nitrate poisoning can result from high levels of contamination (see under Nitrate containing plants for symptoms and treatment).

Fluoride and other metals

Fluoride may be present in high levels either naturally, for example in the northern Cape, or due to contamination by mining activities. Fluorosis is an uncommon cause of poor performance in livestock but has been known to cause skeletal problems in dairy cattle, namely fractures and lameness, and lowered fertility and milk production may also be seen. Mining activities in farming areas can also cause contamination of water sources with other heavy metals such as lead and arsenic which may affect production or cause toxicity.

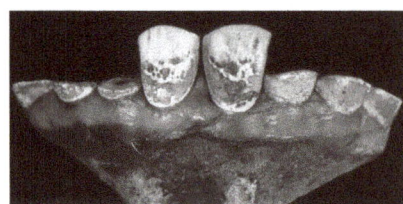

A case of fluorosis in a bovine showing tooth damage.

Suitability of water for livestock

In general, the mineral content of water used for livestock is the same as that required for human consumption, but since the water sources used for animals on a farm are often different from those used by humans, it can be useful to have borehole or river water analysed for its suitability. The table below contains rough guidelines for good quality water.

General requirements for water suitable for livestock

Parameter	Maximum permissible level
Solids	5 000 ppm
pH	5,6-9
Sodium	2 000 ppm
Calcium	1 000 ppm
Magnesium	500 ppm
Chloride	3 000 ppm
Sulphate	1 000 ppm
Fluoride	6 ppm
Nitrate	400 ppm

Ref Casey et al, 1998.

SAFETY ON THE FARM

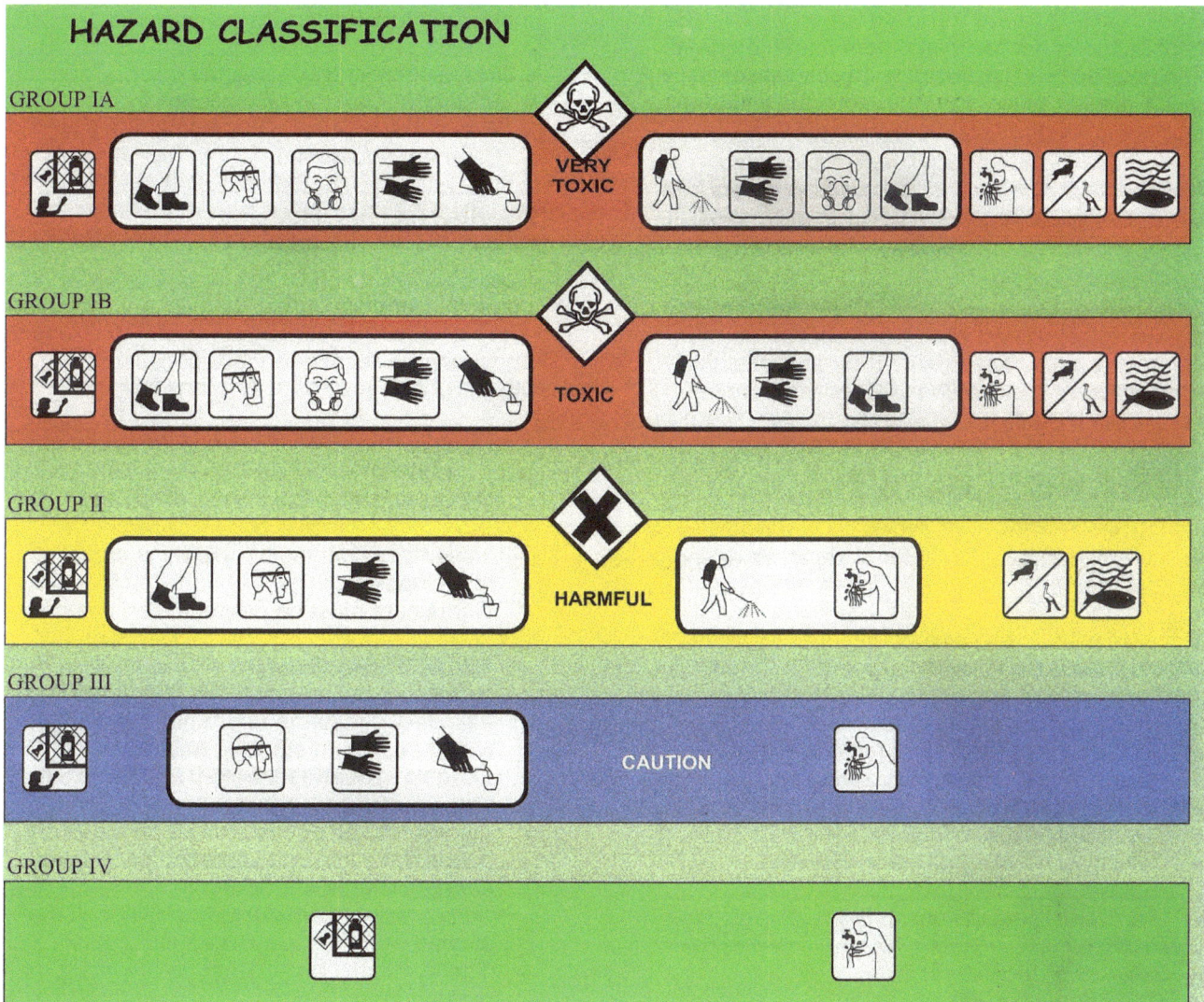

HAZARD CLASSIFICATION

GROUP IA — VERY TOXIC

GROUP IB — TOXIC

GROUP II — HARMFUL

GROUP III — CAUTION

GROUP IV

Hazard diagram

Although the veterinary remedies used nowadays are much safer than those used decades ago, such as the old arsenic dips, some of the current remedies are toxic to humans and the environment if not handled correctly. The remedies currently registered under Act 36/47 are classified for the convenience of users to indicate precautions with respect to storage, precautions and impact on the environment. It is especially the ectoparasite remedies such as dips that are of concern here. On the label of registered remedies is a "HAZARD" classification to indicate the toxicity in increasing order "Versigtig/Caution", "Skadelik/Harmful", "Toksies/Toxic" and "Baie toksies/ Very toxic".

The HAZARD CLASSIFICATION pictograms indicate how the product should be handled (see diagram). For example, from left to right the symbols of Group IA (Very Toxic) are as follows:

"Store under lock and key, wear boots, wear eye protection, use a respirator, wear gloves when handling a concentrate."

At the centre is the key for remedy application:

"Wear gloves, use a respirator, wear boots, wash hands after use." On the extreme right are the symbols which refer to the impact on the environment:

"Harmful for game, birds, fish and water life."

When transporting remedies from a depot or co-operative follow basic safety guidelines: do not load products in the front of the vehicle, make sure that containers are upright and do not pack other objects on top of containers since this could damage the neck of the container and cause a leakage. Do not transport remedies with people, feed or food. If there is a spillage avoid contact with the chemical.

The basic guidelines for personal protection are not eating, drinking or smoking during handling, and washing hands after usage. If the chemical is spilt on clothes remove them immediately and wash the skin thoroughly. The highest risk period is during the handling of concentrates, in other words during opening, measuring out and cleaning up spillages.

Follow advice on the label which may specify the use of more advanced protection such as respirators, boots and gloves. Gloves should be made of PVC, neoprene or butyl rubber, which prevents penetration of the product. Disposable polyethylene gloves or plastic bags can be used as a temporary measure. After using gloves wash them thoroughly with soap and water. Wearing gloves is recommended for the application of pyrethroid-containing pour-ons because these can potentially cause skin irritation.

When diluting products, use gloves and follow the directions on the label carefully. The quality of water used for dilution is important since hard, acid and alkaline water will prevent good mixing. Rainwater is a suitable replacement for poor quality borehole water.

A person who has had accidental contact with a poisonous chemical should be taken for medical treatment if showing one or more of the following symptoms: nausea, headache, light-headedness, salivation, cramps, vomiting, sweating, muscle weakness and anxiety. Ensure that the person can breathe normally and remove them from the contaminated area, remove the clothing and wash skin with water for 10 minutes. If the chemical was splashed into the eyes, wash with water for five minutes. Keep the person warm. Contact a doctor and make the label of the product available for reference. If the remedy has been swallowed, do not induce vomiting unless advised on the label.

Empty dip containers should never be used for any other purpose because of the danger of poisoning. To render the containers safe before disposal, use the triple rinse method as follows: fill the container to a quarter of its volume, shake vigorously and throw the contents into the dip tank. Do this three times (with the first rinse, 4000 ppm are diluted to 40 ppm, and with the third rinse to 0 ppm). Make holes in the container to render it unusable and bury the container in a refuse pit dug specially for the purpose. The pit must be fenced off and must be away from water sources. Alternately the containers can be made available for recycling. Chemical stocks which have expired, been banned or which are unusable tend to be stockpiled on farms, in sheds and outbuildings. According to authorities there are large stocks of arsenic, strychnine and DDT which are either dangerous to the handler or to the environment. Farmers are therefore hesitant to handle these stocks and when they do, sometimes experience incidents of poisoning. It is an offence and it is dangerous to dump chemicals by roadsides, in water bodies or municipal dumps, as this can cause poisonings and environmental contamination. The irresponsible disposal of poisons can cause devastation of wildlife and the impact can be extensive.

Another aspect of safety is the disposal of carcases on farms. In general, animals that have died from any disease condition should not be eaten by humans: in the case of deaths due to anthrax or rabies the carcase presents a risk to the person cutting up the meat and in the case of anthrax to a lesser degree, the person eating the carcase. Animals dying of "krimpsiekte" can cause secondary poisoning if fed to humans or even dogs. Carcases which pose a risk to human or animal health should be placed in a pit, covered with lime and buried.

Ageing Animals

AGEING ANIMALS

AGEING SHEEP & GOATS

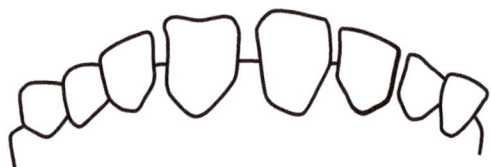

Under 1 year (baby teeth)

1 - 1.5 years (2 tooth)

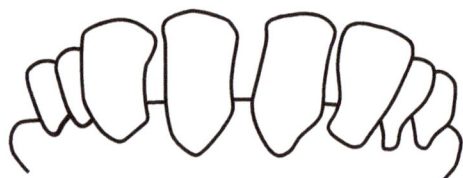

2 years (4 tooth)

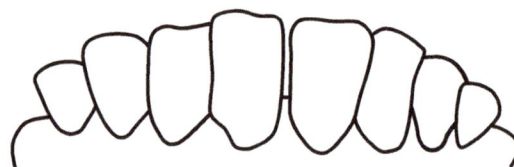

2.5 years (6 tooth)

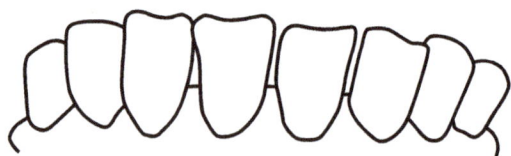

2.5 - 3 years (full mouth)

> 3 years (worn-broken)

old

AGEING CATTLE

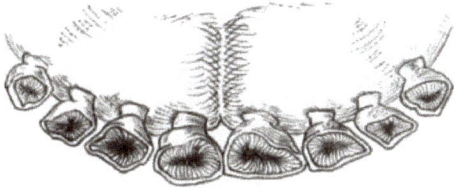

Under 21 months
4 pairs of baby, temporary incisors

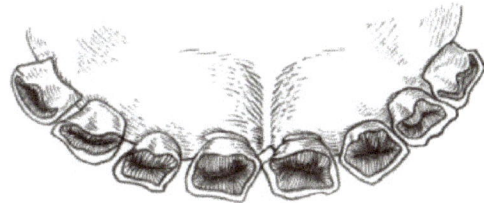

Six years:
All four pairs of permanent incisors
beginning to wear down

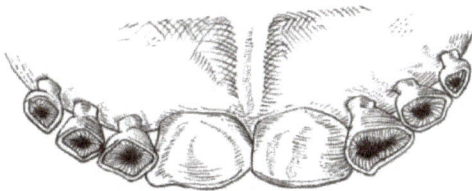

Two years
1 pairs of adult, permanent incisors

Seven years:
All four pairs of permanent incisors worn
Thirteen years:

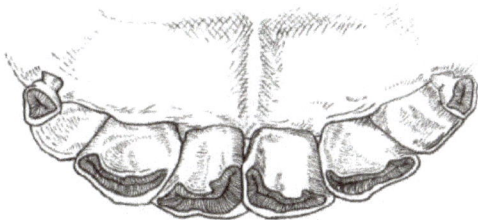

Two to two and a half years:
2 pairs of adult, permanent incisors
Two and a half years to three years:
3 pairs of adult, permanent incisors
Three to Three and a quarter years:
4 pairs of adult, permanent incisors

Thirteen years:
All four pairs of permanent incisors
badly worn and or broken

REFERENCES

A practical guide to diptank construction and management (cattle) Afrivet Training services.

Control of ticks and tick borne disease in Southern Africa PT Oberem (2017). Ticks and tick borne diseases Monograph 4. Publisher: Agriconnect.

Illustrated guide to identification of African tick species AA Latif Ticks and Tick borne diseases Monograph 2. Publisher: Agriconnect.

Livestock diseases of Southern Africa Ed Coetzer et al www.anipedia.org

Livestock Production Systems Maree C and Casey NH 1993 Agri-Development Foundation

Nguni cattle –Breed characteristics and functional efficiency (20 H. van der Pypekamp Publisher Landbou Weekblad.

Plant poisonings and mycotoxicoses of livestock in Southern Africa Kellerman et al www.anipedia.org

Ixodid ticks of major economic importance and their distribution in South Africa. AM Spickett, 2013 Latif www.anipedia.org

Tick borne diseases in Southern Africa AA Latif Ticks and tick borne diseases Monograph 3. Publisher: Agriconnect.

Veld Management -Principles and practices (2015). Frits van Oudtshoorn. Briza Publishers.

Veterinary Helminthology Ed P. Oberem www.anipedia.org

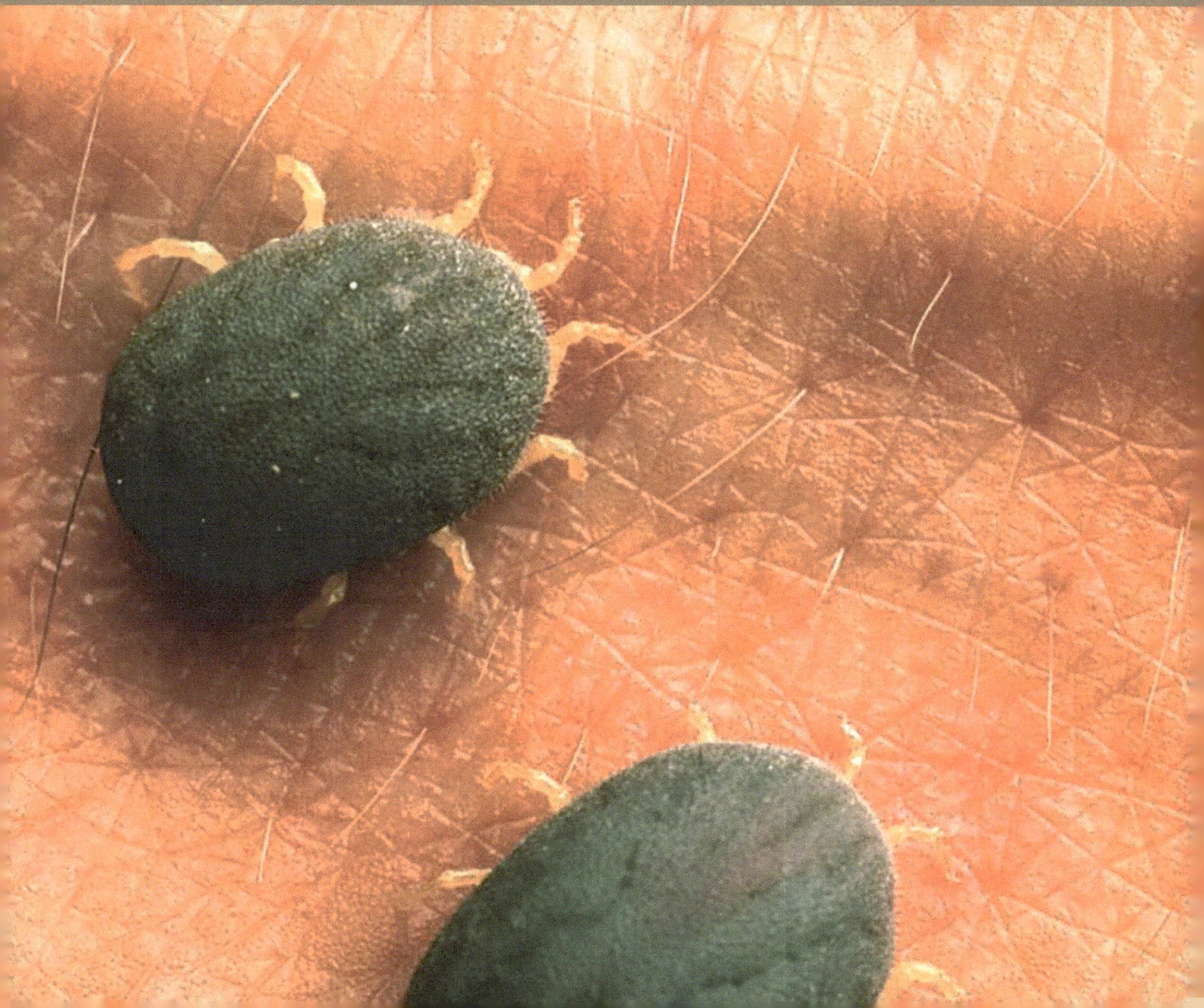

Index

INDEX

www.ingramcontent.com/pod-product-compliance
Lightning Source LLC
Chambersburg PA
CBHW060959030426
42334CB00033B/3289